Uncommon HEROES

Uncommon HEROES

THE HARD MEN AND RAW TALENT THAT BUILT RUGBY LEAGUE

BY JOHN ELLICOTT

hardie grant books
MELBOURNE · LONDON

Published in 2014 by Hardie Grant Books

Hardie Grant Books (Australia)
Ground Floor, Building 1
658 Church Street
Richmond, Victoria 3121
www.hardiegrant.com.au

Hardie Grant Books (UK)
Dudley House, North Suite
34–35 Southampton Street
London WC2E 7HF
www.hardiegrant.co.uk

All rights reserved. No part of this publication may be reproduced, stored in a retrieval system or transmitted in any form by any means, electronic, mechanical, photocopying, recording or otherwise, without the prior written permission of the publishers and copyright holders.

The moral rights of the author have been asserted.

Copyright text © John Ellicott 2014

A Cataloguing-in-Publication entry is available from the catalogue of the National Library of Australia at www.nla.gov.au
Uncommon Heroes

ISBN 978174 270 7655

Cover design by Luke Causby, Blue Cork
Text design by Loupe Studio
Typeset in 11/17 pt Utopia by Kirby Jones
Cover image courtesy of Fairfax
Printed in Australia by Griffin Press

The paper this book is printed on is certified against the Forest Stewardship Council® Standards. Griffin Press holds FSC chain of custody certification SGS-COC-005088. FSC promotes environmentally responsible, socially beneficial and economically viable management of the world's forests.

For those humble in spirit, but who never say die.

Contents

Introduction	1
Chapter One: From the wild	9
PART ONE: THE BOYS FROM THE BUSH	9
PART TWO: CLEALS IN THE THE CITY, PACKER GOES BUSH	29
Chapter Two: 'Humble' Eric Weissel and 'unstoppable' Harry Sunderland	41
Chapter Three: The Maher Cup—Rabbits, floods, fights and fire	74
Chapter Four: Tom Kirk—Making every post a winner	101
PART ONE: FROM THE STICKS TO KING OF THE CITY	101
PART TWO: THE WAR AND THE BUMPER YEARS	123
Chapter Five: Clem Kennedy—The Mighty Atom and Mary's little pin-up boy	144
Chapter Six: Kevin 'Lummy' Longbottom— Raising the flag for his people	171
Chapter Seven: Ronnie Coote—From bunnies to buns	194
Chapter Eight: Laurie Nichols—The Tiger within	213
Chapter Nine: Nathan Blacklock—Running free in Tingha	240
Chapter Ten: Holey Foley and Origin origins	262
Sources	285
Acknowledgements	291

Introduction

They ran onto sodden fields in ankle-length boots and kicked a wet leather ball that felt like concrete. They fell down like flies but rose from the mud in defiance of their injuries to play on—some with broken bones, or badly torn muscles— because there were no replacements. Up to 80,000 people cheered on in the stands, perched precariously just to get a glimpse of the champions. They played for a pittance, and if they finally were given the honour of playing for their nation, they were often away travelling on tour for much of the year only to go straight back into competition when they finally got home. They survived on their wits, natural brawn and the kind of mateship that transcended club allegiances, state lines and national borders.

These are some of the great lives never told from the annals of league. Their names faded like the newspaper clippings of their exploits, kept by friends and fans in dog-eared scrapbooks that few ever saw; great memories kept in the dark. There was little written on who they were or where they'd come from. Many of their famous jumpers became moth-ridden, or their children wore them to school and sport. Others put their famous jerseys away for good in blanket boxes or in the back of cupboards with match programs and medals.

These were the men of little means who grew up in families that couldn't afford shoes for their children or, like Ronnie Coote as a little boy, wearing a sandshoe on one foot and a galosh on the other. Some players came from towns that aren't on the map anymore, from families with fathers who worked in goldmines or carted bread and cut wood to survive. They came from impossible backgrounds to rise into the public spotlight, with their names emblazoned across the sports pages. They became uncommon heroes.

They travelled to training by bike or bus in the hope they could make it to the big time. They dreamed the impossible could become possible. A young man playing in the bush, such as Eric Weissel from south-west New South Wales, could suddenly elevate himself into the realm of international football without ever having played a game in the city. It could happen and it did. Lionel Williamson, raised on a cane farm at the back of Innisfail, could leave his study for the priesthood in Far North Queensland and within a few years don the green and gold for his country and help win a World Cup. Dreams came true, heaven's doors opened up.

The ranks of league from the early years were constantly refreshed. The best city players and coaches played in the country during their career and the young men they taught eventually refreshed league's city ranks. Boorowa, a small town near Yass that was often beset by earthquakes, at one stage had the rumble of Australia's front row playing in its league team. Country players were the backbone of the game. And country teams regularly beat their city opponents.

There was a refreshment of the ranks also from overseas. England and the British Lions would play in Cootamundra, Townsville, Tamworth or Toowoomba as part of a tour and put on great displays as the locals gave them a run for their money. An English international would even take up a contract with Grenfell. Just as a Maori tour from New Zealand, way back in 1907, had helped inspire league in Australia (the Kiwis won all three games), so the great Tests and battles for the Ashes gripped the minds of the sporting public, and kept pub conversations going for decades.

The Kangaroos travelled vast distances to play in England and saw unbelievable sights. On the Kangaroo tour of 1929–30 the players were away for eight months, but what a journey they had—sailing the Pacific and the Atlantic on the best ocean liners, visiting Niagara Falls, meeting the mayor of New York, sitting in the cabinet room at 10 Downing Street with the British prime minister and shaking hands with the Prince of Wales.

England was the mother country for settlement and the mother country for league, but the young Australians, who'd taken up league almost at the same time as nationhood, challenged England's stranglehold on the sport. A tradition was born where players would travel to play for English teams, so many at one stage that the Australian authorities put a ban on transfers. But it was a rite of passage to play with an English club—and the tradition lives on today.

Outside the major competitions in Sydney and Brisbane, there were great league competitions in the regions, followed just as fervently and played just as fiercely. The Maher Cup became one of the most famous cups in any sporting field in Australia and held the attention of a score of towns in south-west New South Wales for 50 years as fans sometimes risked flood and fire to watch games between rival towns. The Maher Cup, known as the Old Tin Pot, was thrown in a river, chucked in a culvert and kept in a police cell as protests raged over who should be its rightful holder. The Maher Cup now sits, lonely, at the bottom of a glass cabinet at the Tumut RSL club, giving little clue to the great celebrations that once went on when a town held it high in the air.

The Foley Shield was the holy grail for footballers of Far North Queensland. The competition spawned many Kangaroos, including Kerry Boustead. Later, its influence on the family of Billy Slater would set the foundation for this amazing footballer, one day voted the best footballer in the world. Slater's dad and uncles played Foley Shield and their guidance helped Billy rise to his great heights for the Melbourne Storm. The Foley Shield was the motivator, the hinge, the fertiliser for generations of footballers. The combatants often played in teeming rain for the right to get into the grand final in Townsville, where a torrid battle always ensued. If Townsville didn't win, the victorious teams from out of town would spend up to a week getting home as they reminisced over their triumph at every little country pub along the way.

The league also boasted vibrant and formidable administrators in its early years. Arch Foley, a friend of Prime Minister Artie Fadden, established league in the north of Queensland. The irrepressible Harry Sunderland led the league in Queensland and then co-managed three Kangaroo tours while also working as a journalist along the way. He helped kick off rugby league in France, pushed for the word 'league' to replace the term 'Northern Union' to describe the game in England, and even tried to promote league to the Americans. They were men of grand ideas and big plans before their time.

Then there were the coaches who turned gangly youths into rapid-firing engines. Jimmy Craig's expertise fashioned Canterbury into the formidable team that won the club its first premiership in 1938. League legend Clive Churchill coached South Sydney to its glory days in the late '60s. Bobby Fulton took the helm at Easts and Manly after his distinguished career on the field, winning a premiership for Manly. Souths player and Kangaroo Clem Kennedy returned to the game to coach Souths' President's Cup team, securing a booty of premierships with his hard training schedules. The retired top players returned to the game time and time again to help the new generation of players.

League was much more than a weekend game and a points table. It was a family, one that included not just the players, coaching staff, officials and administrators, but the wives, the mothers, the fathers; those who watched their sons or husbands go out and do battle every Saturday. The wives of Kangaroo players had to survive on a small ten-shilling-a-week wage while their husbands were away in the 1930s. But they stuck and supported them through thick and thin. Each weekend Preston Campbell's dad drove his son 400 kilometres, each way, from Tingha to Newcastle at the start of his career. Kevin Longbottom's mum watched every game he played at South Sydney. And Billy Slater's dad, Ronnie, was always punching the air as Billy performed his magic tricks on the field, from his little place out amid the cane fields, at Garradunga by Eubenangee Swamp in Far North Queensland. League was a communion of people, families and faiths.

Aboriginal players slowly but surely made their mark on the game, breaking through the wall of discrimination and a White Australia policy that didn't even recognise them as citizens. It is now as if Aboriginal Australia, at least in New South Wales and Queensland, has made league its own and it's become the glue for social strength in many communities.

But who were the pioneers? It wasn't until 1960 that the first Aboriginal player was selected to represent Australia; one Lionel Morgan. Kevin 'Lummy' Longbottom was one of the great Aboriginal footballers, but his story has hardly ever been told. The amazing long-distance kicker from La Perouse paved the way for his relative and fellow Souths clubman Eric Simms to become one of the game's great kickers. Aboriginal footballers started emerging from the country competitions and claiming their place in the top ranks of city clubs. The Tingha Tigers, a club in a small town in north-west New South Wales, helped propel Owen Craigie, Preston Campbell and Nathan Blacklock into the big time in Sydney. The former St George winger Blacklock now returns to Tingha to coach and teach the young men of the Anaiwan and Ngarabal people the right paths to the future through respect for customs and respect for sport. He's now an ambassador for tackling domestic violence in country communities.

League was the conduit to many unlikely friendships. Who would have thought the bearded Cleal brothers, raised at 'Poverty Flat' at Warialda, would one day be out shooting pigs, fishing and sharing jokes with Kerry Packer, Australia's richest man? Who would have thought a knockabout like Laurie Nichols would become the very symbol of league? Born and raised in humble conditions in freezing Cooma, Nichols, a shearer, became the eccentric figure on the sideline punching the air for his beloved Balmain Tigers. This man in his Jackie Howe singlet became a pillar of the club, a confidant to the players and, though a Labor man, he'd enjoy the friendship of Liberal stalwart, football fanatic, coach and radio host Alan Jones. When Balmain merged with Wests his heart was broken, and he passed away shortly afterwards. Among the coffin bearers at his funeral was one of his best mates, Artie Beetson, the nation's first Aboriginal Kangaroo captain, who loved Nichols like a brother and often put him up when he called into Beetson's place after a night out on the town.

These were days when training was hard, but not yet a science. And it was all to do with fitness for the day, rather than building players into mountains of muscle so that any slight tweak would send their whole body into spasms. There were drugs, but only mild ones like salt tablets or Aspros. There were no peptides, steroids or supplement programs or club-appointed sports scientists. The muscles players had were not gym built, but made from hard work on farms or from loading materials onto trucks.

And these were times when players were also larger than life. Newtown's forward Herb Narvo could run riot through the rucks of Sydney's league competition on the weekend and then, on a weekday, rise to become heavyweight boxing champion of Australia. But they were often crude and brutal days, days before the league judiciary was appointed. Players would king-hit an opponent without punishment. There were many ugly moments, brutal acts left on the field that stained games. There were rorts, betting stings that left the public wondering if games had been played fairly. But time eventually had to catch up with the rough diamonds. Television cameras aimed at every point of play made it that way.

The face of league changed dramatically with the advent of television rights, and then the dramatic takeover of league by News Limited in the Super League coup of 1997 created a whole new ball game. The players changed too. Islander players took to the game with great passion, bringing their hulking strong-legged play to the fore. Kiwis such as Benji Marshall have also buoyed league's ranks and now New Zealand regularly defeats Australia in Tests, just as they did way back in 1907. League has never been more multicultural and, in many ways, due to the coverage and media, more exciting, more universal.

The influence of pay television and huge $600,000 a year–plus contracts for the best players has changed league forever. More is expected of today's players than in days gone by. Money and the media demand it. Players can't disappear back into quiet lives, and when things go wrong, as they almost inevitably do for young men with lots of money and time on their hands, it is there for everyone to see. But every day they play, they are carrying on a tradition Australia can rightfully call its own. Australia re-fashioned league and made it the game it is today: fast, unpredictable and exciting to watch. It's been a very long pass down the ages, but the ball is being carried confidently forward. But one day the modern players may reflect that this wasn't all an accident, a dream created by media moguls or publicity agents, but a grassroots phenomenon, instilled in generations, and loyally followed. If they care to look they will discover that the game they play today is a vital part of Australia's cultural identity.

CHAPTER ONE:
From the wild

PART ONE: THE BOYS FROM THE BUSH

Harvey Cleal sits on the front porch of the house in which he's lived for most of his 78 years and faces a road that rarely sees a car. You can be sure, though, that anyone who drives by gets a wave from Harvey on this pleasant day at the end of summer. A honeyeater flits through the branches of a heavily lopped gum beside the house, and in the surrounding paddocks the grass is fence-high. Only the tails of the cattle are visible as they flick up above the verdant summer growth.

But the pastoral idyll belies the disaster that fell upon the region only a few weeks before. A great wall of water came down the river valleys and stranded thousands of people as it flooded in and about Moree, just 80 kilometres from Harvey's house, along the black soil plains. The floods rose as high as cars along the Gwydir Highway and the tops of bridges trapped floating logs like giant sieves.

Warialda, in the hills, escaped the floods. So did Harvey, who is not about to be swept away by anything, including circumstance, although he's had a fair bit thrown at him recently. While sitting outside he contracted an airborne virus that is now attacking his muscle system.

'I've gone from 115 kilos to 75 kilos,' he says, his bright blue eyes darting about, as if hoping someone may soon appear on the road. He's also got fluid around his heart and takes a multiplicity of pills. His back is as sore as hell and a couple of discs down the bottom of his spine have been ground so much there is hardly any tissue left between them, the result of 30 years of back-breaking work as a shearer out on the plains. He can't fully lift his head and he's only comfortable sitting down.

His old weatherboard house leans rather than sits on his block, a bit creaky like him, as if it's trying to stay with the movement of the earth, but can't quite cling on. The house—which is just around the corner from the site of the house in which he was raised by parents Ernie and Ivy—has an old brick fireplace that fits awkwardly among the wood panelling, and it has many dark quiet rooms where hang the old photos that warm Harvey's heart, now that he's the last one left at home.

It's the same house where his two famous football sons grew up: Les and Noel Cleal, the bearded brothers who frightened the life out of many an opponent from Warialda to England in the late '70s and '80s. It's where, for Harvey, memories of their famous exploits rise each day like the sun, as he sits on the porch listening to his battered old radio that he has tied to a verandah post, amid all his odds and ends. It's where family life began humbly fifty years back when Harvey married Jess.

This has been the Cleals' slice of rural New South Wales for more than a century. But entering their patch there's an indication that very few from around here rise above tough times. As you clear the bridge over Warialda Creek and turn left towards the small houses hidden among the pepper trees, a large home-made sign hangs from a tree and rudely announces: 'Welcome to Poverty Flat.'

Prosperous times have come and gone like a flood down on so-called Poverty Flat, where once the bullock drivers camped because they couldn't afford to stay anywhere else. Harvey's father, Ernie, once owned the whole of Poverty Flat, but time and family carve-ups left the Cleal clan with just two bits of the patch.

Ernie Cleal left an enduring mark on Warialda. The line of the highway that brings travellers over the hill from Inverell was carved out of the ground by old machinery pulled by Ernie's team of 18 draughthorses in the early 1900s. It's nice to know that new roads are built on old lines.

The modern Cleals are big men, befitting Warialda's reputation as the home of big men. But Ernie was no heavyweight. 'You wouldn't believe, looking at me and Les and Noel, that my father was an amateur jockey,' says Harvey with a raised eyebrow.

'In those days you could own a horse and ride it yourself. He had a great career until the day when someone tried to fix a race. Put it this way, he wasn't supposed to win the race and nearly did,' says Harvey, with a wry smile. 'He was suspended for two years for that.'

Ernie was a horse lover, earning quick loyalty from his charges. Even after catching a wild horse, remembers Harvey, Ernie'd have it eating out of his hand after just two days of captivity. 'He'd always say, "Good grooming of a horse is as important as the feed it's given." He'd always clean them down, give them a roll.'

Harvey's own contribution to the racing industry was significant: he spent forty years, without missing a meeting, as the senior barrier attendant at Warialda Racecourse. Born on 21 December 1933, Harvey grew up with his two brothers and sisters on the back of the Depression years and skipped school as much as possible as 'we always had something to do for the old man' which mainly led to caring for the working horses. He quickly learnt that anything gained beyond the basics was a bonus.

Harvey kicked off the family's run in rugby league in fortuitous circumstances, all to do with the luck—or for others, the misfortune—of a flood. It was 1952 and Warialda were playing away at a sodden Moree for the Spicer Cup (the main challenge cup in the north-west), donated by Moree bookmaker Bill Spicer way back in 1922. Prior to the cup match, Harvey, in the forwards, of course, was playing for Warialda in the reserve grade match and they lost heavily, 33–5. Then word came through that a number of Warialda's first-grade players from up North Star way couldn't get through the floods to the big game, and six young reserves were called on take their places. Harvey was one of them. 'Us young fellows all ran on as green as grass, but we ended up winning 9–8, the feeling was unbelievable,' recalls Harvey.

Celebrating the town's first Spicer Cup win in 21 years Warialda put on a huge reception for the victorious team, but Harvey quickly found out that Spicer Cup fame wouldn't change his life. 'We were promised the world and got nothing,' he says drily. That's what often happens down on Poverty Flat.

The Spicer Cup, set up by a bookmaker with rather loose rules, was as important to rural towns as the Maher Cup was to the South West Slopes and Plains of New South Wales. Just as with the Maher Cup, the Spicer Cup brought out all kinds of jealousies, shenanigans (one side once imported six Western Suburbs players from Sydney in order to win) and tantrums. Once, in disgust at a result, the Narrabri team threw the cup into the Namoi River. The Maher Cup once met with the same fate in the Yass River. The Spicer Cup was eventually located, but its old gold lid was missing and it's presumed it still lies somewhere buried in the Namoi's muddy bed.

For Harvey, after marrying Jess and roaming all over the plains shearing, his football career dried up. At times he'd be away for weeks at big shearing contracts all the way out to Mungindi and St George (Queensland) on the huge sheep stations when wool reigned supreme on the plains. He'd drive out to his jobs in a Morris Mini-Minor, regularly clocking up to 100 kilometres on the rough back-country roads. When he was home in Warialda, it was quite a sight to see all the beefy Cleals packed into the tiny car.

Harvey and Jess fell in love after meeting at a dance. Funnily, it was his new wife—who was raised on a farm—who taught him shearing. Jess had learnt shearing the hard way, with old scissors. With the modern electric shears she could do 200 sheep in a day. So Harvey, from Poverty Flat, learnt the trade, feeling he had to prove himself for the marriage to be approved considering the rivalry that existed between graziers and those who lived in town.

After losing a child soon after birth, Jess and Harvey eventually had three boys: Les, Noel, and the youngest, Bill. It was on Christie Street that the young Cleals grew up as typical bushie all-rounders, skilled in animal husbandry and physical challenges. Life was an endless football field with no sidelines. 'It was always tip [football] on the road, and tackle on the grass,' Harvey says looking directly at the place where the skills of Les and Noel in particular were honed. 'You could see when they were playing with the other kids they had something special.'

He remembers the time he came home half-cut from the pub, and Les dared him to kick a ball over the power line outside the house. The ball skewed off his boot and into old man Clark's house next door, breaking every pane on a set of louvre windows. Harvey hunches his back as if he can still recall the crescendo of the breaking glass. Either because of the glass incident or something else, Mr Clark wouldn't let the boys retrieve their lost cricket balls from his land. 'They had to wait until I got home and I'd lift them over the fence,' says Harvey.

The Cleal household, already echoing to the thumps of three strong boys, suddenly had another one, even larger, running down the corridor. Bob Barker was sent to live with relatives in Warialda by his father in Bathurst because it was hoped that time at Warialda High would smarten up Barker's attitude to school. He quickly became best friends with the two older Cleal boys and when Barker's relatives moved on, the Cleals offered him board for his final years at school.

The boys proved a formidable trio on the football field for Warialda's under-18s team. As Barker, a front-row forward, set about becoming a punishing presence on the field, Noel became known as 'Blossom', something to do with the freckles he had as a kid, and Les was known as 'Precious', a most unlikely moniker that remains unexplained.

At one time the Warialda under-18s team also starred Stan Plunkett Jurd, who was born and bred in Moree but moved to

Warialda when he was 15. Jurd would go on to fame while playing at the highest level with North Sydney and then Parramatta, with whom he'd win the 1983 premiership over Manly, a team that coincidentally featured Noel Cleal. With 15-year-old Jurd playing alongside Noel, 16, and Les, 17, Jurd recalls that Warialda under-18s side as 'pretty good', yet while they made a grand final Barker reckons they 'lost more often than not'.

Ray Lindsay, who was a player in the Warialda Group 5 team that won five consecutive premierships in the 1960s, and was awarded the Clayton Cup, saw the young Cleals growing up. 'They were both big boys at that stage, and very fast,' he says. 'I thought Les probably had more initial talent than Noel, but he didn't apply himself as much as Noel. But they both stood out in every game they played. Their game plan pretty much followed the pattern of Les kicking the ball 200-foot high and then Bob [Barker] and Noel would run on to it and Noel would race away for a try.'

As the boys began to show great promise Harvey got some bad news concerning his back. A doctor told him he'd have to have an operation and if something went wrong in the procedure he could lose the use of his legs. 'There's no way I'm going to risk that,' Harvey remembers saying. 'I've got two young footballers and they are going places.' So he started a strict exercise regime of 30 push-ups every morning, took a heap of cortisone and headed off to his shearing duties.

As young men with an interest in girls, football and drinking, the trio decided to seek their football future outside Warialda, selling themselves to potential teams as an irresistible trio of league talent.

*

Leaving, moving around and returning is part of the Cleal mindset, especially with Les who is always, as his brother Noel and mates attest, caught between 'marriages, jobs and postcodes'. Everyone says they broke the mould after Les was created, and you could believe there is nothing but pure eucalyptus oil running through his veins. For Les, some would say from the evidence gathered, there is nothing more off-putting than the sight of civilisation. People say he runs a sawmill somewhere in the bush and that he does some painting work. They tell you not to bother to ring him as he never answers his fixed-line telephone, nor would he ever buy a mobile phone. He's quite a sight, Warialdans say, when he drives into town, with his big beard and old car, dragging a pall of dust behind him.

Despite his peregrinations, Les has been Harvey's fallback since Jess died in 2006. He's always there when Harvey needs to go to the city for check-ups or treatments. Harvey can't travel on the train and can only be happy sitting up in a car, with Les in the driving seat taking him on the back roads as only Les knows how. They stay at a simple motel in Sydney, one of those old-style ones with an open verandah, where Les plonks himself in a chair and, with a few beers in hand, talks to anyone walking past, with no intention of visiting any city attractions. When Harvey's appointments are over, he hightails it back to the bush.

On this summer's day, Harvey says Les has shot off to Goondiwindi on the Queensland border after his dog was hit by a car overnight. 'The dog's got a broken pelvis so I'm not sure why he's bringing it back here if it's not going to make it,' says Harvey. No-one's quite sure how many addresses Les has, and it's not worthwhile asking too many questions about his abodes, as you'll probably only end up chasing your own tail, if not a dog's or pig's tail. He has been known at times to live in the deep bush for long periods, just surviving off what he hunts down.

Les, however, does have one known residence. He owns the house across from Harvey's, where two sedans sit among the tall grass. Les's house is well kept, but there is no sign of recent human activity and the curtains are drawn on all the windows. Someone, maybe some local Warialda rascals, has lit the roughage on the side of the tall cabbage tree palm at the front of the house, burning its entire trunk, making it look like one giant burnt matchstick.

At the side of the house is Les's pig meat operation, with a large sign depicting a black boar at the entrance. At certain times of the year, when the pig orders come in from Brisbane, the small paddock is a hive of activity with pig and kangaroo hunters dropping off their catches in the early morning to be stored in the Cleals' chiller boxes that sit like space modules that have landed in the middle of the block. For a long time the operation was managed by Jess, who found herself mixing it with the big, hairy pig shooters and their wild mongrel hunting dogs in wire cages on the back tray tables of their trucks. The pig meat was a short-term bonanza when the orders came in. The meat was destined for Germany, where consumers love the taste of wild Australian boar.

The Cleals are synonymous with the art of pig chasing. Harvey started the tradition many years ago and his three sons followed in the pursuit of the wild and angry beasts. With the number of pigs the Cleals have caught you'd think the feral pig problem in north-west New South Wales would have been solved decades ago. Harvey boasts that in one period in 1971, he and his mate caught 1260 pigs in six weeks, with the use of 16 traps. While pig meat attracts about one dollar per kilogram in the 2010s, back then it was eight cents a pound, laments Harvey. Though he notes 'they aré just as frightened of you as you are of them' Harvey bears the scar of one close encounter with a pig, after a large boar cut up the inside of his right forearm.

One day a half-tied-up pig escaped and hobbled away, and Harvey's mate got lost in the heavy scrub trying to find it.

'Where are you?' Harvey shouted.

'I'm in here,' shouted back his friend. 'It's that friggin' thick in here you can't even change your mind,' he declared.

In another pig-chasing escapade, a pig dog chased a boar through the scrub and ran so fast into a small hole in the fence that 'his ring nearly ended up near his face', Harvey recalls.

Noel and Les also bear scars from close encounters of the pig kind. Noel lost part of one finger after putting his hand straight into a pig's mouth while trying to retrieve it from under a shed.

Of course, with pigs come pig dogs and no dog was closer to the heart of the Cleals, especially Les, than a bull terrier–labrador cross called Scamp, which almost met its maker during one chase. A big red-hued boar had given Scamp a terrible beating and Les was afraid he'd lost his favourite dog. He picked up the bleeding Scamp and took the dog to the truck to get it to a vet as quickly as possible and told Bob Barker to stay with the pig until he got back. The big red boar was chomping its jowls looking straight at Barker who knew for sure it hadn't given up the fight. 'You're not leaving me here,' he shouted and jumped straight in the truck.

After seeing the vet, Les took Scamp back to Warialda that night and lay with it out on the porch in Christie Street. When he awoke, Scamp was gone. Les thought it had hobbled off to die somewhere, but later that morning he found Scamp up and limping about, on the mend.

Scamp became the Cleals' symbol of hope, an inseparable buddy and faithful mascot as they headed off for football fame. 'Scamp would run up and down the sidelines while we played and the kids would follow him,' Barker remembers.

The boys had by then fashioned their skills in the under-18s competition and with no obvious career calling they, and Scamp, headed off on a wild adventure with just beer, rugby league, pig chasing and girls on their minds.

They first landed in Wondai on Queensland's Burnett Downs in 1976, where Les would end up captain-coaching the team to a premiership. That they ended up in Wondai was down to former Warialda league official Fred Hodge, a foreman on Wondai Shire Council and an executive of the Wondai Rugby League Football Club. Hodge had moved to Wondai, about 250 kilometres north-west of Brisbane, and he'd told the local officials about the boys' skills and a package was put together to entice the trio over the border.

When they arrived the boys were fortunate enough (as far as their master plan was concerned) to secure lodging at a local pub, the Wondai Hotel, one of three pubs in Wondai. 'At that stage we all thought we were 10-feet-tall and bullet-proof,' says Barker.

The boys were everything Hodge promised they would be and the team rolled through the season with the Cleal brothers in the centres; Noel, at outside centre, fed off Les at inside centre and scored nearly 50 tries. On the back of their combination, Wondai made the grand final where they'd come up against Kingaroy, coached by Tommy Slater, the uncle of future star Billy Slater.

Slater thought Kingaroy had the grand final in the bag after a strong season, and Wondai were long odds to win despite the presence of the Cleals. But in the last minute of the tense match Wondai were leading 13–8 when Kingaroy's Dave Brown—a heavy-duty prop who would later play with Noel at Easts in Sydney and, like Noel, represent Australia—scored under the posts. Incredibly, Kingaroy's goal kicker, Russell Tessmann, the brother of Queensland representative and Kangaroo Brad Tessmann, missed the conversion attempt from right in front, failing to send the game into extra time. Only the week before, he had kicked seven goals from impossible positions while playing in strong winds. Tessmann was inconsolable and later Slater had to track him down so that he could come and commiserate with his team. Wondai, meantime, had won their first premiership for nearly a decade.

Football commentator Wayne Kratzmann says the Cleals lifted the Wondai team from out of nowhere. 'It was a very strong competition in the South Burnett. A lot of the players would go on to representative honours and at the time South Burnett could have easily beaten Brisbane, such was their strength,' says Kratzmann. Indeed the Cleals played in the South Burnett representative side that beat Maryborough in the final of the 47th Battalion Carnival.

'So the Cleals,' continues Kratzmann, 'were actually playing among the best. But no-one had heard of them before they arrived and they were straight out of school. You have to remember also that Bob Barker was an excellent forward.'

There was also quite a lot of money riding on Wondai winning the competition. A publican, who knew early on that the Cleals were on their way, had a sizeable bet at juicy odds on Wondai clinching the trophy for the 1976 season. He must have had his heart in his mouth when Kingaroy almost stole the final in the last minute.

Word of the Cleals' success was widespread. Sawtell Panthers official Rex Hardaker had heard about the boys from a friend in Wondai and made an offer for them to come and play for the struggling club on the New South Wales north coast. The three boys offered themselves as a package deal and they were all hired for the 1977 season. (At one stage it was believed the Cleals sought more than $4000 to play for a rival team, Taree United, but were knocked back.)

The Cleals and Barker quickly worked their sorcery on the down-at-heel Panthers, who'd taken out the wooden spoon the previous year. In their first year the boys helped take them to fifth on the ladder. Then, in 1978, Sawtell became premiers after winning the grand final in extra time. To cap off a remarkable turnaround, Sawtell were then awarded the prestigious Clayton Cup as the best regional and country team in New South Wales.

Coffs Harbour Advocate journalist Greg White played league in his early years for Taree United and says that when he first saw the Cleals run onto the field for Sawtell he and his teammates couldn't believe what they saw based on the reputation that preceded them. 'They had a roll of guts hanging over their shorts, with big beards and they looked like they had just walked out of the bush and could hardly run a yard,' White says.

'Noel played at fullback, and Les was on the wing. But they were so big and so fast no-one could stop them. They cleaned up our best player and he had to be taken off the field and from then on they just ran over the top of us,' White remembers.

'And when they were playing you sort of never knew which one was which.'

Les was appointed coach of Sawtell at just 19, even though the rules stipulated a coach had to be at least 21. Stan Jurd—who would often make the trip over from Warialda to see the boys play, and to enjoy the Cleal hospitality by the sea—says a ruse was concocted that year, so that when Les turned 20, they made out that it was his twenty-first birthday party.

White says appointing someone as young as Les to a major coaching role was 'completely unheard of' but it paid off. 'He was a genius as a coach,' says White. 'He brought a whole new way to playing the game, light years ahead of what was going on. It used to be just play your four tackles and kick on the fifth. Les changed playing. You know, a bit of kick and chase and thinking ahead. So if the fullback isn't in position, kicking on the first tackle and then [chasing] the ball.'

Often the opposition were so concerned about Barker and the Cleal brothers looming down on them that they'd let the ball bounce, only to find Noel or Les swooping on the pigskin. It was nothing for Noel to score five tries in a match. Blossom, Precious and Barker, nicknamed 'Ralph' after a Warner Bros. cartoon character, were proving an unstoppable combination.

Sawtell Panthers hooker John 'Tank' Mackay told the *Coffs Coast Advocate* that Sawtell was no more than a competent team, one close to going bust before the Cleals and Bob Barker arrived. 'Everything they say about the Cleal boys is true. They were so big there was a huge gap between their shorts and jumper, but they were light on their feet, strong and powerful,' he said. 'In their first year things were rough and ready and we all mucked around. People forget Les was young and liked a good time but he grew up and we got fair dinkum for the next season.'

That was the year Sawtell won the grand final over Smithtown—but only just. At Brelsford Park in Coffs Harbour, the scores were tied at 8-all when Smithtown were awarded a penalty kick with just seconds to go. The Smithtown kicker missed the easy goal and the game went into extra time. Both sides scored a try in extra time but Sawtell clinched the game with a drop goal with the referee just about to blow the full-time whistle. 'Noel won the game for us,' Mackay told the *Advocate*. 'With 20 seconds left he dropped the field goal and the place erupted.'

Some say, however, that it was actually Les who kicked the field goal, but Barker agrees with Mackay that it was Noel. 'I know, because we had a kick-off at training the day before to decide who'd take the shot at goal and Noel won it,' he says.

Not surprisingly, former Panthers official Kerry Hales remembers the Cleal brothers well. 'Noel was unbelievable in the centres; they were extremely talented footballers. Les wasn't a very sociable person and he was doing a bit of [house] painting on the side to get by. Noel did whatever he could but he didn't get out of bed very early, but he survived.'

The trio had left their mark on Sawtell—and not only because it would be 31 years until Sawtell won the Group 2 competition again (and in almost identical circumstances, with one of the two brothers playing kicking a field goal to win the grand final). While Les shacked up with a girl, Noel and Barker shared an apartment and enjoyed their young life on the coast with plenty of beach fun and Tooheys New on tap. They started their own bush cook-ups and had parties that lasted into the small hours. At one party, according to Greg White who lived nearby, a whole kangaroo was cooked on a fire on the front lawn, to the amazement of the reserved Sawtell neighbourhood.

But Sawtell couldn't hold the Cleals and Barker for long. The trio had helped put the name Sawtell on the lips of many rugby league enthusiasts (the team was even featured in *Big League* magazine), but they were keen to move on to a new patch. And as it always seemed to do, fortune smiled their way.

Attending a rugby league presentation in Dungog, Don 'Bandy' Adams, a former Kangaroo representative and Scone Thoroughbreds legend, ran into a cousin of the Cleals'. He told Adams that the boys were keen to move on and Adams saw his chance to bolster the Scone Thoroughbreds' stocks. 'I'd seen them play when they were young so I was keen to get them,' says Adams, who quickly rang Les and secured the trio's services, for an amount believed to be around $10,000 a year.

When they arrived in Scone—unwittingly moving ever closer to the city, where their skills would soon be in hot demand—Les and Noel were a hulking 15 or 16 stone, though it wasn't all muscle. As they'd discover, Scone had a fine crop of under-18s coming through, and Adams's plan was to merge the Cleals' power with the vibrancy of the juniors. Les took on the coaching role and Adams stood back, becoming a selector, working as Les's man on the Scone selection committee.

Scone were one of the most successful clubs in any sporting code in Australia, but they hadn't won a premiership for some time. The Cleals made an instant impact, however, and the season went along fantastically, Les becoming an inspiration to the younger players.

Adams, who describes himself as a 'savage coach', found Les was more into bonding sessions with his teammates; sessions that involved drinking together or pig chasing. But there was a complete ban on drinking the night before the game unless it was a Les-sanctioned event.

Once, during the 1979 season, one of Scone's best players had had a skinful before the game and was confronted by Les and Adams who went around to his house and gave him a full dressing down. The player heeded the advice and didn't do it again.

Despite thriving in Scone, Les was often itching to return to Warialda to go pig chasing. Before an important sponsors' night for the Thoroughbreds, Adams had to convince Les, the team's star, to put his pig-chasing ambitions on hold. Les begrudgingly came along to the dinner, hating anything to do with formality. But during the course of the night he convinced a guest to go pig chasing with him the next day.

Early in the morning, Adams was asleep at home with his wife when suddenly he heard a booming voice at the bottom of the bed. 'Hey, Bandy, do you know where McCarthy lives? I've got to pick him up to go pig chasing.'

Adams was relieved to know that the voice at the bottom of the bed was Les's. While the two men worked out the address, Adams's wife went and made Les a big breakfast to help him on his way. 'That was the Cleals: come right in the house without knocking. But I kind of like that,' says Adams.

Les took a lot of people west and once arrived at Adams's house to say he was leaving for Warialda. It was a hot day and Adams could see something moving or shimmering in the back of Les's '68 Holden.

'What's in the back of the sedan there Les?' he asked.

'A little calf I'm taking home,' Les replied. And there it was, perched on the back seat doing what little cows do, all over the vinyl.

Les worked on a cattle stud near Scone teaching young bulls to be led by a rope. One day Adams went out to watch what he was doing and was surprised to find Les watching as one of the bulls was tethered to, and being led by, a donkey. 'That's the only time in my life I've ever seen that,' says Adams, who'd spent much of his life around cattle, living on a dairy farm.

Once Les almost missed a Sunday match after going pig chasing the previous day and losing his adored Scamp. 'There was no way I was going to leave Scamp out in the bush,' an exhausted Les told Adams when he eventually turned up with Scamp just before the game.

It was during their time in Scone when the Cleal brothers' football careers reached a major turning point. It was 1979 and the Great Britain Lions were touring Australia and as such were playing many regional sides.

It was one of the toughest and best line-ups of English players to play Down Under.

Amazingly, when the Northern Division selectors sat down to put their team together they left out Noel and Les, even though Scone were blitzing the competition. Adams was Northern Division coach and he couldn't believe the decision of the selectors. 'They just didn't want them,' remembers Adams. '[But then, before the Great Britain game] we played the North Coast and lost a few players with injury, and I said, "Why don't we try Noel and Les Cleal?"'

So, belatedly, the Cleals were drafted into the North Division side for the big game against Great Britain at Scully Park in West Tamworth on 5 June. More than 7600 supporters turned up for the game and, according to *Northern Daily Leader* reporter Ann Newling, Tamworth retailers reported up to 10 per cent of their employees hadn't turned up for work so that they could go and see the game. Northern Division were given no chance against the big Brits, but within minutes the Cleals, playing as wingers, were into the action, with Les scoring an early try.

At one stage, Northern Division led the Brits 7–5, and when half-time was called, Great Britain were leading just 10–9. The large parochial crowd sensed a boilover. In the hurly-burly of the second half, famous British player Roger Millward hurt his leg as 'the Cleals hurled themselves like human battering rams' with 'constant raging bursts' against Great Britain.

The battle raged for the full 80 minutes and although Northern Division lost 20–11, to the excited crowd it was like they had won after giving the Brits such a big fright. The *Northern Daily Leader* said Northern Division could have won if it wasn't for 'anxiousness' and a lack of big game experience. 'Great Britain won the game but Northern Division won the crowd and with no amount of luck would have won the game as well,' the *Leader* reported. Unseen in Tamworth, a major traffic jam ensued as the fans piled out of the Scully Park arena.

After the game the British and Northern Division players got together at a Tamworth pub. 'You twins are unbelievable,' one of the Pommies said at the bar to the Cleals. 'We're not fucking twins,' replied Noel, who often had to clarify the siblings' status. One of Britain's walking wounded then declared 'Fook me, how tough are you?' Earlier, Les had sandwiched him up against the uprights as he attempted to go over for a try.

But it was fortuitous day for Noel. In the crowd watching the game was *Daily Mirror* league writer Bill 'Break Even' Mordey. Mordey was astounded by the way the Cleals played and got on to his mate Bob 'Bozo' Fulton, the legendary Manly halfback and then coach at Easts, telling him he had to sign up Noel Cleal. Fulton had already heard about the Cleals' prowess—

and he'd tried to sign them two years earlier—but Mordey's recommendation was the best confirmation he could get.

Within a week Easts made an offer for the Cleals to play in Sydney, and Noel warmed to the chance to play in the big league. Easts offered to buy out Noel's contract at Scone to get him immediately but, amazingly, Noel said he wanted to stick the year out with Scone, a great show of faith in his country origins despite a lucrative Sydney deal just waiting for his signature.

By the end of the year, however, Noel was preparing for a new life in the city: 'Bozo offered me $5000 and I had never seen so much money in my life. I agreed and came down in January, 1980, aged 21. It was daunting; I'd never been to Sydney and the place could be scary. But I'd been out on my own since I was 16, so I was used to fending for myself.'

If Bill Mordey hadn't flown up to watch the game that day maybe Noel would never have gone to the city. At the time Mordey had many rugby league contacts, from his best mate, St George legend Johnny Raper, to Fulton, whose column he was ghostwriting in the *Daily Mirror*. He was the first type of journalist-entrepreneur the game had known, and he eventually moved into boxing promotions. But not before he almost had his comeuppance after writing a critical few paragraphs about the Welshman John Mills, who played for Great Britain in the 1979 tour and also had a stint with North Sydney in the early 1970s.

One of international league's toughest players, Mills was famously told by a coach once to count to three whenever he thought his blood was boiling. 'Unfortunately sometimes I only get to two,' Mills told an interviewer. Stan Jurd played against him in the touring side, when Stan was in Queanbeyan and representing Monaro, and said Mills had a head like 'a three gallon drum'. One day in the '70s, the day after he'd written a poor review of Mills, Mordey was having a quiet drink with his journo mates in Surry Hills in Sydney after the first edition of the *Mirror* had hit the stands. Suddenly there was a big clud on the steps of the Clock Hotel. A big angry voice announced in a broad Welsh accent, 'Which one's Mord-ay?' As Mills approached the bar there was no sign of 'Mord-ay', only a half-drunk schooner of beer.

When the 1979 Northern Division season ended, before Noel headed to Easts, the Cleals had brought glory to another team. Scone won the grand final and were awarded the coveted Clayton Cup—making it two years running for the boys from Warialda. But with Sydney-bound Noel leaving behind brother Les and mate Bob Barker—who'd met a local girl and decided to settle down in Scone—the famous three mates were splitting up. Ralph was handing in his bundy card; Blossom was turning into Crusher; and Precious, well, he and Scamp would always have itchy feet. It was the end of a grand partnership and a wild road trip that had taken three unlikely country youths right around the north with parties, good times and famous victories.

PART TWO: CLEALS IN THE CITY, PACKER GOES BUSH

The city quickly proved a happy hunting ground for Noel Cleal. Instead of any trepidation at his sudden thrust into big-time football and the heady life of the city, he immediately took his amazing chance by both horns, and never looked back.

Without any fears, Fulton put Noel straight into first grade and Noel lived up to his faith playing with distinction in the early midweek cup matches. Fulton obviously saw something special in Noel, and quickly warmed to the Cleal culture, eventually enjoying their company and becoming bush buddies. Easts were hoping to restore lost pride after several disappointing years after the premiership wins of 1974 and 1975. The 1980 season was shaping up as a big year, with the likes of Royce Ayliffe, Kerry Boustead and John Lang among the talent pool.

Noel was one of several players working in the Eastern Suburbs Leagues Club, with his job to move the kegs. In fact, a number of Easts players were listed as a 'cellarman' in the Easts Leagues Club's annual report.

'Blossom' Cleal was soon re-invented as 'Crusher' Cleal by his city mates as he tore up the opposition through the middle of the field and out in the centres. He was also proving dangerous from dummy half. Easts defeated the Brisbane Broncos in Brisbane at Lang Park in April by 14–4 in the first game of the Tooth Cup. Steve Crawley wrote in the *Sydney Morning Herald*: 'An individual try against the run of play by the burly centre Noel Cleal after 12 minutes silenced the Brisbane raids temporarily.'

The next week the press was alive with excitement at the upcoming clash between Mick Cronin and Noel as Easts took on Parramatta. 'Mick Cronin versus Noel Cleal—it's a heavyweight clash if ever there was one,' wrote reporter Tom Bishop. 'The clash of the two big centres should be a thriller for fans at Cumberland Oval. Cleal, a new recruit for the Roosters this season, has really impressed. He had a strong game against two good centres from Brisbane on Wednesday night. The youngster is big and strong with a bit of pace.'

By the end of the season Noel was earning numerous plaudits and a rave review from one of the game's greats, Artie Beetson, who was in the last year of his playing career in Sydney. He was convinced Noel would be the new superstar of Sydney football.

'Generally the game lacks personality today, especially with the loss of form by Graham Eadie and Steve Rogers,' Beetson said. 'But if ever I've seen someone ready to step into their shoes, it's big Noel Cleal. I've never seen a player his size run as fast and yet able to step off either foot at the same time. Cleal has the makings of becoming the game's number one personality next year.'

After losing the first three games of the year, Fulton's boys turned it into a great season for Easts, finishing with the minor premiership on points difference over Canterbury. Easts then made it through to the grand final, and Noel ran out onto the Sydney Cricket Ground in front of 52,000 people, the biggest crowd he'd seen in his life. In his first year at Easts, just like his first years at Wondai, Sawtell and Scone, he had the chance to lift a premiership trophy, but this time it was the most prized in the land. Noel was given the honour of kicking off in the grand final. But Canterbury proved too good on the day. Steve Gearin scored 15 points including one amazing high-flying try to seal an 18–4 victory for the Bulldogs. Noel had come to the brink of glory in just his first year in the big smoke.

Easts were the best-performed team during 1981, again winning the minor premiership. This time, however, they were knocked out in the semifinals. Les, meantime, playing now for Werris Creek, was still tossing up whether he would join Noel during the year. Ian Heads wrote in June in the *Herald* under the headline 'Second Cleal Just Waiting' that, 'after Noel scored two tries against St George, he was in the dressing room towelling down when he confirmed that big brother Les, in the railway town of Werris Creek, is itching to get to Sydney'.

'Les wants to come down in '82 and he wants to come to Easts,' Noel told Heads. 'And if he does come to Sydney they'll knock up scoring tries off him. He was always a more creative player with the ball than I was.'

Later in the year, Les finally made the big decision to come to the city, and his arrival in Sydney's well-heeled Bellevue Hill must have brought to mind television family the Clampetts' pulling in to Beverly Hills in *The Beverly Hillbillies*. He sported a big unruly beard and came with an entourage of favourite animals, including pig dogs.

Fulton was amazed when he saw Les for the first time: he seemed a spitting image of Noel. Les's first request was a big place in which to put all his pig dogs and country paraphernalia. No such place existed in the upmarket eastern suburbs, but Les took some convincing. 'Eventually we had to find five acres for him out at Liverpool,' Fulton remembers.

Les found the transition to first grade a lot tougher than Noel. There was no quick path to success and he was made to go through the grades. He played firstly in third grade as a prop, a position totally unfamiliar to him. He was used for a time as a replacement in reserve grade, but eventually made the start-up squad for first grade.

Alan Clarkson wrote of Les's reserve grade game: '[Les] Cleal grabbed his chance with a display of power running that prompted Fulton to have him on standby as replacement in first grade.'

Les made his first-grade debut against Manly in early May, 1982. Watching from a distance was Australia's then richest man, Kerry Packer, the big mover and shaker behind Easts, but one who always kept a low profile. He often watched games from the stands, or popped into the dressing room to cheer on the players after a game. He was even known to turn up at training to join in touch football. Fulton once told a reporter that Packer had an allegiance to Easts because 'he just lives up the road'. Packer, who was originally a Souths supporter, became best buddies with Fulton after Fulton went to Easts in 1977 as captain-coach, and they often had lunch together in Packer's city office. The media mogul loved to go shooting with his mates around his country property Ellerston, situated in the Hunter Valley. From the homestead verandah they'd fire volleys at targets set up on an expensive wooden fence. (The Ellerston fence maker was livid one day when he discovered holes in his newly crafted fence and demanded to see Packer at the front door.) It wasn't long before one of the unlikeliest of friendships occurred: the richest man in Australia became mates with the Cleals from Poverty Flat.

Packer had two trips up to the country with the Cleals. Harvey Cleal remembers the first trip with great pride and as a social success, despite the vast gap in wealth and experiences. Packer flew up in his private jet to Goondiwindi on the New South Wales–Queensland border looking forward to some country comradeship. Fulton flew in with Packer, and the Cleals' younger brother, Bill, picked them up at the Goondiwindi airstrip. He then drove them out to join the other Cleals in the bush to go pig chasing. When Bill Cleal told Packer he had the same calibre rifle—fitted for .243 Winchester cartridges—Packer told him if he'd known that he'd have brought a barrel full of bullets for him. In any case, Packer still gave Bill 300 boxes of bullets.

The party went out hunting and while walking along the Macintyre River looking for some pig action, Harvey stopped and put his fishing line in the river. Packer asked why they were stopping. Les explained to him: 'Dad likes to take a fish home to mum.'

'If I knew you were that hungry for fish, I would have brought a plane load up for you,' Packer replied.

Packer celebrated his birthday while he was on the trip, enjoying yarns around the campfire and sharing jokes with his rugby league mates. After a hard day's shooting and fishing, Packer jumped in the river with the boys for a swim. He then settled down in the shearer's hut on the side of the Macintyre River and after a solid night's sleep in a bush swag, Packer, used to staying in the best hotels in the world, turned over in the morning half-naked and announced, 'That's one of the best nights I've ever put in'.

The Cleals, Packer and Fulton had one more shooting adventure together, this time at Fulton's property out in the bush at Quambone, on the plains near the Macquarie Marshes in central northern New South Wales. Fulton loved to live life rough there, just like the Cleals. Fulton refuses to discuss anything in detail about his relationship with Packer but one of his mates heard the story of the great pig-shooting rivalry that overcame the hunting party. Packer warmed to the pig-chasing prowess of the Cleals and was keen to beat them at their own game. But how far would he go?

On the first day of the pig challenge the party headed out on their motorbikes. Unfortunately, Packer's bike had a governor (speed limiter) on it. He tried to keep up with the Cleals to try and find where the pigs were, but he couldn't see them for dust. At the end of the day the group sat around the campfire. 'How'd you go?' Packer asked the Cleals. 'Got about 20. Yourself?' Noel said. 'Three,' Packer replied gruffly. Coming out second best was not a situation Packer was used to.

The next day at sunrise, the Cleals heard a low burr of an idling engine near the camp. When they looked up they saw a large Land Cruiser, open at the back with bars across the top, similar to vehicles used by hunters in Africa. Packer smiled and said, 'Ready for the shoot today?' and off they went. The Cleals luckily came upon a fair mob of pigs and came back with a tally of 40. Packer, firing from the truck, had just 20. There was an air of silence in the camp as they all went to bed that night out in the bush.

The next morning there was no burr, but the Cleals suddenly thought they were in a James Bond film set. A huge whirring sound was heard not far from the camp. Packer had called in his helicopter. Off the boys went on their bikes, while Packer took to the sky. When they got back to camp they all proudly said they'd shot 50 pigs that day together. 'How'd you go, Kerry?' one of the Cleals asked the mogul. 'I stopped counting at 200,' he said with a big toothy smile.

Packer had another more subtle influence on life at Easts. He introduced his own personal trainer, George Daldry, to the club to give the Roosters a winning edge. Daldry was a solidly built man who always said he would do whatever he asked his fitness clients to do. He'd helped train Prince Albert of Monaco and US President George Bush. He'd survived the horrors of the Changi prisoner of war camp and he knew the meaning of tough.

Daldry was a blunt talker. If someone came up to him and said 'G'day', he'd just reply 'Fine thanks', to bypass the 'How are you going?' Daldry had Les in his sights when he first arrived from Werris Creek. Les was a bit overweight and Fulton told him to stick to steak and lay off the bread and potatoes. Daldry backed up Fulton's advice and soon Les took the hint, as Daldry mapped out a training program that would get Les up to peak performance.

'A whole great bullock came down from the Cleal farm at Warialda to be stowed in a giant freezer,' Daldry told *Sun-Herald* reporter Dorothy Goodwin. 'Les is an enormous eater,' he continued. 'But he has stuck to a spartan program. I wouldn't have given two bob for him at first.'

Daldry was then amazed at a fitness session at Bondi Beach when Les shot past him in the swim leg. 'There I was waist deep in the surf when Les, who I considered a lumbering kind of bloke, shot past me like a crocodile. It turns out Les still holds country swim records. He's got a beautiful stroke.'

Daldry used to make players piggyback teammates up hills and go on strenuous stair runs. His idea was to eat right and stay fit until your final days. Noel kept using Daldry for training during his career even after he moved to Manly.

Such a tough regimen was strange to Les. He was used to training and then heading straight down to the pub. As the end of the season approached he was already getting itchy feet, tired of the first-grade pressure-cooker. He said in a rare interview: 'I resisted [coming to Easts] for years. Then suddenly I decided to find out if I could make it before I got too old. It certainly wasn't for the money. But one more year, that will do me.'

But Les would bail out after the finals, though not before he was part of an amazing try, featuring 11 different players, scored by Easts against Manly on 21 August. Noel lamented he wasn't considered part of the movement. 'I played the ball [that started it off],' he protested.

When Les played first grade in May he was part of the Roosters' resurgence, helping them win 14 out of their next 19 games. Easts thrust themselves right into finals contention, thanks to the brilliance of the Cleal brothers working in unison.

Noel said it was fantastic to play with his brother again. 'Brothers in a side is like having an extra man on the field. Les and I give each other confidence. I get a great buzz out of seeing him on the burst and it's the same with him. We try to back each other up all the time.'

Asked which Cleal brother was the better, Fulton said it was a tough question to answer. 'They were both very different styles of player. Les had a lot of ability but he didn't adapt to the high pressure of city first grade despite his great skills.'

Noel was fashioned in the same mould as Souths' second-row legend Bob McCarthy. A lot of Noel's strength came down to his strong gluteus maximus, says Fulton. '[His arse] was as strong as they come, and no-one could get a hold of it,' he says. Noel, despite his hefty bulk, was the second-fastest player at Easts after the lightning-fast international winger Kerry Boustead.

Les put in a man-of-the-match performance when Easts defeated Norths in the 1982 semifinal. Easts looked like they were good enough to make the grand final before a rampant Parramatta knocked them out in the preliminary final. So the 1982 season ended in disappointment for the Roosters and soon the major core of the team would leave, including Fulton.

Fulton had had enough of the disappointing run at Easts. Team manager Ron Jones had assured the press midyear that Fulton would be coaching Easts in 1983, but this was not to be. Fulton foresaw a new era brewing at his old club, Manly, and he was keen to return to the place he had so sensationally left after his brilliant career there as a player. It was a case of the prodigal son coming home—and he came bearing gifts, taking with him to Brookvale not only Noel Cleal, but also Kerry Boustead.

For Noel it triggered the best success of his football life. Put into the second row he became an instant great, one of the most mobile forwards of the modern era. In 1985 he'd win his first Kangaroo cap, and in 1987 he'd be there with Fulton when Manly beat Canberra to win the grand final at the Sydney Cricket Ground. Off the field, Noel would win too, making lifelong friends at Manly, friends that would endure right through his working life.

Les, on the other hand, bolted right out of Sydney. He went to play for a short time with Brisbane Brothers before returning to country New South Wales. After a stint with Widnes in England—which he enjoyed due to the simpler lifestyle and reduction in pressure when compared to Sydney—Les eventually went west, actually south-west, ending up in Tumbarumba, a lonely little town nestled into the side of the Snowy Mountains. Bitterly cold in winter, it was wild and rough, its big yearly attraction being a rodeo. It suited Les to a T.

Eventually Les would help perform another miracle and take Tumbarumba to a Group 13 premiership and win the Clayton Cup twice for them in 1986 and 1987. After Tumbarumba—for whom his son, Josh, would play 25 years later—Les returned to coach the Scone Thoroughbreds where, of course, he instituted a unique training method for his players: a weekend chasing pigs outside Warialda. After stints at many other country clubs, Les would coach the women's touch football team at Warialda in 2010.

Noel would also head overseas after his distinguished career, which featured 11 games for New South Wales and eight Tests. He played for Hull and then coached the English side to a premiership in 1991. His son Kane also played first grade in Sydney.

After his playing days finished in 1989, by which time he'd racked up 195 games in first grade, Noel became a recruitment guru for several clubs including Parramatta, Manly and Canterbury. With his contacts throughout country New South Wales and Queensland he had not one or two talent scouts on call, but hundreds.

At Manly, he re-ignited his great friendship with his old teammate Des Hasler and they both enjoyed huge success. When Hasler went to Canterbury in 2012, after falling out with Manly's hierarchy (despite winning the 2011 premiership), Noel followed him. The Cleal–Hasler management team was almost unbeatable. From almost nowhere Canterbury powered through the season and made the 2012 grand final when, unfortunately for the pair, Billy Slater's Storm proved too good on the day. Fulton, the long-time Australian coach and one of the wisest heads in league, says of Noel's ability as a talent finder: 'He's the gun recruitment manager in the game. He's the Billy Slater of recruitment.'

Watching all these peregrinations from afar was his father, Harvey, who hesitates to stay at Noel's place in Sydney because he finds it hard to negotiate the long stairs up to his front door. So he awaits news of where his boys are and is always confident Les won't be far away. When he's pressed to nominate who was the best player, Noel or Les, he pauses and, despite Noel's premiership for Manly, his success in State of Origin and his ten Test caps with the Kangaroos, he leans a little towards Les.

And when he's asked about the greatest game he saw his sons play, he doesn't bring up an Ashes win or a Sydney premiership or Les's amazing four Clayton Cups. No, what wins his vote is that damn fine performance the bearded brothers from Warialda put in when, playing for Northern Division, they scared the hell out of Great Britain at Scully Park in Tamworth way back in 1979. It was the game that put the boys from the bush on the map and had the name Cleal ringing around the world of rugby league.

CHAPTER TWO:
'Humble' Eric Weissel and 'unstoppable' Harry Sunderland

Eric Weissel was about as country lovin' as you can get. Born and raised in the bush, he played all his club football out in the sticks and spent most of his working and retirement years amid the gum trees and magpies of Wagga Wagga. Even when he was offered the great honour of captaining New South Wales to play Queensland, he told league authorities he couldn't lead his state onto the field because he had to play for his home side of Temora against Canowindra! And when he was offered a huge contract to play in England, the ultimate carrot for any league player, he decided he couldn't leave his family and Australian rural paradise.

Eric Leslie Weissel was the youngest of 11 children. He was born on 16 February 1903 in Cootamundra, sharing the birthplace of cricket legend Don Bradman—and the two keen sportsmen were destined to meet. His father, Edward, born in 1857, was a German immigrant who came out to help build the railway from Cootamundra to Tumut, and later worked on other country railway lines that gave the state the infrastructure it so desperately needed. Edward worked as a chief fettler, enduring long hot days on lonely country track lines. Many German migrants settled in the Murray and Riverina areas, and at one stage Albury even had a German-language newspaper. Some German migrants suffered during the war years due to anti-German feelings and some were even interned during the first and second world wars. During the Great War, German place names had to be replaced by law, including Germantown, south of Wagga, which was renamed Holbrook after a First World War hero. The Weissels, though, escaped most of the wartime backlash and life went on as normal for them. Edward and his wife, Ellen, were in charge of the Brawlin railway platform for a time and later its post office. The Brawlin community gave the couple an inscribed silver teapot, a silver shaving mug and brush when they left to start a new life in Cootamundra, just a bit north.

Edward did well out of the railway, built his own home for his wife in Cootamundra and had a vineyard alongside the house, and a sausage smoking room, as many German migrants loved to have.

Edward had bought six blocks of land in 1902 around Cootamundra and, while he continued to work on the railways, his sons worked the land to support the large family. But life in the bush was not all milk and honey. There were droughts, heatwaves, dust storms, rabbit and locust plagues ... and snakes. One time the family made headlines, even in Sydney, when a large brown snake slithered inside the Weissel home when Edward and his wife were away. Three of the Weissel's dogs leapt in to defend the children as the snake was about to strike them. The dogs killed the snake but not before two of them died in the tussle, one of them a beloved sheep dog Edward took to country shows. A fox terrier was found dead lying on the reptile when the parents returned.

The Weissels, fortunately, escaped most of the wartime backlash and life went on largely as normal, allowing the Weissel children the same opportunities as their peers. Edward's youngest son, Eric, was a sprightly lad who was good at anything he put his hand to. He grew up loving tennis, cycling, cricket and golf, and he was a dab sprinter. At the age of 14, Eric Weissel won the 100 yards boys' championship after the Anzac Day commemoration in Cootamundra.

Despite his all-rounder skills, it looked like Weissel would settle on cricket. When he was 17 he was playing grade with much older players and excelling. 'Dad just loved his cricket,' says his son, Bruce, who lives in Kiama on the New South Wales south coast. At one stage, Weissel held the one-day batting record of 220 runs at the country carnival. At country week, representing Southern Districts on 22 November 1926, Weissel had the most thrilling moment in his cricketing career when he caught and bowled the great Sir Donald Bradman—with whom he shared his birthplace—for 43 at the Sydney Cricket Ground.

Bradman wrote about the moment later in his memoirs: 'The country matches were played every day from Monday to Friday. My highest score was 46, my lowest 21, and I obtained a few wickets. There were such figures as Eric Weissel, who became one of the greatest rugby league five-eighths Australia has known. Weissel's magnificent catch to dismiss me when we played South could hardly have been surpassed.'

Considering his success on the cricket field it was a surprise Weissel would end up choosing rugby league as his preferred sport, especially since he didn't start playing the game until he was 17. But straightaway he demonstrated the skills that would turn him into the complete player: pace, judgement, and excellent hand-eye coordination.

These skills were obvious to all when, in 1921, he first ran on the field as five-eighth for Cootamundra, a club embroiled in various protests over results in the Maher Cup—one of the most hotly contested league challenge cups in Australia, in which whole towns would travel to another town to watch a game. Weissel's fame soon took off. Catholic priest Father John Walsh Morrison, who played as a front-row forward and later refereed Maher Cup matches, said of Weissel: 'As a sportsman there was never anyone better … Weissel was the most elusive and cleanest player I have ever come up against.'

Cootamundra rated Weissel as its most outstanding footballer from 1921 to 1926. Indeed, league observers rated him the best player in the Maher Cup in the 1920s—if not the best ever. By 1923, at age 20, he represented Southern Districts in the annual Country Week competition in Sydney. He was part of several Riverina teams to take on New Zealand and England. In 1924 he excelled, scoring 13 points for Cootamundra as they overran Goulburn in a best-of-the-best Group final. Weissel joined eight district players in Sydney for Country Week. Later that year, the touring English side arrived for a game against a composite Riverina side and Weissel was part of the team that held the English at bay for some time, until they were beaten 31–4 in front of 5000 screaming country fans.

Weissel moved north to Temora in 1927 and became the town's rugby league captain and coach. The next year he married his sweetheart, Margaret Eileen Cashman, whose well-respected parents ran a refreshment store in Cootamundra.

Weissel and Eileen, as she preferred to be known, started their family with their first-born, Betty. Bruce and Jenny soon followed.

At home, as on the football field, Weissel was a gentleman. He enjoyed the odd beer, but never abused the drink. A jack-of-all-trades, he was closely involved with the Church of England and, what with his wonderful voice, he was a stalwart of the church choir. A good, kind person, he never had a punch-up in all his years playing the rugged and heated football typical of Group 9 and the Maher Cup, nor did anyone ever have a bad thing to say of him. He was often seen shaking the hand of an opposition player and even at times giving them advice on how to play. When he travelled to Sydney with his country league teammates he was a father figure to the younger members.

As well as being a devastating runner on the football field—and a master at picking up the ball from the ground while running at high speed—Weissel kicked goals, with either foot, and he could make the ball screw so that he could find touch from the most difficult of angles. These skills were bound to be noticed outside of Maher Cup territory, and it soon proved the case.

Weissel's rise to prominence started in 1928 when he was voted the best player as South-Western Districts took on the English in his former hometown of Cootamundra in May. The English captain, Parkin, described Weissel as 'the greatest player he had ever seen'. Weissel was everywhere on the field and, reported the *Sydney Morning Herald*, 'his passing, his resolute straight running and his ability to seize an opening were excelled only by his remarkable tackling'. Weissel's team stunned the tourists on their first game of the tour, holding them to a 14-all draw. Weissel then gave a man-of-the-match performance in the City versus Country game in Sydney.

Fortune then smiled his way. Western Suburbs player Jerry Brien was selected to play for Australia at five-eighth but was injured in a club game. On the advice of New South Wales members of the national selection body, Queensland selectors agreed to select Weissel to fill Brien's spot for the second Test on 14 July (Australia having lost the first test 15–12 in Brisbane). The *Herald* said the injection of Weissel would bring 'variety' into the Australian attack.

Before his debut as a Kangaroo, Weissel was part of a surprise victory when, with a try and two goals, he engineered Southern Districts' 28–19 beating of Sydney's league leaders, Eastern Suburbs (who later that year went on to contest the 1928 Sydney grand final, which they lost to Souths). The *Herald* celebrated Weissel's performance: 'E. Weissel was easily the outstanding player … [he] proved he is a polished inside back. He stands deep in an ideal position for an outside half so that he can take the ball when moving at high speed. Across the field movement does not appeal to him. The goal line is his objective and he races straight with a slight deceptive swerve past an opponent ready to pass with either hand and to come round again in support. He can kick with either foot and is a clean, hard tackler.'

Ahead of the second Test, one Harry Sunderland wrote in the Brisbane *Courier-Mail* that 'all eyes would be on Weissel' who had already impressed Australian captain Tom Gorman, a Queenslander, and a big Toowoomba mate of Sunderland's.

As Weissel was making his name in the game, Sunderland was re-inventing his after the debacle of the split in the Queensland

Rugby League. His overbearing style angered Queensland players who initially went on strike and then formed the breakaway Brisbane Rugby League in 1922.

The son of an English-born train driver, Sunderland grew up on the agricultural rolling downs outside Brisbane. Born on 23 November 1889 in Gympie, he was the eldest of three children. He went to school in Toowoomba and later worked as a journalist on the *Toowoomba Chronicle*. He was involved in a multitude of sports from swimming to boxing, and he competed in the Australasian Swimming Championships in 1909. At various times he worked as an administrator in the sports of boxing, wrestling, league, cricket and athletics. He bankrolled the Queensland Rugby League (QRL) when it was in strife, before the big split in the 1920s. After a stint in Melbourne working for the *Sun News-Pictorial*, he returned to a re-unified QRL as coach, selector and secretary. His chance to walk the international stage came with his appointment to Australia's peak league body.

Sunderland was never afraid to ask a favour from a mate. When he was pushing for the manager's role with the Kangaroos for their 1921 tour to England, he wrote to his friend J.C. Davis, the editor of sporting newspaper *The Referee*, in Sydney, asking for his help: 'Speaking privately—and not for publication in any way—I am still keen on being appointed as one of the two joint managers of the next Aussie rugby league team to England. If there are any kind words that you can justifiably say regarding me during the cricket season, and my work for the game here, it may help to boost my chances. I am tempted to take the view that modesty is a big handicap rather than a virtue in these matters.'

Sunderland didn't get the job but he did go on tour as league correspondent for the *Sydney Sun*, allowing him to get close to the action, a place he always liked to be. In a later letter he berated the performance of the two appointed managers, S.G. Ball and Billy Cann (both league legends in their own rights), saying they lacked 'the power of inspiration and have not risen to the occasion and made the players a happy family'. Sunderland was all fired up to show how he could run things when he was finally given the nod as a co-manager with Lorne Dargan for the Kangaroos' 1929 tour.

Prior to that tour, however, the enthusiastic Sunderland was secretary of the QRL, as well as chairman of selectors of the national team. Given these dual roles it was perhaps hardly surprising that Sunderland was nearly always at odds with his New South Wales counterparts. He once claimed the league powerbrokers in Sydney didn't know rugby league was played in Australia beyond Parramatta, and that they thought Queensland was 'further away than China'.

Queenslanders, however, featured prominently in the national side, with nearly half the Kangaroos team, including the captain, coming from Queensland sides, including Toowoomba, a town close to Sunderland's heart. While Sunderland had his say, there was no doubt Queensland would have a voice.

Ahead of the second Test against England in 1928 Sunderland believed the game would smash the Test crowd record in Australia (set when an estimated 65,000 people saw the English team play 'Metropolis' in Sydney in 1920), but he lamented that most Tests were a shemozzle, with no proper seating and spectators unable to get a clear view of the action. He said it was terrible for a man of middle age to have to get a tram to Moore Park and then find he has to 'fight his way through thousands at the stiles and then crane his neck to see past the shoulders or over the heads of others who have arrived early with their lunch in a bag ... That is why the football authorities in Australia will have to, before very long, make arrangements for the proper booking of seats as is done at Wembley, Hampden Park, and Twickenham and on the baseball parks of New York and Chicago.'

As it turned out the record wasn't broken, but it was a huge crowd nonetheless—some 44,500 people—particularly in light of the awful weather. If Sunderland, who was short and stocky, thought getting a good view was a problem on a fine day, it became a nightmare on a wet day with a sea of umbrellas unfurled around the circumference of the Sydney Cricket Ground. The tough English forwards outplayed Australia to retain the Ashes, winning 8–0. Due to heavy rain the previous night, the field 'resembled a swamp ... [and] on a swamp, Australia will always be at a disadvantage against England', according to the *Herald*.

Despite the result, and the weather, Weissel was a shining light in the gloom and he was singled out by the *Herald*: 'Weissel made a glorious debut. In defence he was ubiquitous. His ability to kick with either foot saved the side repeatedly, and in attack or defence his punting was judicious. His great run toward the end of the first half, when he chose at the last moment to pass out to Byrne, instead of kicking over Sullivan's head, will be remembered by all who saw it.'

Australia exacted quick revenge a week later when they downed England 21–14 in the third and final Test of the English tour, also played at the Sydney Cricket Ground. Weissel had a good game, in which Australian centre Benny Wearing starred, scoring 12 points, at that time an individual points record. Amazingly, it was Wearing's only Test appearance as he was forever after ignored by the selectors, even though his Sydney club record was outstanding with 173 games, 144 tries and seven premierships for Souths.

Noted by the media, Weissel also impressed the opposition. Later in the year, he was offered more than £6000 to play in England. Remarkably, given the sum, which could have set him up for life, he refused. Bruce Weissel explained his father's reticence to leave his beloved Riverina: 'He just didn't like the city, he loved the country.' Weissel would go to England as a Kangaroo, however, when he was selected to be part of Australia's 1929–30 Ashes quest, a grinding eight-month tour of duty. The Kangaroos' squad at that time included such greats as captain Tom Gorman at centre, second-rower George Treweek, centre Cec 'Dicky' Fifield, and halfback Joe 'Chimpy' Busch. Sunderland, now co-manager of the tourists, described his new five-eighth, Weissel: 'A clever five-eighth from Cootamundra [who] played against the Englishmen in the drawn game there last year. He is a great all round sport, an ironmonger, and was an immediate success in the Test last year, when Australia won the third game. He played well with halfback Busch.'

Kangaroo tours back then were arduous affairs, and not only for those on tour. Weissel's new wife, Eileen, had to stay at home with their newborn, Betty, during Weissel's epic time away. League authorities gave her ten shillings a week as compensation for losing her husband to the business of league. Sunderland, meantime, was paid £100 for the tour and a five pounds a week as his wage as a co-manager, while the players received four pounds, ten shillings a week while on tour.

The mammoth trek took Weissel around the world. With a flotilla of boats in Sydney Harbour to farewell them, the Kangaroos left Sydney on 25 July on the RMS *Aorangi*, a beautiful liner only four years into service. Their first stop was Auckland where they were feted with a motor ride around the city, a visit to the zoo, a banquet and, finally, a night at the theatre.

On their next leg to Suva, Fiji, a few players suffered seasickness, or '*mal de mer*' as Sunderland expressed it, as the seas picked up. Outside of green gills, the players were quick to get involved on the ship, arranging a sports and social committee for all passengers. They were conspicuous as they got about the boat deck in their 'gum green and wattle gold blazers', and after their meals they fast-walked around the deck to keep fit.

Making a further impression on board, the players rehearsed the Kangaroos' war cry, based on an Aboriginal war dance, which started '*Wallee mullara choomaroo tingal*' (loosely translated as, 'We are a race of fighters, descended from the war gods'). Weissel even put together a team choir with Arthur Martin, duly noted by Sunderland who wrote reports on the tour for the *Brisbane Courier*: 'Eric Weissel is a tenor who has helped make all the boys blend in melody,' Sunderland related.

The *Aorangi* docked in Vancouver, Canada, and the tour entourage travelled by train across the breadth of Canada, visiting Niagara Falls along the way. They saw wealth and riches beyond their wildest dreams, firstly through the 12-million-pound bequest to Toronto University from the Massey farm machinery dynasty, which was used to build Hart House in Toronto, and then, when they reached New York, a tour past millionaires' row on Fifth Avenue, which they found to be unsightly because of all the security shields. In New York City they also took a boat trip around Manhattan Island and received a mayoral reception, during which they found Mayor James Walker—who registered instantly with the young

Australians and Sunderland—an impeccable host. The players then boarded the famous Cunard liner, the *Aquitania*, for the last leg of their voyage to England. It was a life of luxury if you travelled with Sunderland.

On arrival in Southampton in late August, the Kangaroos were welcomed by the English Rugby League Council before they were whisked up to Wembley in London—not to watch football or soccer, mind, but greyhound racing. The players were amazed by the antics of the 'tic tac' men who relayed bookmakers' odds with unique hand signals.

Distractions aside, it wasn't long before the ubiquitous Sunderland got down to business with Wembley officials, arranging an Australia versus Wales match to be held at the famous stadium towards the end of the tour. Sunderland was committed to making the tour a financial success. The first Kangaroo tours to England had ended in financial disaster, with some players forced to find work to pay for meals and even afford their way home. As part of a way of preventing such disaster, Sunderland's Kangaroos sometimes performed their famous war cry at special events to earn extra money.

Given the long duration of the tour and inevitable homesickness and grouchiness, Sunderland found it important to establish a settled routine, so the team based itself in Marlborough House in the Midlands township of Ilkley, and travelled by bus to all their various matches. The 1929–30 touring party was considered one of the most bonded in history, something underlined by their motto, 'When we move, we move in a body'.

The bespectacled Sunderland had a unique way of keeping calm in the team. At certain times he would divide the squad by sending some on a mini break, which, he said, built up great camaraderie when they returned to the Kangaroos' fold. By setting up a rotation system among the players he was also going some way to prevent injuries, otherwise inevitable in the hard slog of the Midlands where the grey gloom hung low over the sodden fields.

Sunderland sometimes found time to get away from tour duties himself, visiting air shows and taking a look at a display at the Empire Marketing Board, after which he lamented that Australian produce was being subsumed into English products without due recognition in the branding. He went off to the Selfridges store to verify a rumour that Byron Bay's Norco butter was being sold there. He felt the English butter lacked taste compared to the Australian fare.

Food was a recurring interest, and many players complained about the taste of the meat served on tour. In addition, 'they have also sworn to hang and quarter the man who invented semolina pudding', wrote Sunderland. The Australians did, however, find some fine fare when they were guests of the English prime minister, Ramsay MacDonald, in the gardens at 10 Downing Street in London. MacDonald was Britain's first Labour prime minister and he was keen to show his affection for the Australians and his empathy for the working-man's sport. As such, the Kangaroos were received in the cabinet room. The tourists also met the Prince of Wales, the future King Edward VIII, before their game at Bradford, after Sunderland had made representations to Buckingham Palace. He was even getting the Royals involved with the rugby league phenomenon.

After such attention—and convincing tour wins in their opening five fixtures against Rochdale, York, Batley, Widnes, and Broughton—the 'buoyant' Kangaroos were well buttered up for their first big assignment: the first Test against England on 5 October, at Craven Park, Hull. Brilliant sunshine greeted them on their arrival in Hull the day before the game, setting up perfect conditions for the Australians' running game (although the greyhound racing track and assorted rails around the pitch seemed worryingly close).

Wearing jerseys featuring a large white square on the back (enabling a letter to be attached to denote the player), the Kangaroos ran onto the ground and found themselves immediately on the back foot. But Joe Busch and Weissel then helped engineer two blindside moves that resulted in two tries, with Australia up 8–0 after just eight minutes. Weissel 'tackled like a demon' and his unerring goal kicks put Australia into a strong position early on. Sunderland couldn't hold himself back in his rapture for the performance as the Australians ran away with the game, winning 31–8: 'With the speed of a high-witted cattle dog rounding up cumbersome fat bullocks, Australia's representatives in the first Test ran all around and through England's thirteen with brilliant passing,' Sunderland wrote in the *Brisbane Courier*. Sunderland praised Weissel for his 'ferret-like' ability to stop the English runs around the scrum, while Australia's forwards 'never gave England's rugged men, a heavy six, a moment's respite'.

As the chairman of the England Rugby League praised the Kangaroos for their 'glittering football' the English press lauded the wonderful Australian team, saying the only hope for England in the next two Tests was for wet weather to arrive and slow down the Kangaroos' running game. The *Mail* opined: 'It was a wonderful Australian team, without one weak spot.' *The Daily Telegraph* said Australia's Tom Gorman was the best captain Australia had ever had. *The Manchester Guardian* got in on the love-in declaring, 'The Kangaroos are comparable with any team, amateur or professional, which has ever visited this country.'

Weissel told his son, Bruce, that the playing conditions in England were often treacherous. 'Dad said he played in ankle-deep mud and by the end of the game they were exhausted after having to drag their feet through the slush.' The condition of the fields was added to by an exhaustive schedule, as Australia's 28-man squad had to play every club side in England. Sunderland was always there to guide them along, and offer them relief, arranging day trips to Blackpool to watch the great illuminations by the sea, or a weekend trip to Paris for those not wanted for a tour game.

After thrashing the top club side Hull 35–2, the Kangaroos were confident they could win the next Test. Sunderland had warned them, however, that the tail of the English lion would wag dangerously following the first Test trouncing. Then a severe thunderstorm, just hours before the second Test in Leeds, turned the Headingley ground into a bog. The conditions seemed to give England the edge and with England's stonewall defence and spoiling tactics frustrating Australia they ran out 9–3 winners in a dour match played before 31,000 spectators.

For once, Sunderland was not at the game. In the lead-up he had been in a motor accident and suffered a bad head injury that required 15 stitches. The sore Kangaroos gathered around the bed of an even sorer Sunderland at the Oldham Hospital to tell him of their sad loss. England had regrouped before the second Test, they told him with their heads held low, and devised a way to negate the Aussie game. Observers commented that if England had played football, Australia would have won. But if there was any silver lining for the

Aussies and Sunderland it was the large gate takings of £4719—which had the tour on track to record a profit. (Australia took a large percentage of the gate takings—nearly 70 per cent—as did England when they toured Australia.)

The deciding Ashes Test was played at Station Road in Swinton on 4 January 1930. Some 34,700 fans crammed into the small venue, a ground described by Sunderland as like 'thin ice on a village lake'. On a grey and dreary day, Gorman won the toss for the Australians and after the war cry, the players skipped off to their positions hoping to be the happy holders of the Ashes within 80 minutes. The atmosphere was explosive with such an important trophy on the line.

Neither side were able to dominate and, after Weissel missed a penalty attempt early on, the two sides proceeded to cancel each other out. But the Australians were certainly praiseworthy. 'Gorman's captaincy and leadership was a factor of the game,' the Australian Press Association reported. 'His play was brilliant throughout and not one man shirked his job. The brilliance of Busch, Gorman and [Frank] McMillan was allied to the daring of [Bill] Spencer and [Bill] Shankland, and the cleverness of Weissel and [Cec] Fifield.'

McMillan, Australia's fullback, had a particularly good game and played wonderful football throughout the first half, in which Australia had the run of play. 'Not only did he beat Sullivan [the brilliant English fullback] at distance kicking, but he opened many good moves.'

Unfortunately for Australia, their attempts to break the 0–0 deadlock fell short. Shankland missed two penalty goals in the second half, one of them by mere inches, while Weissel missed another. In the excitement a spectator dropped dead. As the game wound down Gorman exhorted his players to find 'the will to win' and with just two minutes left they appeared to have done just that. From a scrum 20 metres out from the England line, Busch picked up the ball and raced straight through the defence and toward the England try-line. Pursued by England lock Fred Butters, Busch dived for the corner just as Butters collected him. As Busch touched down, the corner flag was taken out. An impassive linesman, Albert Webster, ruled no try.

Busch, however, was adamant he got the ball down before he was bundled into touch, and he told the press as much after the game, supported by all his teammates. Busch also said the referee Bob Robinson had commented, 'Fair try, Australia, but I am overruled.' Australia's Victor Armbruster, however, reckoned the referee said 'tough luck, son'.

In the wild scenes that followed at the end of the game—which ended in an historic 0–0 draw, meaning England had retained the Ashes—McMillan was sent flying in a late tackle. Moments later he was cheered off on the shoulders of the Australian tour party for his fine display. Butters, meantime, was awash with blood after he suffered, in the process of tackling Busch, a big gash to his ear requiring ten stitches. To those observing the game, Butters' injury suggested it was he who had actually hit the corner flag. Either that or he'd collected Busch's boot. *The Yorkshire Post*'s comment on the match spoke of its unrelenting nature: 'To call it a game is a misnomer. War is a more appropriate term.'

Overseeing the incredible game, of course, was the now slightly sore but still irrepressible Harry Sunderland. But the Australian manager hadn't been sitting on the sidelines to watch the match. He'd landed a third job (apart from team co-manager and correspondent for the *Courier*) as a broadcaster for the BBC, which had erected, at no small expense, a temporary eyrie for Sunderland to see the game. From such a vantage point he could see every corner of the field and he had a bird's-eye view of Busch's run for the line.

Accordingly, this was how Sunderland saw the critical incident: 'Busch, after running diagonally towards the corner, around the blind side, evaded Smith and Parkin, and with Sullivan out of position, dived in at the corner, ground the ball about a foot inside the corner post. Almost simultaneously, Butters had dived across at him but Busch had slipped underneath, Butters carried away the corner flag and the ball rolled free from Busch's hand. The touch judge ran down raising his flag and the central referee, Robinson, had no other option than to disregard Busch's touchdown and order a drop out.'

The Australians were furious. Only inches from clinching the Ashes on English soil, the players were torn between being bitter at the touch judge or treating such a mammoth turn of events as just bad luck and following the 'sporting way'. Sunderland added: 'Thousands near enough to see the incident realised what happened and it is with people like these that the Australians will be regarded as the virtual victors, but not the holder of the Ashes.'

With so much controversy over the game there was a sensational move to quickly set up another Test while the Ashes contest gripped the public's imagination. This unscheduled fourth Test would also give the visitors a chance to rectify the disappointment of Swinton. The Swinton game had brought in an additional £4170 at the gate, a record for a Test match in England. On hearing the move for a fourth game, the former chairman of the Northern Union, Harry Waller, wrote to the Rugby League Council accusing it of being beholden to 'mammon' and if a fourth Test went ahead, he said, it would make the Ashes 'worthless'.

(The Northern Union was the original name of the Rugby League Council, but it had been changed after representations, including by Sunderland, that rugby league was a much better term to define the game. Australia played a pivotal role in the adoption of the term 'league'.)

Sunderland doubted the Rugby League Council would approve a fourth Test, although from the English point of view, Sunderland—who'd already scored the extra match against Wales at Wembley—was doing a lot of the pushing. But many were unsure if the Ashes would actually be up for grabs in a fourth match. If Australia won would England hand back the Ashes it thought it had claimed after the third Test?

The fourth Test was approved by the Rugby League Council and scheduled to be played at Rochdale on 15 January. The game attracted 16,000 people and was another grinding tussle. But England received the deciding edge when Fifield was carried off after breaking his fibula. At the time, rugby league had a no-replacements rule meaning Australia went a man down. With Fifield off the pitch, England scored a try, the only points of the game, and won 3–0.

After the game, despite his disappointment, Sunderland was proud of his men and he applauded Gorman's play saying he had joined the lofty heights of league's greatest captains, including Dally Messenger and England's Harold Wagstaff. Weissel also had a marvellous tour, ending as the Kangaroos' highest points scorer. His 127 points, which included five tries and 56 goals, equalled Harold Horder's 1921 tour record.

The Ashes were gone but the tour endured, and it snowed during the last few games, giving many of the tourists their first chance to play in a winter wonderland (but probably not Weissel, who had surely played some Maher Cup games in the snow, especially midwinter games against Tumut).

Australia's final tour match was against Wales at Wembley—where the famous Australian aviator Bert Hinkler took a ceremonial kick-off to start the match. The Kangaroos' 26–16 win allowed the gallant Kangaroos—who had won 24 and drawn two of 35 matches—to leave England as winners. English league officials farewelled them for their long voyage on the steamer *Hobson's Bay* back to Australia, a voyage that would chart a course through the rough seas of the Bay of Biscay, across the Mediterranean, down the Suez Canal, and into the Indian Ocean.

On returning home Sunderland was pleased to inform the players that because of the large gate takings on the tour they would each receive a bonus of £150. 'The Kangaroos have failed in their mission to regain the Ashes,' he wrote in his final piece on the tour for the *Courier*, 'but their effort has been grand and praiseworthy.'

Sunderland was back to his busy best as QRL secretary, putting in place plans to host the England team in two years' time. Weissel, on the other hand, returned to his long-suffering family and life in south-west New South Wales. But if Weissel thought he'd melt quickly back into country football he was in for a rude shock. Events suddenly thrust him into the greatest league controversy of the year.

While Weissel at times appeared to be a shrinking violet, perhaps in order to keep close to his young family, it was his unbelievable skills that kept thrusting him into the public spotlight. He'd stamped his class again when he led Country to a major victory over City, scoring 17 points in the classic 'bushie meets city-slicker' clash. He was then given the honour of captaining his state for the first interstate clash of the year on Saturday, 7 June 1930 in Sydney. But Temora put its foot down, refusing to release him for the game, stating Weissel was needed for a Maher Cup fixture against Canowindra the following day.

Weissel's guarantor, Norman Bland, was a Temora stalwart and told the New South Wales Rugby League (NSWRL) that Weissel would not be available, the small township all but thumbing its nose at the league hierarchy. Bland sent a letter to Sydney explaining in blunt terms the club's stance: 'Please notify selectors that Weissel is not available for selection for city fixtures under instruction of his guarantors at Temora, to whom he is under contract.'

It was a classic battle between country and city powerbrokers, something that had its origins in previous disputes. For Temora, it seemed obvious that to lose their very own Kangaroo player, one of the best in the land, was a terrible blow as they fought to win the Jack Hore Gold Cup, a smaller challenge Cup played for in the Riverina and south-west New South Wales, for the first time. After all, they paid Weissel £150 per season to be their captain and coach. For the state selectors, it seemed obvious they should have one of their best players in the team to take on Queensland. Who, they figured, including a club, could refuse such an honour unless a player was injured or there were extenuating family circumstances?

Bland's letter threw the league hierarchy into uproar. At times, country teams had defied rulings on appeals and the outcomes of games by the Sydney body, but they'd never come across a team refusing to allow a player to play for the state or his country. NSWRL secretary Horrie Miller sent back a letter explaining in no uncertain terms that they expected Weissel to play for his state, and if he did not, he was banned from playing for anyone. 'If Weissel is unavailable he must not play anywhere during the period he would have been away if he had been available.' The league threatened to enforce its ruling if Weissel didn't play.

Weissel, however, was taking Temora's line and not budging himself. By the Wednesday before the clash he'd told the press that he would stick with his promise to play with Temora. He was wanted for an important cup match and wouldn't walk away from his home team. Weissel, the *Herald* reported, was 'feeling the position keenly and [was] very worried about the matter'. Two days before the game there was a breakthrough, albeit after a very direct threat from Sydney. The NSWRL had gone to the opposition, not Temora, and warned it would take sanctions against Canowindra if Weissel played and also prevent the city referee from officiating.

But in an amazing turnaround, a compromise was arranged on the eve of the match. The NSWRL was desperate to have Weissel on the field, knowing he was a big crowd-puller and a big money spinner (at a time when everyone was struggling through the Great Depression). The league decided, on Miller's insistence, that if Weissel played for NSW, it would do everything in its power to get him to the Canowindra match the next day, at no expense to Temora. It seemed as if Temora, not the Sydney league bosses, had won the day.

The interstate clash went ahead with Weissel as captain. In a hard-fought game littered with talented Test players, New South Wales defeated Queensland 16–11. Weissel put his heart into the match and was applauded by commentators for his inspiration on the field. More than 35,000 people—including the new New South Wales governor, Sir Philip Game—turned up at the Royal Agricultural Ground, giving the league the motza it had hoped for. Weissel scored two goals and had a blinder—almost literally when he suffered a blow just above the eye that forced a two-minute stoppage.

No sooner had Weissel finished the game than he was whisked off for the 230-kilometre drive to Canowindra. Sitting in the driver's seat was not a hire car driver but Horrie Miller. What a surprise Temora officials would get when Weissel hopped out of the car with the NSWRL secretary in tow! The pair, accompanied by referee Dinny Murray, drove through horrendous conditions, including snow, during the all-night trip.

But it might have been all for nothing. Unbeknownst to the travellers it had rained all day and into the night on Saturday in Canowindra, leaving the football field 'almost unplayable'. Sand was brought in to spread over the ground to make the surface tractable. A ten-carriage train from Temora packed to the rafters, and 700 cars full of spectators, arrived to swell the crowd at the tiny country field to almost 8000. The Temora players outclassed Canowindra and with Weissel calling the shots—if a little off his game (he missed two simple shots at goal)—Temora had little difficulty in raising the Jack Hore Gold Cup, winning 26–7.

The next interstate clash was set down for the very next day, but Weissel was not even considered for the match, in which New South Wales were totally outplayed by Queensland, losing 25–11. The league had changed its tune and now Weissel would pay the price for his country allegiance.

Weissel was, of course, first choice for five-eighth as the Kangaroos took on a 'Rest of Australia' team set down for Saturday, 14 June. Naturally, this clashed with an 'important' Group 9 game for Temora. Bland again got on the wires to Sydney: 'As happened last week, when he was chosen to play for the state, he will not be available because of a fixture in which his club is engaged on Sunday.'

By this time league authorities at both state and national level had had enough. NSWRL president Jersey Flegg said Weissel would not even be considered for the game. Fred Laws from Queensland was announced as his replacement. Temora attempted to satisfy the league, saying it would do all in its power to get Weissel to the Saturday fixture as long as he could get back for the Sunday match. But the bridges had been burnt and there was no Miller to step into the breach. S.G. 'George' Ball, a father figure of league in Australia, and then vice-president of the Australian Board of Control, and a member of the New South Wales rugby league management committee, said in no uncertain terms that he was sick of the Weissel shenanigans. Referring to the affair he declared he'd 'never seen such a pandering in the history of the league'.

Weissel would be left out in the wilderness, and away from state football, for almost two years. The following year, 1931, in almost exactly the same circumstances, Temora again told the league that Weissel was unavailable, even for a Country Week game. By this time Weissel was not on the selectors' radar despite his prodigious talent (a talent soon recognised by country officials with the creation of the Eric Weissel Gold Cup, still played for today as an under-18 competition in the south-west of New South Wales). So Weissel simply continued his amazing career out in the bush, and after the 41–18 victory of the Group 9 representative team over Group 8 in April, 1932, the *Canberra Times* lauded Weissel's brilliance: 'The game was a triumph for Eric Weissel who figured in practically every scoring movement for his side. In addition to converting seven tries he showed uncanny judgement and exceptional handling.' One famous run Weissel is remembered for was during a Group 9 match in which he beat most of the opposing side, and as he was running to the try-line he ran back up the field to dodge a few more players before finally scoring.

As the English tour loomed it seemed inevitable that representative selectors would turn again to Weissel for his leadership and goal kicking. With no letter from Temora's Norman Bland to poke a stick into the hive, the New South Wales selectors softened their stance on Weissel, and on 16 May 1932, Weissel captained New South Wales against Queensland. The game ended in a draw but it convinced selectors Weissel was ready for another go in the Test arena. And in the first Test, a tough uncompromising affair played in front of a rugby league world-record crowd of 70,000 people at the Sydney Cricket Ground, Australia narrowly lost to England 8–6, with Weissel kicking all of Australia's points.

The second Test in Brisbane—'The Battle of Brisbane' as it would come to be known—would go down as one of the most brutal league games in history. It would also forever embellish Weissel's name in league folklore. Before 26,000 people at the Brisbane Cricket Ground on 18 June 1932, a battle was indeed waged, and the partisan crowd perhaps not surprisingly found fault with the visitors. 'The vocal Brisbane crowd roared themselves hoarse voicing their displeasure at England's tactic of using an extended stiffened arm to the head of their opponents,' one report said.

Harry Sunderland was back on the sidelines, both managing the team and reporting for the media. In the latter role he described the opening of the game: 'Little Ipswich half, Hec Gee, scored for Australia in the first minute, and from then on the players fought bitterly in one of the roughest matches ever staged anywhere. Seventeen stone English forward Joe Thompson, who boasted he had never missed a minute's play in 261 matches, was knocked out in the first scrum and carted from the field. So much for boasting in this game! Trainers stood on the sidelines with buckets of water reviving men as they were knocked out.'

Later, Australian hooker Dan Dempsey broke his right arm, and 'wept' because Sunderland wouldn't let him go back on the field. Hec Gee was then carried off on a stretcher after his lip was split apart and needed stitching. Gee also cried, according to Sunderland, because he couldn't go back on the field. Sunderland said he came down to the sideline where Gee was being cared for by the doctor, and 'the sturdy little half was crying like a child, and pleading to return to the field. He had lost a piece out of his lower lip, and he looked a sad sight. He was rested, however, and then later sent back to join the other mangled men'.

Another report, however, said Sunderland actually ordered Gee to go back on the field as Australia were losing players by the minute. At one stage, Australia could only muster three men for the scrum, while Weissel was forced to go out to the wing. Forward Frank O'Connor's gashed eye needed stitching and English forwards Les White and Martin Hodgson had gashes to their heads. Another one of the English players, Les 'Juicy' Adams, was 'temporarily crippled'. Australian centre Ernie Norman was hit hard in a tackle and walked dazed from the field, leaving at one stage just ten Australians on the field. At various times fights broke out and players had to be separated. Weissel himself succumbed to the hard tackling on the concrete-like surface and was forced to recover on the sidelines. His injury fired up the Australian forwards who became 'particularly torrid in their forward sorties'. Although the crowd obviously heckled the English over the fisticuffs, it appeared no one side could be blamed for the melees with the match characterised by the 'grimness of the play and [the] deadliness of the tackling'.

Spectators went into a frenzy as the game went down to the wire as the English pushed for a winning score near the Australian line. Australia was hanging on grimly leading 10–6 with five minutes to play, when Weissel, who'd only just returned to the field, picked up a dropped ball inside the Australian half and ran limping towards the English line pursued by four players. Weissel's leg had been smashed in a tackle, and he could hardly raise his foot, though he scampered up the ground regardless. The crowd rose in their seats and cheered him on, drowning out a supporter who had been endlessly playing his cornet to the tune of 'Australia Will Be There'. Weissel's game run ended metres from the line when he was tackled, falling face down on the ground. But he was able to rise and play the ball, which ended up in the hands of Gee who dived over the England line to secure victory for Australia, 15–6. The Brisbane crowd hurled hats and seat cushions in the air as wild celebrations ensued.

In setting up the game-clinching try, Weissel had run about 75 yards with an ankle injury, later diagnosed as torn ligaments. 'He had given his last gasp for his side,' wrote Sunderland.

After what had happened during the match it was little wonder Sunderland was amazed that same night to see the Kangaroos (at least those who could walk or weren't in hospital) fraternising with the English players at a dance and reliving the torrid Test like old mates. Both teams went to a jazz evening in Brisbane and later the Carlton Cabaret. 'The most remarkable thing about it all was that the players who were participants, mingled together and laughed and made merry later in the night, as if there had never been any undue spice in the game,' Sunderland wrote.

Weissel's son, Bruce, reflects on the Test that had written his father into league annals forever. He says the injury to his father was taken to further extremes as the years went on—from a broken ankle to a broken leg. 'Eventually some said he ran with a broken ankle, which is ridiculous, you couldn't even possibly run.' In any case, Weissel became forever known as the man who had limped most of the way down the field to set up a courageous victory for Australia.

Courageous as it was, Australia needed to win the third and deciding Test to clinch the Ashes—which they hadn't held since losing the 1921–22 series. But even with Weissel recovering from injury to play, Australia's hopes were dashed again at the Sydney Cricket Ground on 16 July. Weissel did all he could, kicking five goals, but England were too strong, running out 18–13 winners in front of 50,000 people.

The third Test would prove to be Weissel's last hurrah from the representative arena. In March 1933, he said he would not go on the tour of England and would be hanging up his number six jumper. 'He said today that it was the wish of his people that he should not make his trip to England,' the *Townsville Bulletin* reported. 'He considered that if he did not aim to get the trip to England, he should get out of big football, as he was only taking the place of someone else.'

Weissel told the press his family had to come first and he would retire to Maher Cup football and life in the country. Over the rest of his career he played for Barmedman, Narrandera, and eventually the Wagga Magpies. In Wagga, where an oval was named after him, Weissel managed the vacuum oil depot, supplying fuel to the region, and to the airfield during the war years. It later became the Mobil depot. Outside of work, he became involved with the Spastic Centre (now called the Cerebral Palsy Alliance), helping build their residential home, and in later years he pottered in his vegetable garden and made preserves.

But having spent 18 seasons playing football it was hard for Weissel to get it out of his system. Even when coaching—and Weissel coached Country for one year—he couldn't stop his urge to get on the field, and he used to sneak his boots along when accompanying the Magpies in case someone didn't turn up. Sometimes he took to the field well after he'd officially retired. He also kept thinking about the game, and coming up with a few interesting ideas, including asking the referee to feed the scrum, and even doing away with the scrum altogether.

There were few people who didn't know Eric Weissel, even after he'd long retired from the game. In 1972, almost ten years after Weissel's death, the Wagga *Daily Advertiser* held a vote on who was the most famous sportsperson the Riverina had produced. Weissel received 54 per cent of the vote—almost 50 years after he had stopped playing football.

*

Harry Sunderland, meanwhile, continued to be a larger-than-life figure, although eventually that wore a little thin in Australia. He accompanied the Kangaroos on their 1933–34 and 1937–38 tours, again as manager. But by 1937 some of his habits were testing the players' patience. His disciplinary style, exhibited in his habit of blowing a whistle to summon the players together, didn't wash with some. And during the acrimonious 1937 tour the team was divided into the troublesome 'pickles' and the less-disruptive 'spiders'.

Sunderland knew no boundaries. At times he even was known to enter the English dressing room to tell them how the rules should be played. He used a blackboard to coach the players and fined them if they were late for the tour bus. Once, in England, he employed a system of beer bottles to help identify how many minutes were left in the game. The players would look over to the bench to check out how many beer bottles there were and if there were five, it meant five minutes remained in the game. Ray Stehr, the Easts front-row forward, was playing for Australia in 1937 and he blames Sunderland, for losing the first Test in England through a beer bottle mix-up.

'Sunderland did a lot for league, especially in Queensland, where they needed someone with his enterprise,' Stehr once said, 'but by 1937 in England, when he had his third trip as an Australian manager, he had been in power too long. He helped lose us the first Test through an extraordinary mix up with an improvised signalling system. England led 5–4 late in the second half when Australia received a penalty kick just inside halfway. Sunderland was on the sidelines with five beer bottles, which were supposed to indicate the final minutes of the game. When our captain Wally Prigg looked across to see how many bottles were still standing, there was Sunderland jumping up and down and pushing two fingers into the air. Prigg interpreted this as an order to punt high and follow on. England got the ball and kept it and we lost our chance of victory through kicking a penalty goal. "Sundy" later said his two fingers meant there were two minutes left but he didn't explain why he had forgotten about the bottles.'

(Bruce Weissel also said he knew of a few tricks in the era when players were kept in the dark on how much time was left in a match: 'I knew a timekeeper at Werris Creek who used to take his hat off with five minutes to go.')

The 1937–38 tour ended in a massive stand-off between Sunderland and his co-manager, Bob Savage, and the league hierarchy. The league bosses ordered the tourists to return on a boat from France at the end of the tour after their final game in France, to save costs. But Sunderland and Savage dug their heels in and said such a trip would be a logistical nightmare as the players' tour luggage was still in Britain. They decided they would leave from England. Heated cables were exchanged and Savage was sacked during the course of the voyage home.

When the ship arrived home Sunderland refused to shake hands with Jersey Flegg. It was a bitter parting for Sunderland and his Australian supporters. He'd been one of league's great promoters, but in the course of his adventurism he'd collected enemies, some of whom had worked to undermine him on the 1937 tour, pitting Savage against him. Through his journalism he had added great spark and flavour to the game. There was no doubt that a lot of the folklore that grew up around league came out of Sunderland's lively pen. In a sense, he was a man before his time. Although a self-promoter, underneath that broad-barrelled chest was a great love for league and its continuing survival.

After the shifting sands in Sydney, Sunderland took himself overseas. He'd already lined up a job there while on tour and was appointed manager of the English club Wigan in 1939. He also kept up his sports reporting, this time for the London *Daily Mail* and also with the BBC. He moonlighted for other newspapers. But trouble was never far behind. He'd made an extraordinary bid to get Wigan to tour Australia using his old networks, including his old mate and *Referee* journalist J.C. Davis, to make the tour possible. Back then it was unknown for a club to travel so far overseas, but the potential cost of such a venture caused acrimony within the Wigan club.

Sunderland wrote to Davis (a.k.a. 'The Cynic') urging him to get behind the Wigan venture and promote the idea of a World Cup in Australia. 'I need it *now*,' a frustrated Sunderland emphasised. 'I will not need it in the years to come … I need it *now*. If I can make a success in Wigan it will establish me and help me have the goodwill and respect and reputation that will enable me to tackle London and elsewhere. If I fail, well, I never think of failure. But if I have to win without the aid of that invite to tour Australia and have a World Cup in late June and early July of 1939, then I suppose I can still win without the aid or help of the very people who will receive help themselves by helping me, and Wigan, and rugby league football in general, at the present time.'

Sunderland—whose son, Sydney, would go on to become a world leader in neurological studies—told Davis that he was doing well in England as a correspondent for various media outlets and didn't need the Wigan or World Cup ventures to survive. 'I have no need to worry about keeping the wolf from the door. Life has been kind to me, but I do want to see our rugby league game prospering—and doing enterprising things.'

His stint at Wigan was over after just six months and the tour didn't go ahead. But Sunderland continued to live in England, writing about rugby league, until his death on 15 January 1964. The English, who had warmed to him, eventually named a trophy after him, one given to the man-of-the-match in the Super League grand final.

Australian league powerbrokers came to honour him too, awarding the Harry Sunderland Medal to the best player in an Ashes series against England.

Sir Sydney Sunderland would become a great enthusiast for medical research in Australia and hold many senior positions on boards and academies. Harry would have been proud, if not a little jealous, of his son's ability to influence powerbrokers. Like his son, Harry had a keen heart, and very close to his heart was always rugby league.

CHAPTER THREE:
The Maher Cup—Rabbits, floods, fights and fire

Ted Curran was on edge. He was the designated player—the man muscle—to accompany league officials on an 80-kilometre drive east, deep into enemy territory to reclaim the prized Maher Cup.

It was a cold June day in 1955 when, around midday, Curran and his gang rolled into the main street of the cherry capital of Australia. Young, a sweet, tree-lined town nestled in the rolling hills of south-west New South Wales, represented nothing but the pits to the boys from Temora. The dust had never settled on a long-running feud between the towns after an on-field punch-up three decades earlier. As they pulled up outside W.H. Kearney Menswear, one of two places in Young that housed the cup (which was awarded on a challenge basis, like a title belt in boxing), the Temora boys copped some icy stares. Young's football faithful knew exactly why they were in town, and it wasn't to order suits.

Tough Bill Kearney, the town's 'Mr Footy', a long-time player and coach, and a leading Group 9 official, placed his hands firmly atop the shop counter and stared straight at them as the Temora boys strolled in as if they were in a Wild West showdown.

'We've come for the cup,' one of the Temora gang said to Kearney, who was schooled in the art of winning, and was one of the two famous 'wizards' that played in Young's backline in the 1930s and '40s. There was silence all around; you could cut the air with a pair of tailor's scissors.

'I've got too many people to serve. Come back when we close at five,' Kearney said flatly. The Temora boys looked around the shop. No-one was shopping. Anyone there was just eavesdropping to see how the confrontation progressed. Curran stood for a while, thinking. Kearney, he surmised, figured Curran and the boys wouldn't wait around, that they'd head back to Temora. Curran thought carefully about his reply. 'Okay,' he said, 'we'll be back at five, see you then.'

The Temora party whiled away the next several hours in a pub of no cheer, not realising the goings-on that had preceded their journey to Young. Earlier, a Young supporter had stolen the cup from the shelf of the Great Eastern Hotel (where it was housed when it wasn't in the front window at Kearney's) and dumped it in an unknown place. He was disgusted at the New South Wales Rugby League (NSWRL) disputes committee stripping Young of the cup after it upheld a Temora protest (which claimed Young had used an ineligible player in a match between the two towns, won by Young, in May).

The furore surrounding the appeal took the towns' shared hatred to new depths but when emotions cooled, and Ted Curran and crew were on their way to Young to claim the cup, there was a mad rush to find it. The perpetrators, conveniently, had forgotten where they'd dumped it. After a frantic search, it was eventually located in a culvert near the Young Showground, 2 kilometres out of town, glinting in the sun, waiting to be claimed. By the time the Temora posse had pulled into town it was sitting in the shop window at Kearney's, as if nothing had happened.

Young were viewed as the silvertails of the Maher Cup, the Manly of the competition, and were openly despised. And because Young was seen as the Catholic centre of the region, an old Protestant–Catholic friction came into play. 'There is no doubt we hated them,' Curran says. 'Especially the officials.' The feeling was mutual, according to Bill Kearney's son, Bill: 'Nobody liked us … we were always too good.'

The illfeeling was also partly due to Young's capacity to cherrypick talented players from the city and bring them to the country. It wasn't that it was illegal, it was just that Young worked the system the best.

Bill Kearney Sr, who himself had been brought to town on a two pounds, ten shillings wages-and-board deal in 1932, and snubbed a chance to play first grade at North Sydney just because he loved the country, was the main talent finder for Young. He had a direct line to his great old friend Frank 'Chunky' Burge, one of league's all-time great forwards, who had moved to the St George Rugby League Club in the twilight of an amazing career in which he had scored 146 tries in 154 premiership games. Burge had an eye for talent like no-one else.

But back to the Maher Cup showdown where, at the designated time, the Temora boys returned to Kearney's store not knowing if it was a set-up.

'We've come back for the cup, Bill,' Ted announced, while feeling uneasy due to a swelling, and not altogether happy, crowd. Slowly, Bill Kearney emerged and thrust the cup towards Ted's chest. 'Okay, it's yours for now, but not for long.' The crowd bristled with anger as the Temora boys walked back to their car. The prized Maher Cup was theirs; the treasure had been retrieved.

It wasn't as if Temora didn't have form themselves when it came to flouting Maher Cup rules. In 1932, the feisty town refused to hand over the cup to Tumut after a ruling by the league hierarchy. Temora faced expulsion from the competition but their defiance wilted at the critical point, and the cup was given to Tumut—this cup that, over the years, had been thrown in a river, tossed into a drain, plonked on a toilet, kicked down a street, stolen, lost, chained to an anvil, locked in a police cell, and held aloft by thousands and revered in council chambers.

A symbol of pride for the handful of towns that played for it since its inception in 1919, the Maher Cup was 'a religion' says Curran, whose father, an Adelong hotelier (at The Commercial), played Maher Cup before him. It was certainly a bloody, fierce and sometimes crazy football competition. Whole towns set great store by it, travelled to watch it, and players would often ignore a chance to play for New South Wales or Australia to play in the Maher Cup, such was its pulling power and fame.

For most of its early existence, the Maher Cup was played on a Wednesday, and towns would declare a half-day holiday so townsfolk could go along to barrack for their team. The Maher Cup was a golden egg every time it landed in a new location, bringing a quick fortune to local shops and businesses. If it stayed in the one place for a long time the town's coffers swelled enormously week after week until they lost the cup. It wasn't uncommon for up to 6000 people to come and watch a game, and in the early days they'd travel by special trains and horse and sulky, and later on in long lines of cars. And they'd all be hungry and thirsty after long trips.

Teams would do anything to get their best players to a game, even if it meant hiring an aeroplane. In July 1935, supporters of the Young Cherries organised a light plane to get their prized player, James McMenamin, to a Wednesday game at Tumut. McMenamin was the only teacher at a tiny village near Young and he had to get his handful of students packed up and sent home before he could get away. So the train was out of the question. The plane landed on a field near the school, picked McMenamin up and flew him to Tumut in time for the Maher Cup match. But the mammoth and costly effort was all in vain. Tumut defeated Young 5–3 thanks to a try and a goal from Tumut's young Tom Kirk, who two years later would win a premiership with Canterbury in Sydney.

The money kept pouring into the towns during the cup matches. 'Cootamundra took a gate of £600 one day,' says Curran. At another game, Harden grossed £800 at the gate. Maher Cup rules meant the home side took most of the takings, while most players earned just three pounds a game. Sometimes, however, elite players received a sling from punters and bookies for winning, and more often than not they were given free hospitality and goods from small businesses and cafes in their hometown.

Celebrations would go on for days after a win. When Temora won the Maher Cup in June 1924, after Cootamundra had stoically defended it against all comers for one and a half years, the *Sydney Morning Herald* reported the scene at the station when the Temora players returned home: 'As the players emerged from the station, the band played "See the Conquering Hero Comes", and then headed by the band, 100 marched through the street, shouting and cheering and carrying the players shoulder high. It was the biggest night since the celebration of the Armistice.'

Young was renowned for huge victory processions, and brass bands helped welcome back the Maher Cup. In 1934, the *Sydney Morning Herald* reported: 'Scenes of enthusiasm almost without precedence marked the triumphal return home of the Young rugby league team with the Maher Cup, which they had wrested from Barmedman on Wednesday. A procession of cars half a mile long was led by the town band. A dance ensued and the cup was taken to the council chambers where it was filled with champagne and passed around the councillors and players.' A toast was then raised: 'To the Maher Cup, may Young long retain it!'

In 1927, a St George league official travelled to the south-west of New South Wales to see how rugby league was progressing and was stunned by the enthusiasm for the game. Joe McGraw wrote in the *Rugby League News* in August of that year: 'If only we could get the spirit of self-sacrifice so pronounced in country football into district football.'

McGraw met one player who had travelled 168 miles by car and train in one day to play a game. 'Through lonely trackless country, many of these young men travel these long distances by car, or sulky, or horseback, or bike, to play their strenuous game, and strenuous it is on these tough hard grounds in a particularly dry season,' he wrote. 'And then [they] return alone stiff and sore, and sometimes defeated, in the blackness of the night. That they should be stiff and sore is hardly to their discredit. These country players—especially in the real outback—do not play regularly, and their training is mostly done behind the plough or the poison cart.'

A lot of the towns were just tiny dots on the map but they could muster as much football strength as the bigger towns. Who would have heard of Barmedman or Murrumburrah (a twin town with Harden), except for the fame delivered to them by the Maher Cup?

Although some towns drifted in and out of the competition, the main combatants for the Maher Cup were Tumut, Gundagai, Temora, Barmedman, Harden-Murrumburrah, West Wyalong, Cootamundra, Junee, Young, Grenfell, Cowra and Boorowa, and in the early and later years, Wagga.

The cup challenge was the brainchild of Tumut's Wynyard Hotel publican, Ted Maher. He travelled to Sydney where a friend showed him two silver cups, destined for Sydney league competitions, both of which didn't have a lid. Maher bought one of them and originally offered it as a trophy for a rugby union contest in 1919, but within two years, as league became predominant, it was turned into a league challenge trophy. Maher set down stringent residential rules for players and set out how teams should challenge and when they should play—never on a Sunday. The cup cost 15 guineas to make and, although not large or particularly ornate, it had a wonderful lustre and fine handles. It became adored, lusted after, bringing out both the best and worst in the people of the towns who vied to hold it.

By 1927, the Maher Cup was given its own song, penned by W.H. Howard, with music for piano accordion. In the lyrics, Howard made play with the fact that it was a cup with no lid:

> It's the Maher Cup and it's the star cup;
> Though they're calling it the Old Tin Pot;
> For she doesn't wear a lid;
> The Old Girl never did.

While Howard, in his song, encouraged teams to play fair and play 'rugby league as best you can', the Maher Cup was never far away from controversy and people losing their lids.

'The competition was held up all the time by protests; there were a lot of protests, the silly buggers,' says Curran who, of course, benefitted when a protest by Temora resulted in them being awarded the Maher Cup. Sometimes teams would lodge a protest based on the smallest details, from claiming a touch judge was ineligible, to saying a match report had not been properly signed.

Such desperate pettiness came out early in the cup's history and never stopped. Because of the stringent rules there were many protests for the tiniest indiscretions. The Maher Cup rule was even changed to isolate Gundagai in 1927. Gundagai's response, printed in their paper, was 'Who cares?' and they threatened to start a rival cup competition. Of course, Gundagai quickly returned to the Maher Cup mix. It was the Maher Cup or nothing.

By the late 1920s, Cootamundra had enjoyed a remarkable period of domination after it wrested the cup from Tumut in 1922. At one stage, Cootamundra had the audacity to make a ruling that gave it the right to challenge for the Maher Cup, no matter who held it, at the start and end of the season. As head of Group 9, and now the Maher Cup holder, Cootamundra were able to change the rules to suit themselves. According to Author John Madigan in his history of the Maher Cup and Tumut, 'The cup had become [Cootamundra's] property and was put back into competition under their own rules which gave them the right to first and last game each year and if beaten the right to claim a new draw.'

In the four years to 1926, Cootamundra were victorious in 40 Maher Cup matches, losing only three games. In that period they amassed 651 points, with only 231 scored against them. The Maher Cup had essentially put Cootamundra on the map (well, beyond it being known as the birthplace of Bradman), and brought it a localised level of fame and fortune. While Cootamundra attracted the ire of its Maher Cup competitors, it was a golden era in league and for the town's progress. The Cootamundra council derived large receipts from the Maher Cup games and the football club also gave large donations to fund the expansion of Cootamundra Hospital. Maher Cup pennies also brought great power. It seemed fortuitous, if not ultimately dangerous, for Cootamundra to be the overseer of cup disputes.

It wasn't long before the system ran into trouble as the first protests were fired in by aggrieved clubs. The Cootamundra club was accused of cheating by Junee and Barmedman in August 1929. Junee claimed Cootamundra had used a player called Phillips who did not have clearance from his old club, Cowra, to play in the Maher Cup for Cootamundra. Cootamundra claimed Phillips, originally from 'Coota', was never granted clearance to play for Cowra and therefore didn't need permission to play for his old team Cootamundra. Junee and Barmedman then countered, saying that if that was so then Phillips had also not met the residential rule of living in a town for one month before being able to play for a town. Of course, Cootamundra, after hearing the appeal, rejected it, but

Junee weren't taking the decision of a virtual kangaroo court that easily. Junee appealed to the NSWRL disputes committee in Sydney, which ruled Cootamundra had acted illegally. The Sydney bosses also disqualified Phillips for a year.

Cootamundra's response was to immediately thumb its nose at the rulers of the league. The Cootamundra secretary of Group 9, Glen Evans, declared: 'As far as we are concerned, [the] New South Wales Rugby League does not exist. We intend to control the matter ourselves and we shall not take any notice of the decision of the league in Sydney.'

It was an incredible display of brinkmanship. Loyalty to the Maher Cup was threatening to split the administration of rugby league in New South Wales. The Maher Cup competition was postponed for a month while the dispute was resolved. After the serving of letters of demand and intense negotiations, the Cootamundra Rugby League Club was eventually brought to heel, allowing the competition to continue, but it then appealed to the disputes committee over the initial protest ruling. The league upheld Phillips' disqualification and again upheld Junee and Barmedman's appeal, meaning Junee would get the Maher Cup. In the wash-up, the Cootamundra committee was thrown out. Cootamundra's defence had failed and it was on again for young and old with the thrust and parry of the Maher Cup competition.

The Maher Cup brought out a host of sins, such as jealousy, rage, boastfulness, lust, covetousness. Fitting, then, that several priests volunteered to act as referees over this heady mix of emotions. One of the famous priest referees was Father John Morrison. Father Morrison had played for Young from 1933 to 1937 as a front-row forward and later on the wing. Young had the holiest of rugby league teams when Father Morrison played alongside a Presbyterian minister, Dudley Leggett. According to the author of one of the Maher Cup histories, Maurice 'Sinbad' Sheehan, Father Morrison was known to last the full 80 minutes of play without showing the least bit of wilting, and he always showed great sportsmanship in the game, as to be expected from a man of the cloth.

But in his refereeing period later in the '50s, he found he could not maintain a level playing field when it came to his rulings. Ted Curran remembers that in one game between Temora and Young, Father Morrison, who was officiating, was prepared to look the other way to allow a little retribution. 'Bobby Sullivan (who played for Australia) was our coach and player and he got hit late in the tackle,' remembers Ted, 'and all Father Morrison said was "you've been looking for that all day son".'

Nevyl Hand of Gundagai came across Father Morrison one day before the game with the priest-cum-referee eager to get something off his chest. 'Oh, Nevyl, that try that I disallowed the other day, I think, after a lot of consideration, that was a fair try,' Father Morrison told him.

Nevyl Hand replied: 'Father, it's too late to go to confession now.'

Temora player Lionel Wheatley was also dumbfounded when Father Morrison sent him from the field for swearing. 'All he had mumbled was something like "Oh shit",' Ted Curran recalls.

While Father Morrison's presence on the field helped keep a degree of decorum, it was not unknown for matches to descend into rioting among the crowd. The competition was of a very high standard but at times games descended into farce. There were a number of brutish incidents and all-in brawls during the cup's history. Sometimes the brawls involved not just players but spectators and officials. In a 1954 game between Young and Cootamundra the referee was knocked unconscious during a melee that involved officials and players.

Accordingly, police sometimes had to give warnings to players before a game—and once they even put the Maher Cup in a police cell, while a dispute over who had won the match was sorted out. In 1929, a Wagga police inspector addressed Junee and Cootamundra players on the field and warned them that while he understood there was good deal of feeling between the teams, he did not want any fighting. 'Otherwise you will know I am here,' he said.

A riot occurred in August 1931, when Young played Temora at Young. While Temora set about winning 25–10 on the field, its supporters proceeded to lose their heads in the stands as melees broke out amid chants of 'bash 'em and eat 'em'. It was alleged one Temora player chewed a small chunk out of a Young player, obviously taking the crowd's advice too literally. The player, R. Maker, was ordered off the field. It was then that a Temora fan ran onto the field and bit a Young player, sparking pandemonium on the field. Police and officials tried vainly to bring an end to the riot.

A repeat of the violence seemed on the cards when Young earned the right to challenge Temora at the next Maher Cup match and thousands of people turned up at Temora to watch. A police sergeant walked onto the field before the game and warned the players that 'the public pays to watch football, not fighting'. Perhaps his words got through. Temora won again, but this time there was no outbreak of violence—or biting.

Young were again at the centre of an ugly incident after their game against Gundagai in 1952. It was claimed that after the full-time bell, several Young players 'lost all reason' and started thumping into the Gundagai players. Gundagai's Nevyl Hand was thrown to the ground and according to *The Gundagai Independent*, 'Two Young players who had now gone berserk, went into Hand with a will, and while he lay on the ground they punched him here, there and everywhere.' Another Gundagai player was reportedly king-hit and then the crowd swarmed onto the ground and started their own fights.

But Maher Cup scandals were not just about violence as we've seen. There was an account of someone trying to bribe a referee, while another hullabaloo occurred when it was alleged a player lived outside the required residential zone in his hometown. It seemed that the offending team moved a mileage post further afield so that it appeared the player qualified for selection but the opposition team got wind of it and protested.

Not only did the possession of the Maher Cup bring a motza to any town that held it, punters everywhere bet on the outcomes of the matches, including players. Big bets were commonplace between individuals. In Harden, two local businessmen were known to bet up to a thousand dollars a game in the late '60s. In the same era, such was the pulling power of the game, all 'SP bookies' closed at a quarter to three and refused to take any more bets so they could go and watch the game.

In one instance, when West Wyalong defeated Young, it was claimed the townsfolk of Young were wiped out for two weeks because they had wagered so much money on their team.

With the involvement of big bets there were many curious decisions made on the field. In a game Ted Curran remembers, player Len Haskins fell heavily on the ground for Temora against Gundagai in 1952, and then in the same movement placed the ball over the line for a try. He then collapsed. The referee ruled 'no try'. 'We all went up and said, "Hey, ref, that's a fair try,"' says Curran. The ref replied: 'You can't score a try when unconscious.' Gundagai won the cup match 10–6.

In a Temora home game against Tumut, the Tumut scrum-half was having trouble getting the ball into the scrum and turned to the referee and declared, 'You put the fucking thing in.' The referee accepted the offer. Temora won the ball and went off to score a try. All from a referee's feed.

In another unusual result on 1 June 1963, Harden, playing at home, defeated Tumut 4–3 after Tumut led 3–0 with seconds to go. In fact, Harden scored two penalty goals after the full-time siren. Harden forward Tom 'Bristles' Apps (called Bristles, he once said, because of the shocking haircuts his father used to give him as a child, while others say it was more to do with his playing sensitivities) said the first penalty was awarded when a Tumut player caught the ball after it was kicked and just fell on the ground. The referee ruled it was a voluntary tackle, therefore illegal, and awarded a penalty right in front of the posts. After the penalty was converted, and play continued despite time being up, another Tumut player did the same stupid thing, and Harden were given another penalty, which was also converted. So in a manner of speaking, Harden won the game, *after* the game.

A huge row unfolded and, according to Apps, one bloke was 'skittled' in the melee of the players and fans. Referee Mick Jones from Young had to be shielded from the wild crowd as the disgruntled Tumut spectators vented their anger before starting their long trip home.

Another referee-related row erupted when Gundagai took the Maher Cup off Cowra in 1951, when even Gundagai players agreed they didn't win the game legitimately. The two teams were neck and neck and at the end of the game Cowra's five-eighth, Jack Cudmore, drop-kicked the ball for what should have been the field goal. Player Bill Peterson was standing next to Cudmore and said he could plainly see the ball sail through the middle of the posts. 'I was stunned when the referee ruled no goal,' said Peterson. Also during the game, Cowra looked likely to score but when the crowd surged forward the linesman ran onto the field and stopped the play.

Patrick 'Scoop' Sullivan, from Gundagai, witnessed the Cowra incident as an older boy: 'At game's end a female fan attacked Rouse Boyton (the touch judge) with an umbrella and the biggest brawl I have ever seen was on. It seemed to my 11-year-old eyes that some 832 people were involved, but perhaps it was only 823.'

Sullivan's uncle Jim, a Group 9 president, and a friend of the referee, Max Ibbotson, had to pick Ibbotson up for the ride south back to Gundagai. He retrieved Ibbotson from the back of a Cowra pub, where he had been in hiding, and drove out of Cowra with a police escort as wild fans hurled abuse and missiles at their car.

'Such was the fanaticism which the Maher Cup inspired, normally sane and respectable citizens became foaming-at-the-mouth ratbags,' says Sullivan, who also witnessed a bitter fight on 2 July 1960 when Harden-Murrumburrah were finally defeated (by Tumut, 8–4) after holding the Maher Cup for almost two years. Sullivan, the owner of *The Gundagai Independent*, wrote about the scenes of both anger and jubilation that Harden-Murrumburrah had finally been defeated: 'Led by a mob of screaming women, a crowd of [Harden-Murrumburrah] supporters rushed in on John Livermore, the referee, after the game, hurling abuse and threats at him and the touch judges. One female screamed and ranted and cursed with such vehemence that it looked as if she would lead a mass of disgruntled supporters into action against the men in white ... Four police were needed to escort the officials safely from the ground.'

'There was a bit of a blue, but I don't remember it that bad,' Apps says of Sullivan's description of the end of this great era for Harden-Murrumburrah. 'All I remember was that Bronc Jones was the game-winner for Tumut with two fine goals. I suppose our run had to eventually finish.'

That moment in Maher Cup history was the end of the most momentous run of any team. Harden-Murrumburrah had held off all challengers for a mammoth 29 games, starting in late 1958 and running right through to mid-season 1960, breaking Gundagai's 24-game victory streak set in 1951–52. For a whole year in 1959 no team could wrest the cup from Harden's hardened hands.

But there was a secret motivation that encouraged Harden-Murrumburrah to stay on its winning way, and it all came down to the joys of a post-match amber fluid. 'We always ran in the direction of the pub in the second half; that's what gave us our incentive,' Apps reveals. 'The pub was everything, it was where we changed, where everyone went after the game and where everyone celebrated.' On a Maher Cup game day you couldn't get into the Carrington Hotel in Harden it was so packed. Unless you were a player, of course. In that case you had priority entry.

It was an amazing feat for the Harden players to keep their winning momentum particularly since, by this time,

Maher Cup matches were played on a Saturday, meaning the battered, bruised and emotionally exhausted players would have to back up the following day to play in the regular Group 9 competition.

Apps, who played in the front row, said Harden achieved their amazing run with only a pool of 15 to 16 players to draw upon. During their unbeaten run in 1959, three players scored more than 100 points for the season, while their famous goal kicker Bernie Nevin scored 136 points in Maher Cup games alone, breaking the record established by Tom Kirk.

Nevin, according to his old teammate Eric Kuhn, was one of the toughest players to play Maher Cup. Kuhn remembers him playing Maher Cup on a Saturday, going out to celebrate most of Saturday night, and then backing up for Sunday's Group 9 game and playing a blinder. Once, against Temora, he was carried from the field and put in the back of an ambulance and treated for almost five minutes. A doctor told him he'd have to stay for observation, but Nevin refused, broke out of the ambulance and raced back on the football field and continued playing. He later went on to have a few games with Newtown in Sydney.

The most tumultuous game during Harden's amazing run was against West Wyalong on 22 August 1959 when the referee awarded the game to Harden-Murrumburrah because, after a couple of contentious first-half incidents, West Wyalong failed to kick off. The game had descended into acrimony and farce after West Wyalong's centre and captain, Col 'Stiffy' Ratcliff, was sent from the field for allegedly kicking Harden star Bernie Nevin, who required ambulance treatment. But as Ratcliff received his marching orders, West Wyalong officials, believing an injustice had been done, urged all their players to leave the field.

Ratcliff says he then walked back onto the field to apologise to the Harden captain, Matt Grenfell, saying the kick to Nevin was an accident. He then tried to persuade his teammates to play on. Suddenly West Wyalong's Ron Cooper rushed at Harden's J. Dowd and 'flattened him'. As Cooper was then sent off himself, the West Wyalong officials again told their players to leave the field. They never did that but nor did they rejoin the match and the game was abandoned two minutes before half-time, with no-one sure what the outcome would be.

Ratcliff remembers the day vividly and the incident has stalked his very successful career in league. He says he was eventually, and much to his astonishment, escorted from the field by a policeman. He remembers too how the on-field row slowly grew worse and worse, but Ratcliff says it was all to do with a tragic misunderstanding. Ratcliff was renowned for his distinct running style, his legs moving like the wheel rods on a steam locomotive, his knees punching high in the air. When Nevin came running in to tackle him, he copped Ratcliff's knee square on the jaw and was promptly knocked out. The original accusation, however, was that Nevin had been knocked out because Ratcliff had kicked him while he was on the ground. As players milled around accusing Ratcliff of dirty tactics, everyone's blood was boiling. The crowd erupted as Ratcliff protested his innocence.

'I apologised to [Nevin] as soon as he came to … There was no way I was trying to kick anyone. I would never kick a man,' says Ratcliff. 'I didn't do anything but run hard. Bernie was a big strong bastard and he was just unfortunate to cop a knock as he ran in. He tried to tackle me and got knocked out.'

Ratcliff said the incident was overplayed. 'Bernie and I were great mates and he's a lovely bloke and I apologised to him. But then suddenly the linesman came running on and he reports me to the referee, claiming I kicked Bernie intentionally. I protested and said "no way". But the referee told me to go off, while my officials said to bring the other players off the field. The next thing I know I'm escorted off by the police. It was one hell of a day I'll tell you.'

Ratcliff was one of the Maher Cup's great characters, a tough centre feared by opponents because of his strength. Some even ran into the crowd to avoid being tackled by him. He was born and bred in West Wyalong on a farm 20 miles out of town and could carry more than his weight in wheat bags. He was working as an apprentice motor mechanic when he was asked if he'd like to be in a game of rugby league between West Wyalong's shop assistants and a West Wyalong high school team. He was 19 and had hardly touched a football in his life. He played in the forwards that day and impressed everyone with his abilities as the 'shoppies' ran over the students. His league career was launched.

Before long, Ratcliff had secured a spot in West Wyalong's first-grade side for the 1951 season. When he started Group 9 and Maher Cup football he was just 20 and already weighed 14-and-a-half stone. He moved to the wing for most of the year, while in his spare time worked on his fitness, with sprints and weights at home. West Wyalong held the Maher Cup for the first two matches of 1951, but their season wilted away after that.

In one of his games, Ratcliff came to the attention of talent scout Keith Moses from Sydney's Western Suburbs, who offered the young country kid a trial. Ratcliff says he originally went to Sydney just to check out his mate's new Holden, but an offer to play in Sydney was obviously a carrot too good for a young man to refuse. Moses was leading Ratcliff to league's promised land and Ratcliff wouldn't disappoint the faith placed in him. Just two years after starting the league caper he was on his way to securing a fourth Sydney premiership for the Magpies, surrounded by the cream of the Kangaroos team including Keith Holman, Arthur Collinson and Frank Stanmore.

Ratcliff's first game in the big smoke was a blinder. *The Sunday Herald* of 30 March 1952 reported: 'Western Suburbs' new centre Colin Ratcliff starred in his team's 31–30 win over St George at Kogarah yesterday. Ratcliff scored three grand tries in his first grade debut.' Two of his tries were scored within minutes of each other, one of them a darting run from midfield to score in the corner. Wests went from strength to strength under the guidance of coach Tom McMahon and, after taking the minor premiership, they won the grand final 22–12 over Souths, who were controversially hammered 15–4 in the penalties by referee George Bishop.

Ratcliff made the City firsts side and found himself playing against some of his old Maher Cup combatants in the City versus Country match. But fortunes turned quickly. His father became gravely ill, and he returned to West Wyalong to help his family.

After winning the Sydney competition and hitting the heights of league he was back in West Wyalong as a player and coach, though ironically earning 15 pounds a week, just as much as he did while playing with Wests. Later on, in 1957, Ratcliff moved to Griffith after a big transfer offer he couldn't refuse. The move saw him win the Clayton Cup when Griffith hammered Temora at Temora. He retired from football in 1960 and set up shop as a butcher in West Wyalong, carving up meat rather than the opposition.

*

In Maher Cup territory, living out in the sticks didn't mean you were living away from the wide world of league. During his playing career in the bush, Ratcliff, representing the Riverina team, played France at Narrandera and Wagga, England at Wagga and Leeton, and New Zealand three times in the country. The international visitors could be assured of a stern contest. Harden coach Harry Melville, who played for St George between 1949 and 1957, years when the team won three premierships, once vowed after a tough Maher Cup season, 'I don't want to come back here, this is the toughest football ever.'

The Maher Cup competition was constantly refreshed by top city players moving to play in the country, or just great country players who returned after a city career. Over the years, Gundagai could boast almost two teams of Kangaroos. In the early 1950s, Boorowa boasted the Australian front row, including forward Bryan Orrock and hooker Ernie Hammerton, both South Sydney first-grade players. Earlier, Boorowa boasted another Kangaroo hooker, George Watt. He was a two-time Balmain grand finalist before he went to Boorowa. He then moved from the small town straight to England where he captained the famous English league club Hull in 1948.

One of the most unusual league transfers was that of Welshman Ben Gronow, who went from being a dual international (in rugby union and league) to playing for Grenfell in 1926. Kangaroos team manager Harry Sunderland had approached Gronow about transferring while Australia was touring England in 1925. But instead of heading to a major city club, Gronow picked out Grenfell. His first game was against Caragabal, a tiny speck on the map. Gronow, who stood 1.8 metres tall, had had the honour of making the first kick on the new Twickenham rugby union ground in 1910 in London. So there he was, from hallowed English turf to running among the dusty, rabbit-burrowed fields on the slopes of south-west New South Wales. During one match, Gronow was part of the Grenfell team that defeated league's famous foundation club, Souths.

Kangaroo and Souths legend Clem Kennedy was another attracted to the country by good pay, work and free accommodation. Kennedy helped win the Maher Cup for Grenfell for the first time in August 1950, and then helped retain the cup against the next three challengers.

Tom Kirk, one of Australia's top goal kickers, started his career in Tumut as a fullback. He played Maher Cup before joining Canterbury—for whom he kicked four goals in their first premiership win, in 1938—then Newtown, and later North Sydney. He returned to the Maher Cup fold after his Sydney stint and coached Temora, helping them win the Clayton Cup, awarded to the best New South Wales country team of the year. And one of the best-ever Maher Cup players, Kangaroo Eric Weissel, refused every offer to leave the country.

Barrackers also made their mark in Maher Cup history. Young's secret weapon was Dulcie Caldwell who would often race onto the field wielding an umbrella to smack the head of any try-scorer from the opposition team. She wasn't the only umbrella-wielding fan. In 1951, when Gundagai challenged Cowra for the cup, a field goal attempt by Cowra's captain, Jack Cudmore, was disallowed by the referee after one touch judge raised his flag and the other one held down his flag, saying it wasn't a goal. A Cowra fan ran onto the field and started attacking the recalcitrant touch judge with a brolly.

Gundagai also produced a secret weapon. Dudley Casnave became a legend in town when, in the 1940s, as Gundagai were defending the cup against Wyalong, he stormed onto the field in a large army coat to tackle the West Wyalong winger Clive Lemon just as he was about to score a try. In addition to Dulcie Caldwell, there was also a number of famous female barrackers. The McGrath sisters from Harden and the Guthrie women from Junee were the type of supporters not to be messed with.

The elements, and animals, have also played their part in the Maher Cup. In 1929, the game between Cootamundra and Barmedman was played during a rabbit plague, with rabbits running in between the players during the match. At Gundagai, on 7 June 1952, a branch of the Murrumbidgee River rose ferociously as a Maher Cup match between Gundagai and Young was underway. Panic set in as about 4000 people appeared likely to be stranded or washed into the floodwaters. They had every reason to be worried. Gundagai was the scene of one of Australia's worst mass drownings when a flood in 1852 killed more than 80 people.

'Scoop' Sullivan was there as the waters rose higher and higher and the locals raced off to get trucks to ferry people through the rising waters. Back and forth they went for over half an hour, saving the day. However, many of the fans refused to leave as the game carried on, even though the area around Anzac Park was slowly being submerged. 'Eventually a pontoon bridge made of drums and planks had to be hastily thrown up to get an estimated 4000 fans over the murky waters,' Sullivan remembers. He says some 'idiots' dived into the maelstrom to get out, but fortunately no one was drowned. Gundagai won the game 19–12.

That wasn't the extent of the mayhem. In one Maher Cup game the match was running so late (because a politician was allowed to make a speech at half-time) that spectators were forced to light the grass around the field so the players could see where they were running. In Tumut, on 7 August 1965, in a match between Tumut and Grenfell, several centimetres of snow fell on the field before the Maher Cup challenge. Snow had fallen all Friday night and Saturday morning before the game. The Grenfell team refused to call off the match because they had travelled so far to get to Tumut, unaware of what conditions they were about to face. The game went ahead and it wasn't long before the field looked like a scene from the Somme battlefield. Hot soup was served at half-time to the players to warm them up. Tumut were winning handsomely and everyone readily agreed to abandon the match halfway through the second half as the thermometer refused to rise above zero degrees Celsius. Tumut were declared the winners 15–0 despite the shortened game, with Grenfell ruing their decision to play and vowing never again to play in the snow.

When the Maher Cup competition petered to its close in 1971 it was fitting that Tumut, the original holders, would win the last game and hold the cup forever. The lust to hold the cup had waned. A split in Group 9 in 1966 had seen the formation of a breakaway rugby league competition, the Murrumbidgee Rugby League, and it took some time for the dust to settle. New teams joined Group 9 that weren't part of the original Maher fervour. Tumut was part of the breakaway mob.

Time, lack of money and dying enthusiasm meant the Maher Cup had lost its lustre, with only a handful of teams bothering even to make a challenge. (Only teams that were in Group 9 could play for the Maher Cup.) West Wyalong held the cup for two years in 1967 and 1968, playing just ten challengers. When Tumut re-entered Group 9 after a peace deal, it sets its sights on reclaiming the cup for good. Luckily, Tumut's timing was perfect. Their team hit a high point in 1970, and in 1971 Tumut would win every Group 9 game except, forlornly, the grand final. Nevertheless, they were still in great shape for a tilt at the Maher Cup.

Although no-one really knew it at the time, when Tumut ran onto Alfred Oval in Young on 5 June 1971 it would be the last time the 'old tin pot' would be played for. In the week before the match Tumut's coach, John Hobby, had geed up his players, suggesting this would be the last time the Maher Cup was contested. Would it be possible for the cup to return to its original home, a most unlikely outcome after more than 50 years of battles?

Terry Sturt, a second-rower, was part of the Tumut team given the nervous task of bringing the cup back home. He remembers at school that all he wanted to do was play Maher Cup football, an ambition common to so many young male students. The young lads used to watch the Maher Cup players training at the Tumut sportsground and idolised them and dreamed of one day running onto the field for the Tumut Blues. Sturt's time came, although because of the waning in interest he would only play in seven Maher Cup matches. But he was playing in the most profound one—the last one.

Most of Tumut had travelled to Young to watch the match, with the whole business district closing early so people could travel to the game. 'We had a good coach and if you weren't performing he'd give you a dig in the ribs,' says Sturt. 'There was quite a bit of feeling in the game and Young had a number of players who loved to play the game hard.'

After an even start to the game Tumut soon ran away with it, winning 43–4, with Young unable to penetrate Tumut's stoic defence. Sturt scored a try, as did Ray Beaven, who had scored on the same ground exactly ten years earlier. (Beaven was a stalwart, having been selected to play for New South Wales straight from the Tumut side. He also played for Easts and Canterbury and toured with the Kangaroo side to New Zealand.) Tumut fans went wild, and as the Maher Cup was taken back to Tumut people waited in the streets to cheer it home.

The Blues were dropped off at the Old Tumut River Bridge and they walked up Wynyard Street with hundreds of people lining the way. The boys ended up at the Wynyard Hotel and each one of them had to get up on the bar and sink a cup full of beer as the cheers and celebrations went on well into the night. Not only had the cup returned to Tumut, it had also returned to the Wynyard Hotel, where its former publican, Ted Maher, all those years ago, had thrown open the idea of a challenge cup.

The Maher Cup now sits in a glass cabinet in the main hall of the Tumut RSL Club, engulfed by other league memorabilia. Its battered form almost shrinks among the big banners, shields and recent victories of the Tumut Blues. Its finely engraved insignia features only three words: 'The winner is …' But the winners' names were never engraved, as there would never have been enough room to enter all the victors on such a small vessel.

In any case, the winners were not just the teams that held the cup aloft, but all the players and townsfolk and officials who engaged in the battle for the cherished prize. History would show that their victory was the great memories they held close like a football; memories of fierce battles, controversies, of braving the elements, of raging and celebrating. Legends were created over this small tin pot, worth just 15 guineas, yet it was one of the hardiest and most famous sporting trophies ever to exist in Australia.

The Maher Cup song:

Yes the Maher Cup is the Star Cup;
For frills and thrills and spills she tops the lot;
Yes the Maher Cup, she is the Star Cup
It's her name that fans the game red hot
And as the ball is kicked and passed
The rival teams play fast
In a fashion that's not easily forgot
Gives a man a dizzy whirl, dizzier than the dizziest girl.
When hometown wins the Old Tin Pot. Good shot!

CHAPTER FOUR:
Tom Kirk—Making every post a winner

PART ONE: FROM THE STICKS TO KING OF THE CITY

The town where goal kicker Tom Kirk grew up has been punted from the passage of time. If it wasn't for historical maps, or the dying memories of a generation, it's a fair chance no-one would know that a place called Shepardstown ever existed.

There are still signs, however, in the hills of south-west New South Wales, of the remnants of the human struggle at Shepardstown, evidence of fortunes sought, like raised little hills of old mine workings, gouges in the ground left from old dredges, and odd channels where miners diverted the creek, wishing somehow that gold would wash straight into their laps. It's all gone quiet now. Willows cling to the scarred banks, cows are so engrossed in the lush pasture they won't bother to raise their heads, while the crispiest Granny Smith apples grow in the orchards on the slopes. The once-bustling township is a sleepy hollow again.

It's hard to imagine there were thousands of people living along the Adelong Creek on top of each other in small pise huts (made of rammed earth and tin roofs), with large families surviving on their wits, and the meat of rabbits and hares. The town grew after American fossicker A.D. Shepard discovered gold there in 1871. In his first year, Shepard took £500 worth of gold, and by the time he cut out of the mining game in the early 1900s, he'd mined an amazing fortune of almost £180,000 from the creek. At one stage he employed 300 men to work his sluicing operations. The other men in the area also worked for gold in the creek outside Shepard's claim, or else they worked in the underground mine attacking the rich Gibraltar gold reef that fell to a depth of over 300 feet. It was one of the finest gold-bearing areas in New South Wales but as the gold returns inevitably thinned out the families did so too, while the men who stayed, who hadn't made a fortune, sought work on nearby farms and orchards. The people led hard lives and some men would die early from the mine dust they inhaled.

Shepardstown, and the nearby village of Grahamstown, a stone's throw over the hill, were places of great community spirit, and on their soils were born spirited people. From humble backgrounds, some would go on to play sport for Australia; others would become professors and leading businesspeople. The hard life produced a hardiness in their make-up.

At one time, at the turn of the nineteenth century, Shepardstown had a baker, two churches, a post office, a blacksmith and a school. In the early 1900s, at Englishman

George Clements' grocery store, you could buy most items, including fuel and produce, and even firecrackers. Mr Clements would receive orders from the residents in the morning and deliver the goods to their homes in the afternoon—that's if one of his flighty horses didn't race off with all the groceries and the cart while he was delivering. Butcher Frank Young brought cheap meat by horse and dray and cut it up on the spot. Residents would place perishables in the hessian-covered refrigerators called Coolgardie safes, hoping for a breeze to maintain the cooling process. Syrian-born trader Johnny Elias would arrive in his dray full of exotic items, including linen and clothing. He'd haggle with the women, stamping his feet and exclaiming 'Missus!', as he urged his customers towards a more agreeable price. At Mrs Chalker's house, kids bought ice-creams and lollies.

In such an isolated valley, sport became one of the main entertainments. Cricket and football were played in the flat near the bridge at Grahamstown and near the creek at Shepardstown. Tennis was played on two courts on the Shepardstown flat. Although life was mostly quiet in the valley, the residents developed a way of settling scores by arranging boxing matches at the creek crossing on Sundays. Quite often, up to five bouts were arranged and the warring parties would take out their venom with boxing gloves as people hollered from the sidelines.

The area produced a wealth of sporting talent. Grahamstown was the birthplace of one of Australia's great footballers, George Treweek. Dubbed the human windmill or 'Arms and Legs', he was spotted in a local game against the Sydney team Mascot and won a contract with the South Sydney Rabbitohs, forging a phenomenal career as a running forward. Treweek played with Souths through the 1920s and '30s, capturing seven premierships in an eight-year period. He played in seven Tests for Australia, playing major roles in Test victories against Great Britain. League experts rated him one of the game's best-ever second-rowers and, during the centenary year of rugby league in Australia in 2008, he was named as one of the 100 greatest Australian players of the century.

Cec 'Dicky' Fifield was born in nearby Adelong and had relatives throughout Shepardstown and Grahamstown. He played for Western Suburbs and was later picked for the Kangaroos before going on to play, with distinction, several seasons with the English side Hull, taking them to a championship. He was also named among league's 100 greatest players.

Former long-time Australian Rugby League supremo Ken Arthurson, a former Manly player, also had a connection to the area. Arthurson's mother came from Grahamstown and it's where his family went back to live when his family was evacuated from Sydney during World War II (he'd attend school in Adelong). Tennis coach and Grand Slam singles title winner Tony Roche, meantime, was born in nearby Tarcutta, but his father and grandparents lived in Shepardstown.

Aside from their interest in sport, Shepardstown citizens were great inventors. A greyhound-racing track was built at Sandy Gully where Alvy Miller pedalled a stationary bike that motored the lure, which was tied to a wire trace. Punters yelled out 'Go faster, Alvy!' as the dogs were about to catch up to the false hare. There was even a Sandy Gully bookmaker.

Tom Kirk grew up in a small pise house on a ridge directly above Adelong Creek, in between the Price and Funnel families, with 'Ed the Chinaman' across the road. Born on 15 November

1915, he was the youngest child of seven to Sam and Mary Kirk. Sam Kirk worked hard to make a living at the Gibraltar mine. It was a job that would eventually take his life at the age of just 56, when, as the miners called it, 'he got dusted'.

The year Kirk was born the Great War had just started, and many young men enlisted in the wake of the marches that meandered through country towns collecting the most able hands of a generation. In the euphoria of joining the fight for the motherland, the young men from Shepardstown, some of them as young as 16, didn't realise they were getting a quick ticket to an early grave amid the muddy trenches of France. After the war, the towns built a wonderful stone memorial with a sculpture of a soldier in the grounds of Shepardstown Public School to remember their sacrifice. The memorial listed 71 men from the district who went to the war, 15 of whom had died in action or of wounds. But when the school closed, the memorial vanished. It was as if Shepardstown could never lay down any roots, not even keep the memorials to people who had paid the ultimate sacrifice. Not even the gold discovered could offer it any base. Slowly, everything in the town was vanishing.

(Remarkably, in about 2006, the whereabouts of the lost war memorial was discovered by some old-timers. It seems that because the townsfolk of Shepardstown and Grahamstown couldn't agree on what should happen to the memorial following the closure of the school some unknown persons had buried it in a paddock. Unearthed 60 years later, the sculpture had largely survived, except for a soldier's rifle, and it was rebuilt with new plinths and re-dedicated at Adelong in 2008.)

With the local school closed, Kirk had to hop in the carriage with all the other Shepardstown kids for the long bumpy ride into the closest school at Adelong, 7 miles south.

By the age of 13 the sports-mad boy decided that he had had enough of school. His father warned him that he wouldn't let him back in the house unless he went and found a job. But he faced a huge task to find work as the Great Depression took hold. So young Kirk marched off to Adelong and knocked on various doors until the local baker agreed to give him a carting job. Shepardstown boys could turn their hands to anything. At the age of 13 he could boast he was fully employed in an era where many grown men were unemployed. After either walking or riding his horse on the 7-mile journey to Adelong, he'd pick up the cart and start his deliveries. Kirk had three bread delivery runs, from Adelong to Tumblong, a run to Mount Horeb, and a run south towards Tumut. Trundling along the dirt roads in the old baker's cart while whistling songs he wondered what the future might hold. Little did he know that within a decade he'd be the toast of Sydney.

There was no sign of the future rugby league footballer in Kirk's early years. He preferred soccer when he was young and it was only as an afterthought that he turned to rugby league. But when he eventually picked up a football, at 13, there was every sign of a burgeoning talent. By the next year he'd secured the wing position for the Tumut Blues first-division team, which played in both the Group 9 competition and the Maher Cup challenge trophy.

Kirk's career took off as fast as the horses he rode. And in 1935, aged just 19, he was part of remarkable team that took all before it. It was a year that would set him apart from every other player in the region as his fine kicking came to the fore. That year, in Group 9 competition, Kirk scored 13 tries and kicked 54 goals for 147 points. In 14 Maher Cup matches—during which Tumut defeated all challengers—he scored 105 points, a record that stood for 24 years until broken by Harden-Murrumburrah's Bernie Nevin in 1959. The young Tumut Blues (whose players had an average age of just 20) were widely feted, and were invited to Sydney where the team's picture was taken on top of the *Sun*'s newspaper office. Kirk stood in the line for the photo, typically smiling, his hair parted down the middle.

That same year, 1935, Kirk was selected to play fullback for the southern team in Country Week and, while doing so, caught the attention of one of the great forwards of rugby league, Frank 'Chunky' Burge, who linked him up with Sydney's Canterbury-Bankstown. Kirk, by now a strapping 13 stone, joined Canterbury in 1936 as one of six recruits from the country areas. He was part of a drive to lift the club's fortunes after the embarrassment of their debut year in the league. After a long and bitter battle to gain entry to the competition, the 'Cantabs', as they were known in the 1930s, had won just two matches in 1935, finishing second last as a result. But in 1936, with Kirk and others on board, there was a quick reversal of fortune and the babes of the league took it right up to the established teams, finishing third on the table behind premiers Eastern Suburbs. With a host of Test-class players, including Dave Brown and Ray Stehr, in the Tricolours' ranks, Easts won three consecutive premierships between 1935 and 1937.

Kirk stayed with his sister, Esme, at Enmore in the bustling heart of Sydney, a world away from the quiet hills of Tumut. Having his own truck, he found a job delivering seafood for the fish markets and the business supported him right through his time with Canterbury. But after a promising debut year, Kirk's second season started horribly when he broke his leg during a game. As a result, he spent nearly four months with his leg strapped to a board while he recovered. It seemed his foray into the big city league would collapse around him.

Sydney was abuzz when the year 1938 dawned. In January, the nation celebrated the sesquicentenary and, although nothing like the huge bicentennial celebrations that were to follow, picnics, balls and events were held throughout the nation. But not everyone was celebrating. On Australia Day, for the first time ever, Aboriginal people staged a day of mourning to highlight their lack of rights.

Hot on the heels of the sesquicentenary, the third British Empire Games were staged in Sydney, the first time they'd been held in the Southern Hemisphere. More than 40,000 people crammed into the Sydney Cricket Ground in early February to watch the opening ceremony. It wasn't long before Australia dominated the events, unearthing its first great female track star, West Australia's Decima Norman. She blitzed both the 100-yard and 220-yard sprints, and helped win two golds in the relays, while also winning the long jump. Her five gold medals were part of Australia's haul of 24, easily leading Canada and England in the medal tally among the 15 nations at the games.

Horseracing and cricket dominated the minds of sports-mad Sydneysiders, and everyone was excited as Don Bradman's 'Invincibles' were about to head off to defend the Ashes in England during the Australian winter. Radio had created a whole new world for sports fans after its launch in the mid-1920s, and by the 1930s radio was as important as modern-day television. It also made it easier for SP bookmakers to run their operations from hotels and at the back of small shops.

At this time rugby league was facing a crisis of confidence and it had by no means won the battle with rugby union for supremacy in New South Wales. Crowds were down and there was a huge split between the managers of the Kangaroos' touring side and the board of the New South Wales Rugby League (NSWRL).

SP betting was hurting crowds at games and there was a fear the game was falling out of favour in the public's imagination. The game was also losing players to country teams in New South Wales and, further afield, to the English league competition. One of the greats of the era, Easts centre Dave Brown, who had captained Australia at the age of just 22, gave up the Sydney competition and left to play for Warrington in England in 1936, having accepted a massive £1000 sign-on fee, far above anything he could get in Australia.

As the dogs of war were howling in Europe and the Pacific, the slump in the competition could not have come at a worse time. The game was not given much support by the city's leading newspaper, the *Sydney Morning Herald*, which was only too ready to highlight problems in the league if they arose. Often the broadsheet gave boxing more prominence. It was left to smaller-circulation papers, *Truth*, *Labor Daily*, *Daily Telegraph*, *The Referee* and the *Sun* to breathe life into the league.

The league writers of the main newspapers were an enthusiastic and accomplished group and most had played the game at the senior level. They included Viv Thicknesse, whose pieces in the *Daily Telegraph* came with the sidebar, 'former Australian halfback'. John 'Dinny' Campbell, a former rugby union player who played in the first win by the Wallabies over the All Blacks in 1910, and then switched to play league for Easts, winning a premiership, also wrote for the *Telegraph*. Ross McKinnon, bylined as 'star three-quarter', was part of the dominant Easts side of the 1930s and played major roles in eight Tests. He somehow juggled his league duties with writing for the *Truth*.

Writing for the *Sun* was Claude Corbett, a former South Sydney halfback, who'd just missed out on a Kangaroo tour, and had coined the famous phrase 'The Pride of the League' in reference to his old team's domination of the early history of the game. Corbett once lost an exclusive story about Australian sprinter Jim Carlton. Not wanting to put his story on the wires, in case a rival saw it, he held the story back, not knowing that *The World* had obtained the story from another source, and beat Corbett to the punch. Author Isadore Brodsky, who knew him, wrote: 'Claude's complexion, always highly coloured, went an even brighter shade of red upon seeing he had been scooped.' Corbett (the grandfather of Channel Nine reporter Peter Harvey) was considered the doyen of all rugby league writers.

While the Cantabs were not on anyone's radar when the 1938 season kicked off, Tom Kirk's big toe was fast becoming famous. Ross McKinnon reported on 10 April: 'Goal kicking gave Canterbury-Bankstown an 8–5 victory over Balmain in the main trial game at Leichhardt. Tommy Kirk's trusty toe did the trick. The fullback landed a trio of flag-waggers.'

The *Daily Telegraph* saw potential in the Cantabs' line-up: 'Coach Jimmy Craig has the foundation of an excellent team in Canterbury-Bankstown. His astuteness should make these young players a formidable proposition. McCarter and Anderson, halves, are an excellent combination. Mitchell on the wing is improving in every game and Kirk, at fullback, is full of promise. Kirk has a personality, and is always doing the unexpected thing.'

Craig was one of the game's great early players, having spent time with University, Wests and Balmain, playing in almost every position on the field during his career. He had the unusual distinction of having played for both New South Wales and Queensland, after he moved north later in his career. He also played seven Tests for Australia. He then coached Wests to their first premiership in 1930. Dally Messenger rated him one of the best players he'd seen.

Canterbury launched into their first game of the season with gusto and completely dominated the Norths team, sometimes known as The Shoremen. They showed great unity between the forwards and backs from early on, bringing each player's potential to the fore. Bill Corbett, Claude's brother, wrote in the *Sun*: 'North Sydney were subjected to an almost incessant bombardment, and the forwards and backs withered under the attack.

'Incidents during the game indicated that rugby league football is going to be as interesting and stirring as it has ever been. Team members played with their brains, not mere physical assertion. For example, there was the strategy of [Roy] McCarter, the slight Canterbury half. His men were near the North Sydney tryline, the ball came into his arms from a scrum. Infield he went with a supporter calling to him from the blind side. The five-eighth [Anderson], not letting him down, took the pass infield and the irrepressible McCarter, bobbed up inside awaiting the pass. [Anderson] swivelled in a tackle, whirled the ball back to McCarter, who sliced his way through for a splendid try.'

Corbett said the North Sydney defenders made the mistake of 'making the unreliable tackle of leaping for the opponents' collar': 'Kirk of Canterbury-Bankstown played the ideal game of the fullback. He kicked well and moved up to launch an attack or support an onslaught.'

Kirk was indelibly making his mark on the league and his boot could be trusted to get his team home. Not only were Canterbury winning, but they were sometimes steamrolling their opponents. The *Labor Daily* wrote: 'It was not the margin of their victory over Norths, 33–5, so much as the convincing system of their solid forwards and the cohesion and determination of their backs, that confirmed the impression that Canterbury-Bankstown have a most formidable thirteen, and will be serious challengers for the season's rugby league premiership.'

Kirk made his only try-scoring mark of the season in the game against Newtown in early May, helping them win 35–11. Kirk scored two tries, three conversions and three penalty goals. The *Truth* said of the win: 'Nothing succeeds like success. Canterbury-Bankstown boys are on top of the world.' Meantime, the *Herald* wrote: 'Kirk, besides kicking well, combined cleverly with his backs, and scored two magnificent tries.'

Kirk's great performance prompted calls for his inclusion in the upcoming Metropolitan match against Country. 'Fullback T. Kirk, husky, active and a powerful kick, has done splendidly for Canterbury-Bankstown,' wrote 'The Cynic' in *The Referee*. 'Well in the running for fullback [in] the Metropolitan against Country [match]. Rare for a fullback to get two tries as he did against Newtown.'

Coach Jim Craig—who was part of the all-conquering Balmain side from 1915 to 1920, and had played seven Tests— was confident his team was headed for big things. 'You haven't seen the best of them yet,' he declared in May. 'Before the end of the season they will be the equal of the 1921 North Sydney side.'

Craig was an exacting master, the *Daily Telegraph* wrote: 'Many charge coaches to cheat the referee. Not so Craig. He realises that penalties can be costly.' The Cynic also jumped on the Canterbury bandwagon early: 'They are becoming better with every match, stronger in the scrum, determined in the ruck, quick and active wherever the ball is to be got, and much more prone to dribble (when halfback keeps the ball in a scrum) than some of the rival scrummagers.'

By early May, Kirk was the second-highest scorer in the league, with two tries and 15 goals, amassing 36 points. But despite his great record, he was to be denied representative honours at this time. His team was firing, however, and everyone anticipated a great game when, in front of some 15,000 spectators, the Cantabs took on reigning premiers Easts at the Sydney Cricket Ground on 13 May. Easts were hot favourites, but Canterbury ran away with the game, 28–9.

The *Labor Daily* spoke of the game as if it had been an annexation: 'It was a case of soundly-equipped force in every arm. Tank forwards of modern mobility paved the way for waves of united attack. Except for a period in the second session, when every cog in the tricolour machinery worked in unison, Canterbury solidity dominated the game.'

Viv Thicknesse, meantime, wrote that 'Eastern Suburbs rugby league team has fallen from its pinnacle of fame—temporarily at least. It shows that Canterbury were a far better side than most people dreamed … Great credit is due to the young club for a solid display, which was too much for the premiers.'

The *Truth* was confident enough to say that the stirring game had turned around the fortunes of the code. In reference to Canterbury's win it ran three headlines: 'Dreadnought pack irresistible', 'Pupils turn tutors' and 'Rugby league boom days are coming again'.

In controversial circumstances, Canterbury later took on Balmain on 21 May at Leichhardt Oval. But many said the game should have been the match of the day and thus played at the Sydney Cricket Ground, where it could have attracted double the crowd. So congested was Leichhardt Oval—a crowd of 10,686 paid £507 to see the game at a venue that was only supposed to hold 8000—that police warned it would close the ground the next time if the same number of people turned up.

Ross McKinnon said the league had thrown 'hundreds of pounds down the sink by its penny-wise, pound-foolish decision not to allow yesterday's match of the day between Balmain and Canterbury to be played at the SCG ... Sergeants Pemberton and Andrews conferred with H.R. Miller (Horrie Miller, secretary of the NSWRL) and threatened to close the gates. Everybody but the committee of the league knew that the only sensible venue was the SCG. Still, the most appealing fixture of the season was played at an obscure, inadequate, and out-of-the-way place at Leichhardt Oval. A combination of petty selfishness and utter stupidity is the reason,' McKinnon wrote.

League president Harry Flegg was seen selling tickets at the front gate, while 'secretary Horrie Miller, Frank Miller and Harold Matthews were as busy as bees supervising the gates, queues and general disruptions caused by the crowd.'

Horrie Miller said he had advocated the game for the SCG. 'We are badly in need of funds and now the committee is throwing it away,' he lamented, denying he was to blame. Miller claimed at least 20,000 would have come to the game at the SCG.

The league couldn't even pick a winner when it was right before their eyes. They had underestimated the drawing power of the young Cantabs, who were re-awakening the league faithful.

As expected, the match was a thriller, and it was Kirk's Canterbury side that got the spoils, winning 11–3 in a game that 'sparkled', according to McKinnon. 'The league gave of its best,' he wrote.

Kirk played his part in the win, his fine tackling being almost as precise as his goal kicking, while the media reserved special praise for forward Harry Porter and half Roy McCarter. Dinny Campbell at the *Telegraph* liked what he saw in the Canterbury attack, and put it down to great training. 'The class of football all through was a lesson for what coaching can do for all willing players. The opening score was as perfect a piece of engineering as one could wish to see. Canterbury are an excellently balanced side. They have wonderful material and will take a lot of beating this season.'

The Cynic, sometimes verging on the poetic, loved what he saw in the Canterbury team: 'Canterbury, working into the Balmain 25, let loose tornadic ruck attacks that were met with herculean tackling, much of it most desperate. The attackers were like striped devils, silent and relentless.'

As the season progressed the league joined forces with other codes and sporting groups to clamp down on SP bookmaking, which was blamed for keeping thousands of people away from attending games. The NSW Government, in an election year, saw a chance to jump on the anti-SP bandwagon, vigorously supported by the churches, and indicated it would introduce harsher penalties for people running illegal gaming houses.

The NSWRL organised a deputation to the New South Wales chief secretary to secure legislation that would suppress starting price betting, a big ask in a nation that was mad on a bet. The legislation was proposed in April, but would not enter the Parliament until later in the year. In the interim, the league urged police to crack down on hotels that were home to SP operations.

In mid-May, police raided four city hotels and declared them 'common gaming houses'. Undercover police had surveyed almost every hotel in inner-Sydney to monitor SP betting. After the raids, the *Herald* reported that 'SP betting in hotels came almost to a standstill on Saturday, and bookmakers were driven out of hotels'. At the same time, the hotels stopped putting up starting prices on blackboards and only chalked the results of races. Adapting to the sudden change, one bookmaker operated from out of a car, driving from hotel to hotel to conduct his business.

The tough new measures seemed to have a positive effect. 'Increased attendances at football fixtures and Moorefield racecourse were attributed to the inability of punters to make a bet in a hotel,' the *Herald* reported in May. Horrie Miller hailed the police action as a success and said that if 'the campaign continues, within a month our gates will increase fifty per cent'. He also believed the ban would bring many young footballers into the code. These claims are hard to verify, but in its fight against SP bookmaking, the NSWRL led the way for all other sporting codes, and there was a gradual increase in attendances during the year.

On 28 May, prior to a break for representative games, Canterbury took on South Sydney in a game transferred from Belmore Oval to the SCG (indicating that the NSWRL, recognising Canterbury's pulling power, had learnt from their mistakes). Watched by 20,090 fans, it finished 3-all but the low score belied a gripping contest in which South Sydney pounded the Canterbury line in the last 20 minutes but couldn't get through. Kirk stopped many tries with his fine tackling. But considering that performance, and his season's form, his omission from representative teams surprised many, including The Cynic, who thought Kirk a good pick for City: 'The fullback one would have chosen is T. Kirk, the big rugged Canterbury-Bankstown man. He began the season in form, improved match by match, and is now of representative class, as tough and forceful as Jim Sullivan.'

The season proper resumed in mid-June, and Canterbury continued on their unbeaten ways, including, in July, beating country team Cowra 21–3 in an exhibition match, Kirk scoring a classy individual try. 'It is not often that one sees a fullback score,' the *Lachlan Leader* reported, 'however, the visitors' fullback, Kirk, was seen in a scoring role when he secured in his own half and ran strongly, weaving in and out of opposition players to score a brilliant try, which was converted.'

By the time Canterbury came up against neighbours Western Suburbs in late July, they were still undefeated. But the Magpies would be a big test, particularly since Canterbury would be missing two forwards selected in the New South Wales side to play Queensland in Brisbane. And a big test it proved to be. Too big. 'Riled by a 28–3 first round defeat, Wests administered a parental thrashing, 19–9, to their offspring at Pratten Park yesterday and caused the season's sensation,' reported the *Truth*. 'Despite the incredulous astonishment of the success-inflated local Pratten Park enthusiasts, they were not dreaming.'

Wests' D. Gulliver, the *Truth* continued, was 'everywhere the ball went ... Apparently inspired by the feeling he was in the land of the Lilliputians, he towered over both packs ... Of Canterbury much could be said of their mistakes. Failure to seize scoring opportunities were frequent when passes went wide, and when they were accurate speed was lacking.'

It was a most uninspiring performance and Canterbury realised they had to lift their game if they wanted to win the premiership. And lift they did the following week against the premiers, Easts. 'In one of the finest and most thrilling games I have ever had the pleasure of witnessing,' raved Ross McKinnon, 'Eastern Suburbs played a 15-all draw with Canterbury Bankstown at Belmore Oval yesterday. Never have I seen a game so dominated by forward play produce football, under heavy conditions, so inspiring and exciting as that of yesterday.'

The crowd of 4500, he wrote, were in 'delirious delight and consternation alternately, as the fortunes of the game fluctuated ... With the Tricolours playing a man short, and desperately hanging on to a slender point lead, local hero Roy McCarter shot from the scrum base to score amid a crescendo of noise, pandemonium and any words befitting sounds rivalling those of volcanic eruption.'

As the Belmore streetlights came on, ahead of a heavy downpour that had the decency to wait until after full-time, Easts levelled the game with a fine penalty goal. But the draw was hardly seen as a disappointing result. Amid praise for Kirk—who kicked three goals—and Easts' Jim Norton, all were effusive. 'I have never been so excited by a football game than I was by the Canterbury-Easts fixture,' gushed the *Telegraph*'s Viv Thicknesse.

The draw set Canterbury back on track and the following week, in the season's penultimate regular-season game, they secured the minor premiership by defeating Souths 12–8, before 10,592 people. McKinnon wrote in the *Truth*: 'The club secretary, players, coach Jim Craig, and trainers, deserve a resounding slap on the back for attaining such an elevated position in so short a time, and giving a much needed fillip to the code.'

A win for Canterbury in the final game of the season was necessary, if only to maintain momentum, but they only just managed it, defeating Balmain 20–18 at Belmore Oval. The hero of the day was Kirk, who kicked seven goals. As McKinnon wrote: 'Only the unfailing accuracy of Tom Kirk's boot saved the minor premiers from the season's second defeat.'

Canterbury and Balmain met a week later in the first semifinal, playing for a spot in the final. At the SCG, in front of a disappointing crowd of 10,751, Canterbury were more certain of things this time and won 31–24 after a late try by Ted Anderson sealed the match. According to Claude Corbett, who was mystified a punch by a Canterbury player on a Balmain player went unseen by officials, Canterbury had overwhelmed Balmain with 'fire and dash'.

Front-row forwards, and great scrummagers, Eddie Burns, hooker Roy Kirkaldy and Henry Porter, were the cornerstone of the Canterbury attack. The trio played together for almost 11 years and in a unique show of faith, Kirkaldy often refused to play if either of his supporting props were injured.

Eddie Burns, later to coach New South Wales, said Kirkaldy was fearsome: 'He was lightning fast, and he could take and give it. I never heard him squeal, but he sure hated to be beaten for the ball.'

Burns worked as a glassblower at Waterloo, and said it was his trade that helped give him the strength in his lungs to play a full game without tiring.

Henry Porter was born in Dungog in 1912 and later lived in Bombala. In his early years, like Kirk, he preferred soccer.

After joining Canterbury in 1935 he went on to represent New South Wales for five years, before achieving the unusual feat of also representing Queensland, when he moved to Brisbane after the war. His motto was 'play hard and be prepared to take hard knocks'. His game plan was to strike for the ball at the same time as the hooker when the ball was fed into the scrum.

While this formidable front row laid the foundation for the win, Kirk applied the finishing touch with three magnificent goals. Still just 22, Kirk was the leading point-scorer for the season with 86 points and about to play his first grand final. It was a heady time for the young man from little Shepardstown.

In the week before the grand final, the Cantabs suffered a major blow. With their captain Alan Brady already in doubt with a knee injury, the team watched in dismay as their top five-eighth Ted Anderson broke down with an ankle injury at training five days before the big match. Brady was watching from the sidelines and coach Jimmy Craig called him on to the training field to see how his knee would go. Remarkably he showed no pain and, somewhat unexpectedly, Brady, a centre, was picked for the big match against Easts, bringing his much-needed stewardship to the back line.

On the eve of the final, the *Herald* suggested it would go down to the bell. But Canterbury had the advantage, it said, because due to the rules of the day, they could, as minor premiers, challenge Easts again in a second final—a grand final—if they lost. And while the paper wondered if Canterbury's momentum had stalled, it predicted that if Canterbury got its fair share of the ball then Easts would probably pay for it.

On a bright Sydney spring day on 3 September 1938 the Cantabs took on the mighty Tricolours in front of 20,287 people at the Sydney Cricket Ground (the players getting 'two bob' for everyone who walked through the gate). Easts boasted four internationals in their front pack: Sid Pearce, Henry Pierce, Andy Norval and Ray Stehr, one of the greatest props the game had seen. It was a formidable challenge to the babes of the league despite their dominance during the year. But Canterbury hoped that their cohesion that would get them through.

Just before the match Canterbury took an early blow when winger Aub Mitchell had to withdraw due to sickness. And things hardly improved in the opening few minutes when Easts' Aden Cairns scored an unconverted try. But Canterbury settled and soon Kirk kicked his team in front with two difficult penalty goals, and at half-time Canterbury led 4–3.

After the break the premiers struck back with a try to Dick Dunn. But rather than set up Easts, it fired up Canterbury who then, wrote Corbett, 'unleashed its dogs of battle'. Coach Craig would call it 'Test match football'.

Three tries followed for Canterbury, two to pacy winger Joe Gartner—his first a 'high-class' try in which he 'caught the ball and ran down the touchline, side-stepped the opposition and scored in the corner'—and the third to Jimmy Duncombe, a late replacement for Aub Mitchell. And Kirk would play his part, inevitably, landing two penalties and two conversions, one from within a foot of the touchline. 'The last named two were themselves match winners,' Corbett declared.

In the fading light, at almost 6 pm, Canterbury had their first premiership in the bag, 19–6 winners. And to top off the magnificent effort by the young club—which Canterbury club president Tommy Johns called the 'happiest moment of my life'—Canterbury had also won the club championship. Amid joyous scenes, captain Alan Brady was carried into the dressing room by his elated teammates. After the match, the team went down to the referees' 'smoko' in the city for a party, an unusual mix of players and officials unheard of in the modern game.

When the news reports of the game were published they were effusive in their praise for the new premiers. Canterbury, McKinnon wrote, 'were a contrast in all-round solidarity. Backs and forwards had strength and ability. Brady had lost his attacking penetration, but his defence and generalship are still the goods, while Gartner on the wing has real side-step, which leaves them looking as awkward as an elephant in a crockery shop.

'Sponberg, Porter, Kirkaldy, McCallum, McCormack and Burns,' he continued, 'deserve the highest praise for a season of consistent vanguard play which should be emulated in other clubs.'

The 1938 grand final was a huge watermark in the history of rugby league. It gave hope that any team could win the competition, provided of course they had all the ingredients, not least an astute coach like Craig, who had taken Canterbury to a new level of skill and professionalism. All through the year, commentators said that league had been reborn by the enthusiasm and play of Canterbury who, from that point, would forever be a force in the competition. No doubt Canterbury had reignited the enthusiasm of people who may have drifted from the game. And despite the onset of the war, league was given a huge slingshot into the future.

In a rather awkward and unfortunate end to the great year, Canterbury had to play one of the top regional sides in their last engagement on 17 September. They took on Newcastle's minor premiers Waratah-Mayfield, and destroyed them 31–5, but left a sour taste with many people. The melees on the field were so bad that police intervened.

When Kirkaldy was dropped by a punch when he did not have possession of the ball all hell broke loose. Corbett wrote: 'Kirkaldy was struck and some of his comrades went to his aid. Waratah-Mayfield men rushed in and Ling (W-M) was knocked out with a right swing over the left eye. Waratah-Mayfield finished the game with 10 men (out of 13) after one was sent off and two were injured.' 'Furious Footbrawl' was the headline in the *Truth*. 'What started as a game of football ended in a free-for-all brawl,' it wrote. At one stage a policeman walked onto the field to give a warning to the players.

The riotous end to the season couldn't spoil the feeling of elation for young Tom. He was the competition's highest point scorer with 94 points. His career in Sydney would last for another ten years, and he would finally get his representative honour the next year for New South Wales.

PART TWO: THE WAR AND THE BUMPER YEARS

There was, as with most country lads, a larrikin side to Tom Kirk. He became renowned for kicking footballs out of the Sydney Cricket Ground. Nearly every time he played at the hallowed ground he tried the feat and mostly made the distance, normally—despite warnings about such antics—sending the ball on a trajectory over the Members Pavilion just to annoy those in officialdom. Once, dared by someone after the match, he kicked the ball clean out of the ground and onto the then No.2 Oval, a massive distance of more than 100 yards (that field is now the Sydney Football Stadium). He's the only person known to have achieved the feat.

'That was nothing,' says his son Ian. 'One time, when he was at Canterbury, he kicked the ball out of Belmore Oval during a game, and it landed in a goods train on the nearby railway track. The ball probably ended up in Cobar or somewhere.'

Kirk had the chance to make his kicking prowess officially recognised during the war. In an army display at the Sydney Cricket Ground, he, as the best rugby league kicker, was pitted against the best kicker from the US gridiron competition (who was with the US Army and stationed in Australia), the best Aussie Rules kicker, and the best rugby union kicker (like himself, chosen from Australian Army teams). By that time, Kirk was the leading pointscorer in the professional Sydney rugby league competition.

The army crowd roared as Kirk kicked the ball the furthest by some margin. It seemed just a bit of fun, but out of it came an incredible offer. Several months later, he received a letter from the management of US gridiron team the Pittsburgh Steelers offering him the position of lead punter after the war. He thought long and hard about the move, but eventually declined, preferring to pursue his league career in Sydney.

After his starring role in Canterbury's 1938 premiership win, Kirk, dogged by injury, had a quiet 1939—though he did finally make his New South Wales debut in the centres. But ahead of the 1940 season, he was then forced to part ways with the Canterbury club that had been such a major part of his development. The club change was due to the then 'residential rule'. League officials had found out that Kirk's residence in Enmore was actually part of the Bluebags territory, not Canterbury's (the same thing would happen to Kirk in the late '40s when he moved to McMahons Point. He was then forced to play for North Sydney).

So Kirk was forced to become a Newtown Bluebag. Some believe Bluebag was in reference to the early jerseys of royal blue, which looked like cut-out sugar bags. Others thought it a reference to the blue bags commonly put in washing as a detergent during the era. As well as changing clubs, Kirk also changed jobs. He'd left the fish markets for a job at the famous Mick Simmons sports store and sports goods distributor. He was the store's 'league man', which gave him the honour of working in the same store that Don Bradman had helped make famous, when he was the store's cricket man and publicity manager for some time in the 1930s. Kirk was one of several prominent sportsmen, including Bradman, league greats Reg Gasnier and Dally Messenger, and snooker champion Walter Lindrum, to work as department heads at the store over the decades.

Kirk married his sweetheart, Joyce Bell, on 16 September 1941, and three days later he joined the army. In the war he was assigned to a domestic position as a staff sergeant and warrant officer in the 111th Transport Company based at Paddington and Broadmeadow. His first assignment was not, relatively speaking, a difficult one—to captain, and coach, the army's rugby league team.

At the start of the war, the prime minister, Robert Menzies, had given his full imprimatur for sport to continue. But as the war progressed, and home soil was attacked, politicians were forced to reconsider their position. But as some sports waned and many race dates were cancelled, the buoyant league competition only saw bigger crowds. When former Queensland player and rugby league enthusiast Artie Fadden was voted in as prime minister after Menzies resigned in August 1941, he made one of his first official duties a visit to the dressing rooms at the SCG when Easts took on Canterbury in a semifinal. (Fadden was prime minister for just 40 days and in that time he'd also attended an Aussie Rules match in Canberra).

But Fadden was set for a rude shock. Being prime minister didn't necessarily give you access to a dressing room where the tough Eastern Suburbs forward Ray Stehr held sway. Stehr would not let anyone in as his team prepared for a game, and he refused to make a concession for Fadden. League secretary Jersey Flegg warned Stehr that he would never play again at the SCG over the snub.

(After his league career finished, Ray Stehr became a training consultant to many rugby league clubs, including Newtown, in the 1950s. When he trained Newtown's forwards he put in place a harsh 'no moisture' rule. That is, players were not to drink any liquids, including water, between the time they finished training on Thursday night to the time they played on Saturday afternoon. The extreme measure, understandably, wasn't a winner among dehydrated players.)

When John Curtin was elected the new Labor prime minister in September, he made it clear he wanted professional sport to continue during the war. Sport was vital to the well-being of the nation's psyche, he said, echoing the argument from World War I. 'I cannot agree that participation in games and sports in moderation, either as players or spectators, need be in any way detrimental to our war effort,' Curtin told reporters in Canberra. 'On the contrary, all those working through the week have as much to gain by spending their afternoon at a sporting contest as they have by spending a night at the pictures. Reasonable participation in sport not merely includes the physical wellbeing of persons working strenuously during the week, but it also improves their morale. The fact is that our race does not live by bread alone. I would think it would be an extremely commendable thing and a demonstration to the world at large of the spirit of the British race, if immediately after the war ends, England and Australia will resume the Test cricket matches. I think those things are just as important to the British race as a performance of Shakespeare. I think the two things go together in making us what we are.'

But Curtin and his cabinet were forced to act as the war deepened and the economy was put under enormous stress. From the start of 1942, all midweek sport was banned to reduce the strain on manpower, cut fuel use and stop the congregation of people in confined areas. Later there was a ban on sport on public holidays, a reaction to stop discrimination against service people who had lost their right to holidays.

By February 1942, sporting bodies were told further curtailment of sport was 'inevitable'. Much of the management of the continuation of sporting events was left to state governments. The South Australian government moved on its own to ban all racing. League stopped in North Queensland for two years and many councils banned sport on Sundays. The NSWRL, however, vowed to continue on with the Sydney competition despite the logistical nightmare of getting players to games, and it had the support of the New South Wales government. Nevertheless, it seemed the army, who had its own football teams, did all in its power to allow the best in the competition to be available, and many players were spared active overseas service. So as Saturday race meetings were cancelled, rugby league blossomed and record crowds came to watch games at the SCG, some of the biggest seen since the sport started.

Through all this, Kirk settled beautifully into his new career at Newtown. The foundation club had struggled through the previous three decades with just two premierships but Kirk had arrived in its golden era. He was called 'mother' by his teammates and, as it was quite common for the best players to be targeted by the opposition, they did all in their power to prevent him from being hurt during games; mothering him, as it were.

Newtown were brimming with talent, from the tough 95-kilogram forward Herb Narvo, exciting centre Len Smith, talented winger Sid Goodwin, speedy Bruce Ryan, and one genuinely scary character, Frank 'Bumper' Farrell, the big cauliflower-eared forward who was also the most feared policeman in Sydney. Farrell, who was of the mindset that if you weren't injured during a game you really weren't trying, would become embroiled in one of the biggest controversies in league: the famous ear-biting incident of 1945. Kirk saw all of the blood-spattering drama.

Every player at Newtown was larger than life, none more than Narvo. The thickset Novocastrian was the complete sportsman: cyclist, cricketer, footballer, heavyweight boxing champion. Kirk and Narvo became great mates and Kirk agreed to act as his number two man at ringside when Narvo had a bout. The war had stopped most professional fights, but nothing could stop the army from arranging sporting contests, official and unofficial.

Narvo, who worked as a fitness trainer for the RAAF during the war years, stood at 179 centimetres (just over 5 feet, 10 inches) but his reach was about 4 centimetres longer than his height. He had claimed the Australian heavyweight title after stopping Billy 'Wocko' Britt in just 25 seconds in April 1943—at that stage, the fastest end to an Australian title fight. He was one of many league players ready to chance their arm in the boxing ring. Earlier during the war, Narvo, a southpaw, had knocked out Easts' Stehr—the man who wouldn't let a prime minister into the dressing room—in a fight at Leichhardt Stadium in Sydney. Narvo's boxing career subsequently took off and he participated in a number of fights against international opponents, the first, early in 1943, against the 'Alabama Kid', Clarence Reeves. (Reeves, an African American, married an Australian girl but wasn't allowed to settle in Australia because of the White Australia policy.) Narvo's inexperience caught up with him and in the third round of their bout, Reeves knocked Narvo out; it was the first time he'd been sat on his pants.

In June 1943, in Brisbane, Narvo took on the Pacific champion, Al Hoosman, and was again knocked out. But keen as some were to bolster the troops doing it tough in New Guinea and up on the Kokoda Track, a second, unofficial fight was arranged between Narvo and Hoosman. It was billed as the battle of the armies, the best Australian against the best American. Kirk flew with Narvo to Port Moresby for the 'rumble in the jungle'. Amazingly, Narvo held his nerve this time and beat the American to the astonishment and glee of the Diggers. The American soldiers were less amused.

Unfortunately for Narvo, Hoosman was quick to seek a rematch through official channels, and another fight was arranged at Narvo's hometown of Newcastle on 11 November 1944. Hoosman stopped Narvo in the seventh round after pummelling him on what was a hot night. 'Hoosman punished Narvo in the fifth and sixth rounds,' the *Army News* reported, 'and in the seventh, when he sent Narvo down with a terrific right to the chin, the latter's seconds then threw in the towel.'

It was Kirk who had to pick up the sore Narvo from the canvas, and help him, cruelled and beaten, back to his house, not far from the boxing stadium in Newcastle. Narvo lay in his bed for three days while Kirk went off and bought a keg of beer, which Narvo used to drown his sorrows and injuries over the next week.

Despite his pugilistic adventures, Herb Narvo was a gentle giant and very rarely lost his cool. After the war, however, a communist agitator from the wharves at Newcastle pushed him to the limit, foul-mouthing Narvo, in his car with his family, before Narvo hit him with a swift left knocking him to the ground. It cost Narvo a five-pound fine in the courts for his retaliation.

The war took its toll on league's ranks just as it did on the rest of society. One of Newtown's players, Bill Ryan, the brother of winger Bruce Ryan, was killed in action in New Guinea in 1942. He'd played 14 games for Newtown in 1941. His death during battle affected Newtown terribly. Other members of the team went in and out of active service during the course of the war.

But the game went on, and Kirk was an integral part of Newtown's mammoth 1943 season in which they won ten games and the minor premiership. The team was a powerhouse unit and often gapped their opponents. The 1943 season featured good crowds, although it wasn't until Newtown played Balmain for the minor premiership that a record crowd—there were 47,232 in attendance—was achieved. While that was good news for the NSWRL, the bad news was that the scourge of betting was out of control at matches. After Saturday race meetings had been cancelled the punters took their wagering to rugby league grounds instead. At the Newtown versus Balmain match, won 11–10 by Newtown, even the strictly ruled environs of the SCG members area saw spectators wagering on the size of the crowd, while up in the public stands, amid a huddle of bookmakers, there were side bets on the game's first scorers.

Another record crowd was expected at the grand final when Newtown played North Sydney. There was a sensation before the game when Norths lock Harry Taylor failed to show up. It was not until many years later that it was revealed Taylor's unit had been secretly dispatched out of Australia to fight in New Guinea. War injuries prevented Taylor from continuing his career after his return.

Narvo and Bumper Farrell were Newtown's wrecking balls during the season and they took up where they left off in the grand final. Newtown's coach, Arthur Folwell, was worried because Norths were Newtown's bugbear during the season, beating Newtown in all their three meetings.

It was a massive day at the height of the war, and although the official crowd at the SCG was recorded as just over 60,000, it was felt that with all the service people in attendance, who were let in for free, that the actual crowd was well over 80,000, a remarkable figure. A huge wire fence had to be built around some parts of the ground to stop the crowd surging into some areas, but this didn't stop some canny troops who scaled the fence commando style. The famous league player Dally Messenger couldn't even get into the ground until an official recognised him and made a passage through the milling crowd outside. More than 1000 people sat on the roof of a tin shed in the nearby showground to get a glimpse of the game.

Ahead of the match, Folwell made a few tactical changes in light of Newtown's poor season record against Norths. It worked. As Narvo and Farrell went for the throat—Norths' Frank Hyde was knocked out in the second half by a bit of Farrell athleticism and didn't return to the field—the fleet-footed backs carved gaps up the middle. Newtown raced away with a big lead early on and never looked back, scoring eight tries, with Kirk's trusty right boot adding five goals.

'Newtown is coming, hear the Bluebags humming,' the supporters sang as Newtown marched away with the grand final, 34–7. It was, the *Herald* reported, 'a brilliant display of teamwork in the second half'.

In winning his second premiership—Newtown's third—Kirk also became the first league player to kick more than 100 goals in a season: 58 of which he kicked in the regular Sydney competition, the others in army and trial games. It was a tremendous effort considering there were just eight teams in the competition, with very few representative matches.

Newtown were hot favourites to make it back-to-back premierships in 1944, and their season started well. As did Kirk's. In May, Newtown put the cleaners through Easts. As reported in the *Truth*, the Bluebags' backs 'ran riot in spasms, backed up in tantalising fashion, brushed aside weak tackles and crossed almost at will. Tom Kirk's toe was never trustier. He kept the flag-waggers busy by booting the bare nine goals and for good measure galloped across for a grand try'.

During the season, the *Sun*'s Corbett described Newtown as 'irresistible', not quite the adjective that would have been used to describe the brutish Bumper Farrell after he once took fancy dress to extremes, donning a skirt and brassiere (apparently he was a Russian ballerina) on a night out. Farrell, although second-generation Australian on his father's side, had an Irish mother and was as Irish as they came. He often sang rousing Irish songs after matches including his favourites, 'Paddy McGinty's Goat' and 'Ireland Must Be Heaven for My Mother Came from There'.

Farrell headed the vice squad that patrolled Sydney's most dangerous streets around Darlinghurst and Surry Hills, cracking down on black marketeers, brothel- and slave-traders. He was so influential it was believed he told his superiors in the police force what to do. And if the Newtown players had to rustle up some grog during the war years, they knew Farrell could always provide some stimulus for the party.

In June, Newtown smashed St George 52–7, with Kirk kicking an amazing 11 goals as he moved from fullback to the centres to replace Len Smith, who was on military duty. Farrell said he'd never seen Kirk play better and Kirk's huge tally put him on track to win a 25-pound bonus from the Newtown Supporters Club for scoring 100 points before the semifinals. In the interim, he earned five pounds from winning a bet he made with one Bluebags supporter by kicking six goals against Newcastle club side Waratah-Mayfield.

If cheeky wagers inspired him, so did his children. Kirk told an interviewer in July that his son Ian, known as 'little Tom' was, like Kirk's newborn daughter, an inspiration. Little Tom, two, was ill in hospital and a nurse was telling him: 'Be a good boy, your father is coming to see you.' Little Tom replied: 'My dad's kicking goals for Newtown.' Kirk kicked six goals in the next game. 'I couldn't let the lad down,' Kirk later told the media.

Kirk's kicking style was part ritual, part art. He began any goal attempt by placing the ball on a tiny mound of grass, with the ball slanted forwards and the lace of the ball facing down. He'd then get his bearings, putting his right foot just behind the ball and his left foot at the halfway mark at the side of the ball. He'd then pace backwards, measuring his run-up. When he was ready to move in, he'd approach the ball with his arms outstretched like an eagle, before kicking the ball at its apex and following through strongly. No matter how strong the wind, he always aimed above the black dot in the middle of the crossbar, although at the SCG he was a bit more circumspect. He knew the fluky winds that blew through the grandstands like the back of his hand, and he hardly ever missed a kick for goal at the storied ground. That was down to practice as much as anything else, for he'd take 30 or 40 kicks for goal at each training session. When asked what was the best time to practice, he replied, the country larrikin in him emerging, 'preferably in daylight'.

In later years, when he was playing Maher Cup football, a spectator challenged Kirk to put the ball through the goals from a kick taken directly side-on with the goalposts and in line with the corner post. He did it three times in a row, knowing exactly when the momentum of the ball would peter out. The man said he'd been using the wind, and it was a fluke, so Kirk went to the other side off the field and repeated his great kicking feat. The spectator walked off shaking his head.

Party tricks were one thing but, in July, Kirk broke Dave Brown's record for goals scored when, after Newtown again overran St George, he took his tally to 66 goals in 12 matches.

Kirk, who served in New Guinea, was involved in several army fundraising drives at this time, including one in Martin Place where he was brought before a mock 'Court of Injustice' and another when he played in the Army versus Rest of NSW game in August which raised more than £1300 for the Comforts Fund (which distributed Christmas hampers to soldiers). The game also signalled the departure of Len Smith to other war duties, a huge loss to the Bluebags as the finals approached. Narvo would also miss much of the remaining season. However Newtown couldn't be stopped from claiming the minor premiership.

Kirk had always been a much-admired figure in the game up until this point but when Newtown played Balmain in the final of 1944 he became the centre of suspicion and innuendo. It wasn't just that Newtown played poorly in the shock 19–16 loss at the SCG, but that Kirk missed three easy goals. 'Kirk hooted for missing easy goals: display shocks officials,' read the headline in the *Sunday Telegraph*, with the article beneath it adding: 'Newtown fullback and champion goal kicker Tom Kirk was hooted when he missed his third easy goal ... League officials in the Members [Pavilion] did not disguise their dissatisfaction at the standard of the game and the lethargy of some of the players.'

As this suggests, the loss attracted the attention of the NSWRL hierarchy after allegations were made that large bets had been placed on Balmain winning. Several inquiries were held into the game and the conduct of its participants, and the Newtown players were hauled before the league committee to explain.

Arthur Justice, former international and St George club secretary, was one of many people upset by the result. 'This game will put the league back twenty years,' he told one paper (although in another newspaper he was quoted as saying 'ten years'). Justice led the chorus for an investigation. He suggested all future proceeds at finals, including the upcoming grand final, should go to charity. Newtown officials were dumbfounded by their team's performance, but Bumper Farrell assured everyone that all players were 'flat chat' out in the middle. And while Kirk had missed easy goals in front, he'd also kicked an amazing goal from 60 yards out.

Newtown led the game 11–0 after ten minutes before falling asleep. The *Sunday Telegraph's* George Thatcher wrote, 'Some of the errors were inexcusable. Nevin stood flat-footed, Newtown forwards were too tired to chase opponents, and Jacobsen and McKinley missed easy passes. Balmain then scored from an obvious forward pass.'

Kirk, he continued, was 'mediocre', and erred in not kicking in open play more often, although Kirk later said that he'd followed his coach's instructions not to do so, so as not to give possession back to Balmain in the strong winds. The suspicions didn't go away and the *Sydney Morning Herald* ran the story of the poor game in its news pages, alleging that 'the result of the match was widely anticipated'.

Kirk was aghast at all the slurs—and much later he'd tell his son that he just had 'an off day' against Balmain. Indeed he was going to change the course of his army career to shout down the detractors. Although he was supposed to be sent away with the army, Kirk took special leave to be part of the grand final (remembering that, as minor premiers, Newtown had the luxury of a second chance in the form of a grand final in the event they lost the final). Newtown secretary Dave Jolly said Kirk was furious about the smears: 'You should have heard him. I had to get an extension to let him finish what he had to say about his traducers. To say that he's annoyed is to put it mildly. He's boiling mad.' To add to the pandemonium, centre Len Smith was unavailable for the grand final and the whereabouts of Narvo were 'unknown'.

The tanked final claims lost momentum the next week when Balmain won again, defeating Newtown in the grand final. It was the fifth time they'd beaten the Bluebags that year. In a dour muddy struggle, Balmain prevailed 12–8, with Kirk kicking one goal for Newtown. After league officials had time to reflect on the accusations flying out of the final, Newtown's president, Dick McPhillips, declared 'all those who made wild statements about the final should have known better'.

The loss meant Kirk just missed out of claiming his third premiership. However, he once again ended the season as the competition's top pointscorer, something he would do five times in his career, a record that remains unbroken.

The following year one incident was to blow the war off the front page. On 28 July, a cold day, as Newtown played St George at Newtown's home ground of Henson Park, all hell broke loose after St George forward Bill McRitchie's right ear was partially severed during a scrum. As a precursor to the incident there'd been some niggle between Farrell and McRitchie prior to McRitchie sustaining the horrific injury and one of Farrell's mates had claimed McRitchie knocked out a few of Farrell's teeth earlier in the season.

As a scrum was set down midway through the first half, McRitchie came in as the loose head prop, while Farrell was just opposite and slightly underneath him, on his inside. The referee George Bishop was on the other side of the scrum as the ball was put in. Suddenly McRitchie yelled out, 'For God sakes, let go' as the two men's heads were seen to rise up and down in the scrum. The referee came running around and warned them to stop 'scruffing'. McRitchie complained he'd had his ear bitten, then Farrell said, 'Look what he's done to my face', showing scratch marks down the side of his left cheek.

The referee continued play without noticing McRitchie's injury, but it wasn't long before the other players noticed a huge stream of blood coming from McRitchie's ear. At one point Kirk tackled him and came away with blood all over his jersey. Newtown's Herb Narvo then walked over to McRitchie and told him he'd better go and get ambulance treatment. Shortly after, one of the St George players, Dick Healy, noticed a bit of flesh on the ground. But the ear segment was treated as if it was a bit of paper that had blown onto the ground.

McRitchie was bandaged on the sideline before he was taken to Marrickville Hospital, where he also was given a tetanus injection. The laceration was huge. Not only was the whole lobe of McRitchie's right ear bitten off, but so was some of the supporting flesh, with the doctor reporting cartilage sticking out. As a result, McRitchie was looking at a possible 22 weeks in hospital for skin grafts to restore his ear. St George officials, led by secretary Arthur Justice, vowed they would seek a full official inquiry at the NSWRL into the biting of their player.

McRitchie didn't name Farrell at first as rumours spread wildly. A headline in the *Cairns Post* blared 'Rugby "Cannibal" Bit Piece off Man's Ear'. For his part, McRitchie said: 'The Newtown forward opposite me in the scrum sank his teeth into my ear without warning. There had been normal rough play between us, but nothing vicious. When he bit me I tried all I knew to break away, and in desperation I even scratched his face.' Doctors at Marrickville could not believe that the mutilation had happened in a football match. Nor could seasoned players and officials. Even Newtown's stalwart Dave

Jolly concurred 'it certainly looks terrible'. Justice declared it 'the worst looking injury I've seen in football'.

After receiving three reports over the ear-biting incident, NSWRL president Jersey Flegg said in an initial hearing the following weekend, 'nobody seems to know anything'. Justice replied: 'Except me. A feeling of sympathy has arisen over this happening and it exists in this meeting, but I have a duty to perform and I will not shirk it. McRitchie has met with an injury that no-one would expect to see caused in a football game.'

The NSWRL held an inquiry into the biting in late August, but the injured McRitchie was still being treated in hospital and was unable to attend. Stories on the ear-biting incident knocked the dropping of the atomic bomb at Hiroshima off the front page. By this time Farrell had been named as the alleged culprit. But he protested his innocence: 'It is only one man's word against another. I say my word is as good as his and there is no reason to doubt my word.' Farrell said he was underneath McRitchie in the scrum and it wasn't physically possible for him to turn up and bite his ear.

The gangsters of Darlinghurst made merry with Farrell's predicament. As he went to a game the following Saturday at the SCG he found obscenities whitewashed across the footpath at the entrance. The hoons had also swabbed slogans about Farrell in Sydney's subways.

As the inquiry progressed, evidence was given of previous biting incidents. The earliest known in league was when a touring Maori bit off part of player Peter Burge's ear in the early 1900s. Also the well-known Sydney surgeon Howard Bullock was bitten in the arm during a game. 'He accused a tough looking guy, and made the referee examine his teeth. The accused only had one tooth,' the inquiry heard. This was the dilemma in many biting incidents: often the perpetrators had a tooth alibi.

The league committee hit a brick wall every time it thought it was close to establishing the identity of the elusive biter. The referee said he didn't see the incident, nor did he notice the blood from McRitchie's severed ear, nor did the touch judges see anything, nor did an off-duty touch judge in the crowd see anything. The league's doctor, H.C. Finn, also could not say with certainty the injury to McRitchie was caused by a bite, but it was possible. Nearly all the players in the scrum and nearby at the time of the alleged incident were unable to corroborate McRitchie's claims. One St George player, Jim Hales, said he saw Farrell spitting, and he had blood all over the front of his jersey. He wasn't asked if Farrell was spitting blood.

After the long hearing, one of the NSWRL's committeemen declared: 'We are no more enlightened than at the beginning. There is some doubt. I cannot vote for any punishment.' The committee then voted 17–2 to adjourn the hearing until McRitchie could give evidence. A visibly upset Justice shouted angrily: 'You can just forget about the matter. I think it is a disgrace.'

The next hearing into the incident didn't resume for nearly six months. The appearance of McRitchie with his ear still bandaged added new electricity to the proceedings. There were yawning gaps in the questioning of officials at the previous hearing and these stayed as yawning gaps in the next hearing. The doctor said on his second examination that he couldn't see any evidence of teeth marks. McRitchie declared again: 'Farrell bit me severely on the ear.' Suddenly, though, the most sensational bit of evidence was produced. Farrell declared he had no—or at least, few—teeth, and he took out his dentures and showed his bare gums to the committee. He said he left his dentures in the dressing room on the day of the alleged incident. McRitchie exclaimed: 'You still have two fangs on either side at the top. They were enough for you to do the job Mr Farrell.'

Suddenly the inside of Bumper's mouth was the main bit of evidence. Baden Wales, representing St George, submitted the charge against Farrell should be sustained and Farrell declared guilty of the offence. The committee retired and soon after returned to announce that by a vote of 15–12, Farrell was not guilty.

There had been as many holes in the prosecution as there were in Farrell's mouth. By a couple of votes his reputation had been restored, his job in the police force saved, and within a year he'd be playing for Australia, rather than probably being banned for life. He protested his innocence to his dying day. Strangely, no-one had ever raised the quaint little custom Bumper had when out at night in the pubs of inner-Sydney with his mates and associates. His great party trick was to take his dentures out and crack hard nuts apart with his bare gums.

The years 1945 and 1946 were disappointing for Newtown. After finishing second on the ladder in both years, twice they were unable to make the grand final. Kirk continued to star, however, and played for City and NSW against England in 1946, the last of his representative honours. In 1947 he was offered £200 to leave Newtown for North Sydney, becoming Norths' captain. W.F. Corbett (brother of Claude, with same initials as his father) commented on the change in Kirk, now that he was captain of a team: 'Leader for the first time of a first grade team, his responsibility sharpened his football.'

In May, Kirk played the match of his life against his old team. In the comprehensive 27–8 win, Kirk landed six goals, two of them from 60 yards out. Tough play was still part of Newtown's make-up as the Bluebags tried to, as the reports said, 'test the character of their opponents by massaging with fists'. But Norths had an average season finishing halfway down the ladder. It was Kirk's last year in Sydney, but he went out with a bang, celebrating being the first player in the league's history to score 1000 career points.

Done with the big smoke, Kirk packed up his bags and his young family and headed back to where his grand story started, in Maher Cup territory. The war had robbed him of his chance to play for Australia, as it had many players, and his future lay with his old mates in the bush. He landed on his feet in Barmedman as captain-coach. But hard times were soon to hit. A failed hotel investment saw him lose all his money and he had to start from scratch.

In 1955 Kirk and family moved to Temora and two years later he became their non-playing coach on a fee of £108 a year. He got rid of most of Temora's paid players and brought in local talent. The change was extremely effective, and Temora won the next five Group 9 premierships, the Riverina Championship, and the Clayton Cup as the best country team in New South Wales. Kirk also won country coach of the year. And during his time in Temora, Kirk refereed Maher Cup and Group 9 games and was a no-nonsense referee. In one match he sent off seven players. 'That really opened up the game,' his son Ian jokes. 'One of the best free-flowing games seen in a while.'

But Kirk would one day return to the city, or at least its fringes, eventually retiring to Caringbah in Sydney where he often helped goal kickers with their techniques, including Cronulla star Steve Rogers. In his final years he battled diabetes, with the disease becoming so bad that doctors were forced to amputate his famous kicking leg. But Tom never complained about his predicament, and he'd sometimes joke with his son Ian, 'I wonder where my leg is? I can't find it.' And then, as if remembering all those marvellous days of kicking for Canterbury, Newtown and Norths, when he had the goal-posts at the SCG at his mercy, where he kicked from the longest points on the field, or skied those larrikin kicks at the end of the match, way over the grandstand, he would declare, 'I can still feel it, I can still feel it tingling.'

CHAPTER FIVE:
Clem Kennedy—The Mighty Atom and Mary's little pin-up boy

'He was me pin-up boy,' says Mary Kennedy, drawing up a big breath and shedding a tear that she vainly tries to pull back. She's talking about the love of her life, husband Clem Kennedy, a Kangaroo, a Rabbitoh, and a man so quick on his feet he was known as the 'Mighty Atom'.

It's nearly always tender with Mary, but she can get heated too, particularly when jumping to the defence of her pin-up boy. Like the time Kennedy was awarded a national sports medal, but in the shemozzle of Souths being kicked out of the league competition, it wasn't passed on to him by the club for a year. Or the time Kennedy—who used to bring her flowers on his way home from games, hiding them in his kit bag—was forgotten when the oldest living Kangaroo was celebrated at the 2009 Grand Final. Or when, at the re-opening of Redfern Oval, she felt snubbed for the 'flashy types', despite her husband having coached Souths' President's Cup team to nine grand finals.

She feels intensely the various little slights over all the years, and it's as if Mary and Clem Kennedy—who could set each other off, but were always inseparable, and tied together in spirit—were destined to tough out life's battles together.

Mary remembers the day she first set eyes on Kennedy and it was, of course, at a rugby league match. She was brought up in tough surrounds in Chippendale in the 1930s. Her father, Bill, worked on Sydney's tram lines and her mother, Mary, a strikingly beautiful woman, sewed to make ends meet. They all grew up in the cauldron of working-class inner-city Sydney where the hard streets produced the hard men that played rugby league.

League, which she grew to love, was a game into which she was thrust. As a young woman she was sent to a match by her mother, not to watch it, but to stymie the drinking ambitions of her uncles who otherwise would have hived off to the pub after the game. Mary remembers so many scores and players and match details from league's rich history, but she especially remembers a particular game in 1945 when Souths played Newtown.

She had a keen eye for legs, normally more a trait taken up by males. Her first comment at the match was about the whiteness of Newtown fullback Tom Kirk's legs. 'I'd never seen such white legs in my life,' she remembers almost 68 years later. Maybe Kirk was still carrying a 'Tumut tan'.

'Then I said to Uncle Billy, "Who's that player running over there?" "Oh, that's Clemmy Kennedy," he replied.'

'He's got great legs hasn't he?' young Mary then said, not knowing that one day very soon she'd be dancing toe to toe with those very same legs.

Sydney was abuzz after the war. Following the years of deprivation and huge sacrifice there was a sense of elation and frivolity among young Sydneysiders. And there was plenty of entertainment on offer. For Mary, as a teenager, there were the Surreyville dances, bike races at the arena in Surry Hills, and ice-skating at the Glacierium near Railway Square in the inner city to visit.

The Surreyville was a dance hall in City Road, Darlington. Renovated in 1934, it re-opened with a huge dance floor that had special springs underneath comprising almost 11,000 square feet. As was the fashion of the day, smoking was popular, and the smokers' balcony took up 800 square feet. They played mainly traditional dances, which they called fifty-fifty dancing, including the Pride of Erin, the odd tango and a barn dance to get everyone up on their feet and new vogue dancing. The men would politely ask for a dance and more than likely get a 'yes'. There were, as Mary says, in the heightened atmosphere after the war, very few wallflowers sitting and waiting to be asked to dance at the Surreyville.

Mary's friend Margaret had some contact with the players of Souths and she worked alongside Kennedy at the White Wings flour mill in Chippendale. Kennedy—who, at the time, was living with his parents in Waterloo—was a dance hall enthusiast and one Saturday night, Margaret saw him at the Surreyville and introduced him to Mary. Later that night, as they were about to dance the La Bamba to the tune of 'Jealousy', Kennedy came up and asked Mary if she'd like a dance. 'I just said, "Yes."' His first comment to Margaret later about Mary was 'she's a nice little girl'.

They'd planned to meet up again the following week for dancing at the High Hat Club at Glebe Town Hall. But Kennedy was late and Mary thought she might have been given the slip. He turned up later and explained that he'd been to the hospital to see his sister's new baby. At the dance, Kennedy invited her to go with him to a twenty-first birthday party at Alexandria Town Hall for one of his Souths teammates, Frank Bonner. On the big night, their first real date, the big hulking Souths forward Jim Armstrong was there, as was Jack Lawrence. Armstrong was a policeman and would later represent Australia in wrestling at the Olympics. His lone rugby league Test appearance was alongside Kennedy. So there was Mary mixing it with the elites of the Rabbitohs, suddenly moving from spectator to being on the periphery of the South Sydney burrow.

A year later, Mary's move into the Rabbitohs' fold was complete when she and Kennedy married.

Clement Michael Kennedy was born on 25 November 1921, in Redfern, the heart of Rabbitoh territory. His father, Joseph Clement, was the son of an Irishman, and known as Clem Sr. He encouraged Clem Jr to play rugby league as he grew up with two brothers and three sisters. Clem Sr owned a grocery store right opposite Redfern Oval, when the ground ran from east to west, and quite often a football would land in his shop because the store sat right behind the goalposts. More often than not, as Kennedy's career took off with Souths, Clem Sr would place a ladder on the fence of the Redfern ground so he could climb up and watch his son play, and then he'd rush to back to the shop if he had a customer.

Kennedy was educated at Our Lady of Mount Carmel Catholic School at Waterloo; at that stage it was run by the Patrician Brothers. At the age of 12 he was already the captain and playing at halfback. In 1937 Kennedy created an all-schools record, amassing 183 points in just ten games. His team was undefeated through four years of competition in the

Catholic schools' competition. During three of those years, no-one had crossed their line. In total, during Kennedy's time with Mount Carmel, the side scored 1209 points, with only nine points scored against them in those four years. In one game, Mount Carmel defeated Redfern 104–0, with Kennedy scoring 53 points.

Such was the amazement at his football exploits, the *Sunday Sun* wrote a story about the schoolboy's achievements: 'Clem Kennedy has been captain of the team each season and has never missed a game throughout the four years. Quiet and unassuming, this youngster has shown a remarkable football brain and has proved an outstanding leader. This year [1937] he has scored 183 points—twenty-one tries and sixty goals in the ten games played, this creating a record for all-school football. Kennedy finished off the season with a characteristic burst, scoring two tries and adding six goals.'

Kennedy got an early taste of representative football through Mount Carmel, which was chosen to play St James Forest Lodge as the main junior fixture before the first Test between Australia and Great Britain at the Sydney Cricket Ground in 1936. The Test attracted a massive 63,000 spectators, at the time one of the biggest rugby league crowds ever recorded. One of the British players, Gus Risman, the future English captain, gave Kennedy his British stickpin and told him 'One day you might be playing here for Australia', which steeled the young boy in his ambition to achieve such an honour. As it happens, Kennedy would play in the next Ashes series. However, due to various rows in the league and the not insignificant matter of World War II, that would be ten years later.

After he finished up at Mount Carmel in 1937 Kennedy went to night school at the Cleveland Street School in Surry

Hills. While he was there he played C Grade league with Cleveland Street in an under–nine stone competition. Weight limits were strictly enforced. Players were allowed to gain no more than half a stone after the start of the season and officials used to spring surprise weight checks, often stopping a game in progress to weigh players and catch 'cheats'.

Souths Juniors boss Joe Healey came to watch the schoolboys play and spotted Kennedy, and in 1939 the diminutive kid was graded with the club, initially playing in the thirds. Later that year Kennedy, weighing just 56 kilograms, made his debut in first grade, but some felt he was too small and too young to cement a spot in the top flight. Nevertheless, it was a good year to be at the club with Souths making the grand final. But Kennedy was on the bench when Souths got creamed 33–4 by Balmain in the decider. Balmain, he would remark, 'laced the ears off' his team.

Despite being pint-sized Kennedy 'could hold his own' against any opponent, says Mary. Indeed, at one stage, Kennedy almost turned to a boxing career. Top Sydney boxing trainer Ted Milmo took Kennedy under his wing and two or three times a week Kennedy would meet up with Milmo at a friend's place for boxing practice. Milmo rated Kennedy one of the best boxing prospects he had seen, saying he was 'keen and fast and only had to be shown a move and it all came naturally to him'.

But league would remain Kennedy's favoured pursuit and, in 1941, his big chance arrived when he was chosen as the run-on first grade half at Souths. But Souths could only muster four wins for the season, finishing second last in the premiership. Kennedy enlisted in the army the following year and was part of a unit called the Narellan Rifles, which was engaged in militia and civilian work. As the Japanese posed a threat to Sydney, Kennedy's unit was required to erect barbed wire barricades on the famous Bondi Beach to thwart any possible landing by Japanese troops. As Kennedy laid barbed wire on the beach, he caught the eye of an army sergeant who immediately conscripted him, and all those alongside him, to be sent straight to the battlefront. The wheels of the war machine moved fast and Kennedy was taken to the Sydney Showground and given just one evening to go and say his goodbyes before he was put on a ship, the RMS *Aquitania*, and sent (he would later discover) to the Kokoda Track in Papua New Guinea. From the Narellan Rifles to the hastily constructed 39th Battalion in a day. He and his mates' heads must have been spinning, for when he left, remembers Mary, he had little military training, and he carried a rifle with no safety catch, a helmet with no padding and an army haversack without straps.

Unlike many rugby league players, he was not spared front-line service and soon he was running vital messages for a colonel on the Kokoda Track as Australia fought valiantly to stop the Japanese marching towards its own soil. Kennedy was the right size and had the right fitness for the job.

Kennedy—who became well known for his ability to get a fire going in the saturated jungle—celebrated his twenty-first birthday on the Kokoda Track while digging slit trenches. He blew out imaginary candles on an imaginary cake to celebrate.

Kennedy's main role was to operate behind the lines but he soon saw battlefront action. 'I was in the final assault on Gona Beach when the Japs came in and we were waiting for them … and we were lucky enough to get them away', was one of his few comments on his time in Papua New Guinea. After the war he would hardly ever talk about what he saw or what had happened.

After a year's hard slog on the battlefront, Kennedy contracted malaria and was sent back to Sydney. He was given his leave papers and was now free to rejoin Souths, as the league competition continued during the war.

But he was a different man, and had become almost obsessive and somewhat secretive. For a time, the war shattered his sense of wellbeing. He would do extraordinary things in the street, gathering bark off trees into piles or miming the throwing of hand grenades. Later in life, after the birth of his children, Maureen, Gerardine and Clem, he bought three copies of the book *To Kokoda and Beyond*, by Victor Austin, which told the story of the 39th Battalion. Inside each book Kennedy wrote an inscription: 'This I hope gives you some idea how young boys, with no training whatever, were thrown in against the best of the Jap troops.'

On the football stage Kennedy had to start all over again. Someone had taken over his halfback spot at Souths and he had to settle for reserve grade. He didn't make it back into first grade until 1944, and then only sporadically.

His size again made headlines in the *Daily Telegraph* on 11 July 1944 when he was pictured at training being carried in the arms of his Souths teammate Jim Armstrong. Prior to the photo, Kennedy, standing not much more than 5 feet and 4 inches and weighing little more than 9 stone, had dropped Armstrong, weighing over 16 stone, 'like he'd been hit with a mallet' during practice at the sports ground. 'Kennedy is as tough as they come in rugby league,' the *Telegraph* said. 'Kennedy has recently been discharged from the army, after nearly two years in New Guinea. South Sydney selectors consider him the best grade half. They preferred him to Bill Thompson, even after the state selectors had chosen

Thompson for the first City team. Will-o'-the wisp Kennedy is also a deadly tackler.'

Kennedy's small proportions were again illustrated in a story related by Mary. Once, when he returned home from a game at the SCG, his mother was going through his kit bag in order to wash his clothes when she said, 'Where are your boots, Clem? They're not here.' 'I must have left them at the ground,' he said, and he cycled back to the SCG to retrieve them. When he got there the place was almost deserted except for one official. 'You haven't spotted any boots left in the dressing room?' Kennedy asked. 'No, only a ball boy's ones,' he replied flatly. The boots were Kennedy's. He wore a size four, not much bigger than a kid's size.

The year 1945 proved a turning point for Kennedy, as it did for the whole world what with the war ending. Kennedy was selected for the New South Wales side in the match against Queensland, even though Souths were struggling to win a game. His great exploits, as New South Wales crushed Queensland 37–12, were recorded. 'Souths halfback Clem Kennedy was a grand little player and often had the Queensland defence in a maze.'

In April, the *Herald* said Kennedy had boosted his Test chances after his performance in a club match against Newtown, but Souths would finish last in 1945 after winning just one game—and that was lucky, Souths legend Bernie Purcell later revealed, because Kennedy's try to win that single game should have been ruled out for a knock-on. Souths' form in 1946—when again they'd get the wooden spoon, this time without winning a game—was even worse so it was a huge feat for Kennedy to be winning representative selections. It was a bittersweet time for Kennedy because of Souths' woes but, as he said, 'You stick in the bad times.'

But Kennedy stood out amid the gloom at Redfern and, in a roundabout way, he explained how he managed that in a 1946 newspaper article centred around the art of a halfback:

'The halfback is the key of the backline. On him every movement from the scrum base hinges. His duty is to get the ball away to the five-eighth as fast as possible, which means passing from the scrum base. We have had a great lesson in this first principle of halfback play from the visiting Englishmen. Too many halves insist on trying to make ground [but in doing] so bring the opposition on to their backline thereby stifling any effective movement. Rule one says "pass from the base of the scrum".

'The same rule holds good for the half's tactical play from the play the ball, though more latitude is given to him now because he is virtually a five-eighth. Having set his backs in motion, his job has only begun. He should immediately set out to cover the back line for a possible dropped pass and if he is fast enough, try to make an extra centre. Also be on the alert for a reverse pass—a move which enables the half to start those thrusting forward movements which are so often point-scorers. Most halves pay too little attention to putting the ball into the scrum cleanly. Penalties resulting from lack of care have frequently cost matches. The use of the short kick should be very limited. The half seldom has time to kick carefully and careless kicking means loss of possession.

'Since a half will be frequently called on to stop forwards much heavier than himself, he must learn to tackle correctly. Halves who go high usually end up on compensation. In defence the half should aim to take the opposing five-eighth, leaving the half to the lock forward. He must be careful however not to crowd his five-eighth in defence.

'In brief: Get the ball away from the scrum base fast; use the blind side sparingly; put the ball into scrums straight; stay onside; tackle low; play football as a team game; win more matches by letting the other fellow score the tries.'

Kennedy was in a real dogfight for the Test halfback position. His main rival was Western Suburbs' Jack Russell. But as the 1946 Test series approached Kennedy was already being compared to one of the great halfbacks: 'The players who will be opposing [Great Britain] are at the zenith of their careers and if present form is a guide, Clem Kennedy, whom critics say is the best halfback since Duncan Thompson, will be opposite McCue,' wrote Les McMahon in Rockhampton's *Morning Bulletin*.

But yet again fate intervened in Kennedy's life, just as it had done on that day laying out barbed wire on Bondi Beach. Just as he looked certain to bag that Australian jumper he dislocated his right shoulder while playing against Balmain in May, exacerbating an injury he picked up while serving on the Kokoda Track. A doctor told him he shouldn't play against Newtown in June, and this ruled him out of representing Australia in the first and second Test. Kennedy was also forced to forfeit his New South Wales spot to rival Keith Froome.

But Kennedy recovered and he was fit to play in the third Test in Sydney, and on 20 July 1946 Kennedy ran onto the field as a Kangaroo, ten years after he had played on the same field as a Mount Carmel schoolboy.

The return of the Great Britain team to Australian shores after a ten-year absence was organised by lawyer, politician and rugby league enthusiast Herb Vere 'Doc' Evatt. Evatt—who once declared that rugby league was the 'fastest and most skilful form of football'—had brought rugby league to the

University of Sydney in 1920 and became patron of the New South Wales Rugby League in 1944. He was intimately involved in major political events, such as the creation of the new United Nations General Assembly, later becoming its president. Even during these tense and difficult years during and after the war, he always wore his love of sport on his sleeve.

An article on Evatt in *Rugby League Week* once highlighted Evatt's passion for sport and his belief in its transformative powers: 'He can quote extensively from memory, records of individual players and club teams, and in this respect is a veritable encyclopaedia of sporting history. He has even surprised American experts with his detailed knowledge of the statistics of American baseball teams.

'He believes that international sporting fixtures are as essential to world peace and understanding as the diplomatic conferences and international parleys at which he so ably represents Australia.'

When he was Labor's minister for external affairs, Evatt made it a priority on his visit to London after the war to negotiate a return of the Great Britain rugby league team (and also the English cricket team), although British league officials were immediately resistant. Getting the league team to Australia proved to be a logistical nightmare as the war effort had taken its toll on all available transport, and the British rugby league would not allow their players to travel by plane. Not only that, once the tour was finally agreed upon, the British War Office refused to grant leave to a number of the senior English players. It wasn't until representations were made by House of Commons members from the nursery of rugby league in Yorkshire that the players Phillips, White and Ward were allowed to join the tour.

Evatt helped secure passage for the 26 members of the British team on the British aircraft carrier HMS *Indomitable*, which had served extensively in the war and was now running naval errands between England and Australia. A limited number of civilian passengers (100) were allowed on board but this caused an unexpected problem because they bumped from the ship 40 women from Plymouth, all of whom had married Australian servicemen and were planning on travelling to Australia to start a new life with their Aussie beaus.

Four of the British players knew the *Indomitable*'s corridors intimately because they had helped build it at the shipyards at Barrow-in-Furness. The carrier sailed on 3 April from Devonport. The players helped stoke the boilers to keep fit on their long journey, and played cards, basketball and deck quoits. After the Red Sea the passengers endured stifling heat and one player said the ship was 'red hot'. Some players lost 6 to 8 pounds on the journey. An observer said the British captain Gus Risman looked as slim as he did when he toured Australia ten years previously.

The team upped their training schedule on the huge deck of the *Indomitable* after leaving Colombo as the cooler air kicked in. The ship called in at Gibraltar, Malta, Port Said and Colombo before reaching Fremantle on 4 May. The team was accorded a civic reception and saw an exhibition match of Aussie Rules. But the tour schedule was suddenly thrown into disarray. The ship that was to take them on to Sydney had been damaged in the Bight on the way over. Because of the strange aversion to air travel the British rugby league team had at that time, rail was the only other alternative if the tour schedule was to be met.

The only train leaving Perth for Sydney was a naval goods train and special permission had to be given from

Canberra for civilians—the British rugby league team—to travel on it. After permission was secured the team travelled in second-class conditions with no sleeping berths. The team arrived in Sydney after the exhausting five-day journey only to discover that some of their heavy baggage had been lost. Many of the tourists had to then get about in borrowed clothing.

It wasn't all bad news for the English. To this point their travelling expenses from England had been zero because they had travelled entirely on military service transport. And the players were on a good wicket in Australia, not only through pay, but also through all the opportunities they had to dine out. The front-row forward Frank Whitcombe found he was suddenly a stone heavier, at just over 17 stone and 12 pounds, than when he left England. 'Oh boy, that is going to take some shifting,' he told reporters on arrival in Sydney.

In terms of pay the players received a daily allowance plus a tour bonus at the end. The English Rugby League took 60 per cent of the gate takings, and one-third of the money was distributed in bonuses to the players, which came to about £100 each. In addition, they received a daily salary of two pounds, ten shillings (Australian) per day while in Australia, and if they had a wife back in England she received three pounds sterling a day, and another 7/6 per child.

The tourists' first game was against Southern Division in Junee, where they fashioned a penalty-marred 36–4 victory against the cream of Maher Cup players. They punished other regional opponents too, in one game beating Mackay 94–0. With these wins behind them they were on song for the Test series, drawing the first Test in Sydney before defeating Australia in Brisbane in the second Test.

Meantime, Clem Kennedy had recovered from injury in time to make the third Test, on 20 July, and the *Rugby League News* talked up his inclusion in the Australian team: '[Kennedy] will be the smallest man in the game, but also the smartest. Australia has been waiting to see this fellow play in the Tests and now that he has thrown off his injury, he gets his chance. Kennedy's presence will make a big difference to the side and should mean better opportunities for the men outside him. Runs well from the scrum base and will vary his play to suit conditions.'

The day of the Test didn't start well for the Australian team with the loss of captain Ron Bailey with an ankle injury. Then, just seven minutes into the match, Australian fullback Dave Parkinson of Balmain was injured in a tackle. Amazingly, as an X-ray later showed, he had broken his left leg, but played on during the whole Test, so that Australia wasn't a man down. Knowing of his plight, the British, to their credit, didn't tackle him.

If the game began badly for Australia it got better later in the first half when Kennedy—whom the Great Britain team manager Walter Popplewell cited as one of Australia's best players they'd come up against on tour—scored after an amazing run down the sideline. But it was to be the local team's only real highlight. Despite leading 7–2 at half-time the Kangaroos were overrun by Great Britain in the second half, losing 20–7.

Mary has the photo of her husband's scoring effort for the Kangaroos, showing him running down the right wing away from his British pursuers in front of 35,000 people at the SCG. Kennedy is shown out wide and running fast, with the big crowd cheering him on. It would be Kennedy's only moment of international glory. But as much as the photo captures this glory it's also a reminder of what might have been had war, injury and perhaps, as we'll see, religious intolerance, not robbed Kennedy of his rugby league prime.

To mark the end of the series, Australian forward and notorious police hard man Frank 'Bumper' Farrell took some of the British players and a few teammates to the Dolphin Hotel in Surry Hills for a drink and singalong until the early hours of the morning. They deserved it, the Brits, for their Ashes win was an extraordinary performance considering their exhausting travel schedule, and the fact that every player had experienced the horrors of the German bombardment. And in honour of the ship that carried them to Australia, the British touring side of 1946 were forever referred to as the 'Indomitables'.

An unhealthy division in league developed during the years after the war as Kennedy hoped to continue his career. The divisions between Catholics and Masons affected the way some Catholics were treated in representative sides. Kennedy surmised that many in the league hierarchy, and at Souths, had it against him because of his Catholicism (a practising Catholic all his life, Kennedy always attended mass at St Therese's in Mascot with Mary, and before bed each night they would recite the Hail Mary together). He never spoke up about it, nor took anyone on as an enemy, but he came to the conclusion that he wasn't likely to go much further in top grade league, although he would keep trying.

At this stage Kennedy had met most of his goals. He'd played for Souths, New South Wales and Australia, and felt it was time to move on. Anything else would be a bonus, he figured. Mary, who was good friends with the wife of rugby league official Jack Duggan, was told by Kennedy to 'never to repeat anything you hear or we may lose the roof over our heads', such was the air of spite and retribution at the time.

While Kennedy sensed this division, it raised its head in the most public manner with the virtual sacking of Les Smith as Australian captain-coach in June for the 1948 Kangaroos team. Smith, a Catholic, was amazingly left out of the national side despite his great form, having captained New South Wales to victory over Queensland and squared a Test series with New Zealand, and later that year being named player of the year by journalist E.E. Christensen. Author Ian Heads wrote in *True Blue: The Story of the NSW Rugby League* that there was a huge mystery over the snub to Smith, with four players chosen over him for his centre position. Smith himself later said he was convinced that because he was Catholic, the Mason-dominated board of the rugby league conspired against him.

'The mystery remains unsolved,' Heads wrote. 'The five men who picked the Kangaroos of '48 are dead. If there was a set agenda on the table on that night in June, its story departed with the last of them.' In any case, Smith had nothing more to do with rugby league in an official capacity, although he continued to help with fundraisers for the Newtown Bluebags behind the scenes.

Kennedy had itchy feet and luck came a calling just as romance with Mary was blossoming. In 1947, Cessnock Rugby League offered Kennedy £200, and free accommodation, to move to Cessnock as captain-coach. This was just too good to refuse and Souths couldn't match it, so Kennedy soon made the Country firsts side from Cessnock in 1947 and played as captain. A number of Test players missed out on the City and Country teams that year and it was hard to understand the selectors' logic. Test forward Farrell did not even make the City firsts side. Following his Country selection, however, Kennedy was also selected in the New South Wales side in 1947.

A young Clive Churchill was playing in the Country seconds and he came up to Kennedy at training and asked him if he should try out for Souths. 'It wouldn't hurt, but when you do, mention my name,' Kennedy told Churchill. Within weeks Churchill was approached by Souths official Dave Spring soon after the Country versus City matches. Spring travelled to Newcastle to negotiate the signing—an offer of 12 pounds and ten shillings per match. Churchill accepted and would become one of Australia's and Souths' greatest players. He'd also go on to earn a lot more than 12 pounds and ten shillings per match.

While he was in Cessnock Kennedy, who stayed with 'Darky' Johns, one of the famous rugby league Johns clan, drove a truck at an open-cut mine near the town. You didn't need a driver's licence to drive the mine trucks. Just as well, because Kennedy would never have a driver's licence in his whole life, always getting around on a bike. Mary used to go and visit him on weekends.

Soon, however, the need for special visits stopped. First, Kennedy and Mary married at St Benedict's in Sydney in November and then they settled down to a new life in Sydney, at first living with Mary's mother. By this stage Kennedy wanted back in the city competition and he originally tried to join Balmain but their offer came up short and they wouldn't budge. When he started training with Newtown he received rival offers from Young, Harden-Murrumburrah and Bowral.

A report in the *Herald* on 9 April 1948 said: 'Kennedy last night said he had refused an earlier offer from Young of a ten-pound-a-week job and free board and lodging for himself and his wife. Kennedy received a telegram today, asking him to contact Young officials. He said last night that if the offer was increased he might accept. His main object is to gain selection in the NSW side and later inclusion in the Australian side to tour England this year.'

But the Young offer wasn't increased and Kennedy became a Bluebag alongside his Kangaroo teammate Farrell. His move to Newtown, though, sparked a rugby league inquiry. It was alleged that he hadn't been away from Souths for the required 12 months before he could gain Country selection, and his recent move was deemed illegal. The rule seemed onerous as Country players could qualify for City if they had been a resident in the city for just 28 days. But after the inquiry sanity prevailed and Kennedy was cleared to play for Newtown—not that he was assured of a first-grade berth. His opponent for the halfback position was the exciting Keith Froome, a future Kangaroo captain. There'd be a ding-dong tussle between the pair for the halfback position over the next two seasons—though Froome always had his nose in front.

Early in the season, in one game, Kennedy played the first half as halfback, but was outshone by Froome who played in the second half. A precedent was set and frequently during the season Kennedy was forced into reserve grade, only gaining a first-grade spot if Froome was sick or injured. It was a similar story throughout the 1949 season.

Froome was born near Armidale and moved to Newcastle in his early years. He played many sports, and mixed soccer in the morning with playing rugby league in the afternoon when he was growing up. But sooner or later he had to make a choice, and not just between soccer and league. He was going out with a girl who did not like rugby league and she told him it was either her or his rugby. He chose rugby league. Froome would join Wests in Newcastle where he played his junior football before making the move to Newtown.

His career blossomed after that, and Froome—who once abandoned a game to try and catch his three-year-old son, Alan, who he'd spotted running along the top of a perimeter fence—would go on to play eight Tests for Australia, captain a tour to New Zealand, and score 124 career points for Newtown. In 1949 he was named the inaugural *Sun-Herald* player of the year. After he retired from football in Sydney he moved to Gunnedah where he coached and played in the local rugby league team. He would later coach junior teams in Gunnedah and Bellingen.

Before all that, however, he was a Bluebag alongside Kennedy, and in 1948, the year they came together, Newtown ran second in the competition, but won the reserve grade grand final. In 1949 they finished sixth and Kennedy couldn't believe his eyes as his former club, Souths, rose from years of mediocrity to win the minor premiership, only to go down to St George in the grand final.

By this time Kennedy and Mary were living in Rose Street, Chippendale, following the birth of their first child, Maureen. Inner-city living has never been without its drawbacks and Mary was having terrible trouble with noise from the pub opposite, which was keeping up her newborn daughter most of the night. Seems some car transport drivers were arriving late at night outside the pub and then carrying on with some women in their trucks through the night. It was times like this it paid to know Bumper Farrell and Mary called him at the police station where he worked to complain about the disturbances. 'Bumper came down and quick as a wink they got moved off. I think they were getting the ladies of the night up in the trucks with them,' she remembers.

The couple's next move was to the fresh air of a new life in the country. Kennedy accepted a captain-coach role at Grenfell in the state's south-west. The young couple lived at the Railway Hotel in town and Mary did sewing work, made beds and washed laundry to help get by. She also made debutante dresses for Grenfell's young women. They seemed to enjoy the country atmosphere and fitted into the local community like a hand into a glove.

And this happiness had success added to it in August 1950 with Grenfell winning the prestigious Maher Cup for the first time in 20 years. As if aligned to the proportions of their new captain-coach the cup-winning team were one of the smallest by weight and size ever to play Maher Cup. Kennedy worked out the average weight of a player in that 1950 Grenfell team was just 10 stone 7, despite having a couple of huge forwards. No matter. Grenfell held on to the cup for a further four games before losing it in the first game of the following season. They would only win it twice more in the cup's history. Kennedy, it seems, had been Grenfell's good luck charm and the friendships he forged in the township were as strong as any he had made in the city.

Quintin Graham played with Kennedy at Grenfell and they became great friends. 'I loved the man,' says Graham, who played in the centres and on the wing and remembers the grand day Grenfell won the Maher Cup off Junee. Celebrations were in order, of course, but first they had to get home. As the whole population of Grenfell was out in the streets waiting for them, the club president's car kept breaking down on the trip home from Junee and everyone in the convoy had to stop each time it happened. 'We didn't get home until well into the night but everyone was still there waiting, and then they all went mad,' Graham says. 'We were kings for quite some time.'

To beat Junee was a great feat because they were a well-drilled side. But Grenfell's team had many good players including Jack Clare, who played, and later coached, with Balmain, and of course Kennedy. Graham, for one, will never forget him. 'He was a tiny little fellow, but he had a big heart,' says Graham, whom Kennedy referred to as just 'Q'. And for the rest of his life, Q rang Kennedy on his birthday and on Christmas Day; every year for 60 years without fail.

Despite the joy their two years in the country had brought them Kennedy and his family decided on a move back to the city, and a life of hard work. After settling down into their small home in Linden Street, Mascot, in 1955, Kennedy would ride his bike the 8 or so miles (13 kilometres) to Drummoyne to work at the Dunlop factory. He had a set route for the long ride that went through most of the Redfern haunts he'd grown up around. Kennedy worked like a Trojan all his life but Mary always respected his need for a night out during the week—usually a Thursday when he'd go off to the Souths Leagues Club in Redfern with his mates, getting a bus home. (One night with an old mate at the bus stop he was about to be set upon by a group of teenagers, who only relented when he told them he was an old Souths player.)

At the club there were many celebrity entertainers, often old Rabbitohs legends delivering a rousing song or two, like this old beer-drinking favourite:

And now that we're all round the bar
And the captain's declared it's a quorum
We're drinking our way through the night;
And we're having the time of our life.
Throw the empties away, start again
For the boys of South Sydney are together
And we'll drink 'til the dawn breaks again
And may the sessions of South Sydney last forever.

The song was followed by a wild shout of 'Up the Rabbitohs!'

Linden Street was an interesting place for the Kennedys to live. Across the road were the stables of horse trainer Sid Nicholls who'd sometimes reveal a good tip as he was passing. Once he asked Kennedy if he could stick a horse in the backyard for a little while. Working for Nicholls was Ada Lynch, who was also a part-time vet and horse breaker. Mary ended up getting a job through her when she became a machinist sewing together jockeys' colours and caps. 'She could do anything, break in horses or castrate cats,' remembers Mary.

Next door lived the Piggins family and Mary recalls that a young George Piggins would sit at the front fence waiting to see Clem arrive back from work on his bicycle. Piggins' sister and brother still live in the family home next door to Mary. It was Kennedy who later encouraged Piggins to pursue top-level rugby league. Of course, Piggins would go on to be one of the Rabbitohs' best hookers, as well as a tough and successful businessman. He would guide Souths through the dark days when, at the end of 1999, they were thrown out of the competition. And, as chairman of the club, he would then lead them back from oblivion to re-enter the competition in 2002 after their Federal Court victory.

Piggins remembers Kennedy always showing an interest in what he was doing. He recalls Souths' President's Cup team (under-19s) putting on a trial in the early 1960s for new players. Kennedy, then the coach of the team, encouraged Piggins to try out. 'If Clemmy hadn't have been there I wouldn't have gone to the trials,' Piggins revealed.

Kennedy coached junior and President's Cup teams for 11 years, starting in 1951, and during that time eight future internationals came through his teams: Graham Wilson, Brian Hambly, Ron Coote, Bob McCarthy, Gary Stevens, Paul Sait, Eric Simms and Piggins.

Kennedy once recalled to Bill Mordey in the *Daily Mirror* how much he loved coaching juniors and he said he always had their respect. 'And I was able to impart my knowledge to them, the rest they did on the field,' he said. But Kennedy was no pushover. 'I was a bit of a slave driver. My slogan was "If we can't outplay them, we'll outstay them".'

Kennedy said the President's Cup teams he coached were fitter than Souths' first team. 'At the end of any training session they were buggered. And everything I asked them to do at training, I'd do too. "I'm going to keep you sprinting until I run last", I used to tell them.' Since Kennedy was a fitness fanatic, and used to do speed training with top sprinters, that could take a while.

Kennedy's record in the President's Cup was astonishing. Nine times he guided his side to the grand final; six times they came away winners. Although he once overlooked future Kangaroo Ronnie Coote for selection during the early 1960s, Kennedy had an eye for talent. In 1979, when Souths had him working as a talent scout, he was told to go and check out a young player from the Illawarra at a junior match in Wollongong.

When he got back he told Souths' officials that he didn't think the player was much good but he'd spotted someone else he thought had a big future. But the Souths hierarchy didn't want to know about him and Kennedy resigned his scouting duties on the spot, upset that they didn't trust his judgement. The player Kennedy had spotted was Steve 'Blocker' Roach who would go on to great heights playing for Balmain and Australia.

Kennedy remained, however, a club diehard, a member of the Souths committee and he was later awarded a life membership. He was in one of the cars with league great and broadcaster Frank Hyde when special guests were driven to the Sydney Town Hall as 80,000 people marched to protest News Limited throwing Souths out of the rugby league competition in 1999.

But as we've seen his life had more to it than just football. Family, for one. His daughter Gerardine remembers him as a man of integrity. She remembers too being a teenager and receiving her Higher School Certificate results. She was so excited that she wanted to go straight around to her father's work to show him. By this stage Kennedy had been laid off from the Dunlop factory but he'd found work nearby at another factory in Botany. When Gerardine tracked him down there she came away crying, not knowing that he worked in such dire conditions to earn money for the family.

Kennedy moved to a nursing home later in his life when he needed special care. Mary was visiting him on a Friday late in 2010 when the home was having a concert. She got him ready and wheeled him down to the front, although he immediately told her he wanted to go back to his room, which set off Mary.

Back in the room he looked intensely at Mary and told her he was going to see the Lord soon.

'You can't go yet,' Mary said.

'Why not?' he declared.

'Because I want to come with you and I'm not ready.'

Thinking no more of it Mary went home that afternoon. She was called about 7 pm that night by a sister at the home. 'I think you better come in, Mary, Clem's not well.' But by the time she got there, he had passed away. The Mighty Atom had finally hung up his humble boots at the age of 89.

These days Mary has regrets, and she rues the day when rugby league changed from being a big family—where everyone knew each other and socialised together at the leagues club or at singalongs at people's houses—to today's big-business version.

There's still a feeling of indignation inside her about how her husband was treated over the years. He wasn't even invited to the Kangaroos' reunions, she says, because he didn't travel overseas with the teams, having only played in one Test in Sydney. She also feels Kennedy has been left out of Souths' modern history. 'Anyone before [Clive] Churchill they don't want to know about,' laments Mary, who also nurses the insult of being refused a war widow's pension after Kennedy's death.

But Kennedy was not forgotten and when he died tributes filled the Rabbitohs' online forum when the club announced his passing. However no tribute could match the one his daughter Gerardine delivered at his funeral.

'My father was an extraordinary man, like many of his generation, a true gentleman,' she said in her eulogy. 'He was tough but gentle, competitive but fair, confident but humble. A man of his word. Integrity could have been his middle name. [He was] a man of values, [he was] honest, polite, trustworthy and loyal to a fault.'

*

Today, Mary stands at the picket fence where she has watched the goings-on in Linden Street, Mascot, for more than 56 years. Nothing grows too tall in the miserly sandy soils of Mascot, but she has seen many people rise high from difficult starts, and was so proud that her pin-up boy played for Australia. She looks down the street to where Syd Nicholls used to bring up his horses after swimming them in Botany Bay. She sees where a young and wild George Piggins used to kick the ball around the street with his mates, and where her Clem returned most days on the old red rattler Speedwell bike he rode all over Sydney.

But that was then. Now her suburb is almost a microcosm of the United Nations. People speak a variety of languages, and not many people stop to speak. The game of league has changed too, and she's not as happy with the modern version as she was with the old. There are too many players coming in to the tackle, she says, and they're coming in far too high—not like Kennedy who launched himself like an Exocet missile around the legs of his opponents. 'The referees should do something about that,' she says. But she still gets a real thrill when she hears that the Rabbitohs have won a game. Life's small pleasures are no less cherished.

'Two good things happened to me today,' the 84-year-old declares, looking up and down the street. 'The doctor says my heart's got at least another twenty years in it, and the other thing was that I got to talk to you about me pin-up boy.'

CHAPTER SIX:
Kevin 'Lummy' Longbottom—Raising the flag for his people

One hundred and seventy years after the towering barques of the great explorers and colonisers anchored in Botany Bay, a solid, barefoot Aboriginal youth places a football on a mound on the sandy patch of ground known as 'The Flat'. He steps back just five paces and stabs at the ball with his big right toe. The ball sails higher than a tall ship and further than a boomerang and clears the whole field. His mates look on in amazement and cheer him on. The long-range kicker is Kevin 'Lummy' Longbottom and he'll go on to stake his claim as one of the greats of the South Sydney Rabbitohs.

Longbottom was a kid who thought furthering himself in education would only take him further away from his main goals—playing football and golf. After La Perouse Public School, where he received his rather unusual moniker (after lumbago, a painful condition of the lower back), he decided to give high school a miss. In his spare time, and he had a lot of it, he practised football, collected golf balls, worked at the nearby Chinese gardens, and hung around golf courses, unknowingly preparing for a future, post-football, as a caddy (one day he would be the permanent Australian caddy for golfing legend Bruce Devlin).

Longbottom grew up in a small tin shed on the Aboriginal mission of La Perouse in southern Sydney with his three brothers and four sisters. Later the authorities would 'upgrade' them and their parents, George and Phyllis, to a wooden shack before moving them to a fibro house on bricks with a wire fence. But the La Pa residents had the last laugh on the shaky tenements the various authorities built for them; they all ended up with million-dollar views of Botany Bay, living in one of the most picturesque places in Sydney. George and Phyllis's four boys and four girls slept in two rooms, two kids to a single bed, placed, shakily, one above the other. (Two other Longbottom children had died young.) In the 1940s they had no hot water, a wood stove and no showers. Life was tough in the midst of a child's paradise.

La Perouse was named after the great French explorer Jean-François de Galaup, comte de Lapérouse, who arrived there in January 1788 after a mammoth expedition around the Pacific. Lapérouse was perusing the activities of the First Fleet and watching another country fall under the Union Jack. Lapérouse's men built a stockade and buried their dead chaplain, Claude-François Joseph Receveur, 'a man of letters and genius', in a plot overlooking what became known as Frenchmans Bay. Receveur was the first European buried on the east coast. The French explorers stayed for six weeks. But it was the Frenchmens' last taste of land. Lapérouse and his crew were never seen again after leaving Australia, perishing during a violent storm when their boats were wrecked on reefs in the Solomon Islands. The terrible legacy of their stay was a smallpox epidemic that decimated members of the Eora tribe.

In the late 1800s, Christian missionaries set up an Aboriginal reserve at La Perouse—and the missionaries' churches still sit there today, off-white, crestfallen, broken and sad. The influx of South Coast Aboriginal people, who were either enticed or forced by the Aboriginal Protection Board to reside there, quickly filled the gap left by the decimated Eora tribe. Their permanent residency allowed them to receive housing and rations. Segregation of Aboriginal people was the policy of the New South Wales government at the time, and a white picket fence designated the border of the reserve. Other church and charity groups also operated at the reserve. Although hoping to help the Aboriginal people, they were forcing them into further isolation. Indeed, this south-eastern tip of Sydney was often where people were deliberately quarantined, either because they were victims of an epidemic (there was also once a leper colony near the hospital) or their own waywardness (Long Bay Correctional Centre has been open at nearby Malabar in some form or another since 1909).

At the turn of the twentieth century there was plenty of beauty and amenity for pleasure seekers in the area. The La Pa reserve was adjacent to pretty Yarra Bay, a weekend getaway for Sydneysiders until the 1920s. Picnickers would take the tramline all the way south or go by carriage from central Sydney, unpacking grand picnics. The Aboriginal people filled the seafood bar there with oysters from the Georges River, receiving just five shillings a bag in the early 1900s for their trouble. Yarra Bay eventually lost favour to the popularity of Coogee's amusement areas. During the Great Depression, the holiday huts were taken up by the unemployed. When the first migrants came to Australia after the war many of them settled in the area. Many migrants became the best friends of La Pa's Aboriginal community. The displaced often ended up all together.

Longbottom's father, George, was one of the South Coast Aboriginal people who moved north. Born at Coolangatta, near Nowra, he settled in La Perouse in 1937 after marrying Phyllis Simms in Redfern in 1929. George, a handsome, lean and considerate man, worked as a cleaner at the nearby Prince Henry Hospital. On weekdays he sold boomerangs that he'd made at 'the loop' in La Perouse, a coastal walking trail and promenade where visitors enjoyed fresh fish and ice-cream, and watched the La Perouse snake man play his dangerous trade in the snake pit. George also showed off his boomerang skills to visitors and joined the mission's gum-leaf band.

Longbottom was born just before the war, on 8 September 1939, the second youngest of the Longbottom brothers. La Perouse and its bays and bush were his playground where there were plenty of fish to be caught and plenty of places to hide. For Longbottom, who loved golf as much as rugby league, there were the nearby New South Wales and St Michael's golf courses straddling the headland to hang around. It was, in all, a time of unrestrained adventure, though there was always an edge.

'We used to run around a lot together,' Longbottom's older brother George Henry, or 'Sparra', remembers. 'One day he took my bike and he was dinking all the girls on the front of it and I was a bit upset. I chased after him and he rode straight bang into the clothesline knocking out his two front teeth. He had two false teeth for the rest of his life.' The collision had one good and unlikely outcome, however. 'After he lost his teeth, for some reason he just started to grow and grow,' says George. And Longbottom grew into a big, strong and speedy customer.

Longbottom's father, George, meantime, was often the spokesperson for the La Pa community or the man with whom authorities liaised. George also earned some small-scale fame when he featured in pictures on the front page of metropolitan newspapers in April 1948 after his gum-leaf playing attracted the praise of the famous American author and activist Helen Keller, who was both deaf and blind. Keller had made a flying visit to the La Perouse mission during her Australian tour and her visit to La Perouse gave a new spotlight to the Aboriginal people, mostly ignored by the press at the time. As Longbottom's father, George, warmed up the band of gum-leaf players, Keller gently placed her hand on the gum leaf as George played the hymn 'Lead Kindly Light' at the special evening function at the mission's church. 'How delicate it is,' Keller told the reporters keenly recording her every move in Australia. 'I did not know that anything so lovely as this music could come from the gum leaves which you have played for me.'

Longbottom, eight, was one of the excited kids watching his father and the gum-leaf band enjoy their moment in the limelight. It was his first sight of fame and later he would learn just how fleeting it could be. George enjoyed the moment too and he would name one of his daughters Helen in honour of Helen Keller. But it was typical of what often happened at La Pa; important people came and went, but life changed very little for those who stayed behind.

George was still at the mission when the New South Wales Department of Housing took over control of the La Perouse reserve land in 1962. By this time the government policy on

Aboriginal people had turned 180 degrees from segregation to assimilation. The Aboriginal people had to smile as the next lot of officials moved through their mission.

But while things would always change politically and socially, one thing was constant: the locals' love of rugby league, in particular their devotion to the La Pa Panthers who played in the southern Sydney competition and were a de facto nursery for the South Sydney Rabbitohs.

As it happened, Longbottom's football career began at a time the La Pa Panthers had gone into recess, so he joined Kensington United, based in the suburb further north. Very quickly the then 14-year-old became noted as the best long-range kicker in the junior competition. At Redfern Oval in the late 1950s he caused a major boilover with one of his booming kicks. Playing Moore Park in the A-grade junior league, the opposition was so sure of beating Longbottom's Kensington team, or 'Kenso', that the Moore Park players wagered 60 pounds that they could win the game, with the Kenso team matching the bet.

The match was a tight affair and it was never clear which way the result—and the betting winnings—would go. But with just moments remaining Moore Park were leading by a point when the referee awarded Kenso a penalty, 5 metres on Kenso's side of halfway. There were audible gasps when the tall Kenso fullback—Longbottom—indicated he would kick for goal. And kick it he did: between the posts, over the crossbar, out of the playing field and into neighbouring Redfern Park. Kenso had won the game and the money, and Longbottom's reputation as a divine kicker was set in motion.

Before long the La Pa Panthers' recess came to an end, which meant that, while playing in the district competition for Kenso, Longbottom sometimes came up against his own brothers, who were playing for La Pa. On one occasion, his brother George was involved in a barney with some of Longbottom's teammates. Longbottom quickly leapt to his defence amid the melee. 'That's my brother, you leave him alone,' he warned his teammates. Lummy was a big man and people generally listened when he spoke. In another local game, George remembers being creamed by his brother in a tackle. 'I took an intercept off him, and he wasn't too happy with that,' says George. 'I made a couple of breaks but he always caught me, one time he knocked me arse over head.'

Longbottom was an ideal league player, not just for his powerful boot but also his speed and size (he was 14 stone and just over 6 feet tall). With such attributes he was on a one-way ticket to success and it wasn't long before he was spotted by Souths' vigilant scouts and picked up by the club, playing President's Cup in 1959 and 1960, that first year—during which Souths finished runners-up to Balmain in the grand final—in the unfamiliar role as centre.

In 1960 Longbottom's wish to play fullback was granted. Coach Clem Kennedy also offered him the captaincy, which Longbottom accepted, much to the surprise of Kennedy, who had reckoned that Longbottom would decline the honour because of his unassuming nature. But the burden of captaincy didn't affect his form and in the 1960 President's Cup grand final—once again, against Balmain—Longbottom had a day out to remember, as Kennedy once recalled: 'With less than five minutes remaining in that game and four points behind Souths went into the Balmain twenty-five when the Tigers' fullback elected to kick, the ball going straight to Lummy about forty yards out. Beating man after man he crossed fairly wide [to score] and then, taking the kick, put the ball over the crossbar for an easy conversion to give Souths the Cup.'

Longbottom would have many match-winning moments in his career, including in two first-grade grand finals. If he wasn't scoring tries, his massive bulk cutting through the defence like water, he was kicking goals from seemingly impossible angles and distances—distances most kickers would never dare to contemplate, particularly in those days when the ball was made of heavy leather (rock-like when wet), unlike the lighter synthetic footballs used in the modern game. Funnily enough, it was often the kicks close and straight in front that he often missed.

In the 1950s and 60s kicking was a vital part of the game and, like league's version of duelling banjos, opposing fullbacks would often trade massive punts for several minutes until someone knocked-on or found touch. With tries worth just three points and a successful penalty kick or conversion two points, an expert kicker was often the difference between winning and losing a game. Such was the importance of someone like Longbottom.

Longbottom's entry into the President's Cup competition was the start of a six-year period of domination for Souths. That President's Cup era was the nursery for the future stars that would transform Souths' first-grade side from competition easy beats to one of the most feared and revered teams in rugby league history. Longbottom was in the first wave of new stars making it through to first grade, and he proved to have amazing staying power as other great players came and went.

Longbottom was graded for Souths in 1961 and became an instant celebrity at La Pa. It wasn't unusual for people to wait outside his house in order to watch him run out in his football gear and head off to training. Russell Amatto grew up at La Pa and saw Longbottom rise to great heights, eventually playing with him in the top grade. 'He used to cop a bit of flak when he came out of his house in his gear, but it was all in fun, we always looked up to him. He was my hero,' says Amatto, who would follow in Longbottom's boot prints and play first grade for Souths (with Longbottom later becoming godfather to Russell's son, Paul).

Longbottom was just as popular among his own, and the whole Longbottom family were regular supporters at his games, including his mother, Phyllis. Longbottom's sister Helen says he and his mum were very close. 'She hardly missed one of his matches and that meant a lot to him.' Helen was also a passionate fan of her brother and once she almost came to blows with a spectator after he shouted out racial abuse at Longbottom.

In his late teens, Longbottom formed an enduring friendship with a young man called Gabby Stathis. Gabby's family came to Australia from Greece in the first wave of Castellorizian migrants in 1930, and they almost all settled in Sydney's southern suburbs. Gabby met Longbottom at a party in 1957 and they became inseparable. Gabby grew up in a Surry Hills slum and their friendship was bonded in working-class roots. The mates' mantra was 'have a good time out, find a girl, play golf or rugby league and treasure Kenso United'. 'We met at a party and it just grew from there,' Gabby says. 'We clicked just like brothers.'

Chasing girls was always a popular pursuit for the pair (though Longbottom would never end up marrying) as was going out on the town. Gabby found he was always driving Longbottom to parties or dances. 'He'd always get me, the bastard,' says Gabby. 'He used to throw a bit of shit at me, and I'd throw a little bit back again. He was no big head but I'd let him know if he was getting too big for himself.'

The mates often lined up a whole day's drinking. Starting at the Yarra Bay Sailing Club in the morning, they'd end up at the Automobile Club in the city by the early hours of the next morning. Longbottom's favourite drink was a cool schooner of Reschs draught beer.

Gabby—who Longbottom called Werris, as in the town of Werris Creek, because it rhymed with 'Greek'—was also backing his mate on the punt when the big betting plunges hit district football. 'SP was rampant at that time,' remembers Gabby. 'You'd think nothing of putting twenty or thirty quid on a game. All the betting fraternity from the races would come out to the league games. That was part and parcel of the game.' Longbottom himself loved a punt and Maroubra's Pagewood Rex Hotel was their favourite watering hole in which to listen to the races.

Somehow all of these off-field shenanigans didn't undermine Longbottom's football and, in his first year in first grade, he played eight games, scoring five tries and kicking 14 goals. As he did in President's Cup, the 21 year-old started in the centres and it was there he made headlines on 24 July 1961 after his efforts in Souths' 15–4 win over Canterbury in mud-bath conditions at Redfern Oval.

Under the headline 'Speedy Souths Centre stars' the piece read: 'Longbottom showed surprising speed for his size and made many penetrating runs downfield before finally scoring a solo seventy-yard try just before full-time. He again came to light as a goal-kicking find, to land three difficult goals. Longbottom was captain of Souths' winning President's

Cup side last year, and yesterday was his fourth game with Souths' firsts.'

Longbottom's second season of first grade, in 1962, was interrupted after he dislocated his collarbone during a game against Canterbury in July. He'd finish the season having kicked just 12 goals and scored six tries, but he was on the field to witness one of the great displays of sportsmanship seen in the game when, in the last match of the year, Souths played Norths. Fan Norm Blacklock said Souths were fighting out the wooden spoon with Norths when, with the game locked at 20-all with just seconds remaining, the referee awarded a penalty to Souths.

'Kevin Longbottom stepped up to take the difficult shot at goal. The full-time bell had rung when he moved in for the kick, and he sent it sailing just wide of the posts. I was devastated,' Blacklock reflected. But the referee ordered another kick, believing some of the Norths players had moved as Longbottom stepped in.

'Surely Lummy wouldn't miss again,' thought Norm, before he noted that Longbottom wouldn't even take the second chance. 'Souths captain Jimmy Lisle took the ball, kicked it into touch and walked up to shake hands with the Norths players. I was horrified. It was ages before I appreciated what had taken place.' Lisle's great act of sportsmanship consigned Souths to last position on the table.

The 1963 season was only marginally better for Souths who finished second last on the table. The Rabbitohs were suffering through an era of underachievement, a stark contrast with St George who, inspired by the likes of Graeme Langlands, Norm Provan, Kevin Ryan and Johnny Raper, had dominated the competition since 1955 and were headed towards a world-record run of 11 straight premierships. Souths, however, appeared to be in crisis, with the team not winning a game in their first five matches despite having talents such as Longbottom, John Sattler and Michael Cleary. One committeeman railed at the performances in the first half of 1963, saying they were 'making a laughing-stock of South Sydney'.

As was quite often the case, Souths' selectors were ruthless and took a sword to the team whenever they felt they were underperforming. One of the players axed in the early May 1963 purge was Barry Harris, who had diligently worked his way back into the first-grade side, only to be quickly put on the outer again. He simply walked out of training when he heard he wouldn't play that weekend. Longbottom was also axed from the team to play Balmain. The changes appeared to have worked as Souths creamed Balmain 22–9. But the fix was short term. Souths would only win three more games that season, one of them against their archrivals, Easts. Longbottom was back in the side within a couple of weeks, but all in all he had a terrible year, scoring just two tries and kicking just one goal from 12 games.

Things improved markedly for Souths in 1964 as the team finished fifth, thanks to an influx of young talent and the work of new coach, and former Souths player, Bernie Purcell. Before Purcell took the coaching job, training at Redfern had been pretty lackadaisical. The team would train for just 20 minutes on Tuesdays and Thursdays, and afterwards many of the players would head straight to the pub. One of the Souths players' favourite haunts was The Bat and Ball at Moore Park. Another was the Star Hotel at Alexandria, owned by the parents of horse trainer Les Bridge, who was a big Souths fan. Souths' greats Chicka Cowie and Clive Churchill were also regulars at the Star.

It was Les Bridge who would put the cardinal red and myrtle green colours of his beloved team on the silks of all the horses in which he had a share. Famously, when his stayer Kensei won the Melbourne Cup in 1987, Souths' colours were there for the whole nation to see. Bridge hardly missed a Souths game when he was young and it was his dad's mates, Souths players, who took him to the matches. He remembers the 'wonderful atmosphere' of the games and seeing Longbottom kick many a goal from the halfway mark at Redfern.

The 1964 season was one where Souths began to reap the benefit of its junior program, which saw young locals, as opposed to players brought in from outside, form the backbone of the side. Some of the youngsters would become Souths greats, like Ron Coote, Bob McCarthy and Arthur Branighan. In that year only one Souths player was older than 30, unusual for the era. Indeed, almost half the players were under 22.

In April 1964, Longbottom was in the team that beat Newtown 25–12, in what was described as the team's best performance in several seasons. A crowd of 21,563, the second largest crowd up to that time, filled Redfern Oval, with the gate takings a record £3000.

'Souths' bright young team swept aside the opposition with an entertaining display of open football, reminiscent of the club's great sides of the '50s,' league writer Alan Clarkson enthused. Longbottom played in the centres and kicked five goals for the match—amazing considering he only kicked one goal for the whole of the previous year. He also set up McCarthy and Cleary for tries before scoring one of his own, from a 50-yard run, to 'cap an excellent match'. Souths hadn't played like this in years and there was now an inkling around Redfern that something special was around the corner.

If the 1964 season was a portent of signs to come for Souths, it was also the year Longbottom showed he belonged in first grade. As if to underline this, against Balmain at Redfern in May 1964, Longbottom, with a strong wind behind him, kicked a goal from his own 25-yard line—a kick of 75 yards. Like another of similar length against Easts in 1965, it was one that entered Souths' folklore.

Souths' upwards trajectory continued in 1965 and they stormed through the season, finishing fourth on the table. They then defeated North Sydney and Parramatta before setting up a blockbuster grand final against St George. Despite St George being premiers for the previous nine seasons Souths had reason to feel confident, having beaten the Saints twice during the season.

The first of these encounters, at the Sydney Cricket Ground on 12 June, was a fiery match of the day with 'savage scenes' as three forwards were sent off for various offences. One player broke his nose, a Saints player required three stitches in his head, and the towering Saints skipper, Norm Provan, was punched. Longbottom inspired his team with four goals in the 14–4 win, while Souths swooped on the dropped ball quicker than the Saints and their defence held out a late rush by the reigning premiers. Saints may have gone into the match without Tests stars Reg Gasnier, Johnny Raper and Ian Walsh, but Souths weren't about to worry about that. It was their first win over St George since 1957—ending an eight-year drought.

Their next encounter, in August, carried the same aggression, Souths' players having followed coach Purcell's bullish instructions to 'worry the life out of 'em, knock 'em over'. As one league writer wrote, 'sustained bustling tactics with tigerish tackling' set up the 17–8 victory for Souths, who this time were playing against all of Saints' stars. But in what was an omen for Longbottom's future career, the scorecard for Souths read in part: 'E. Simms four goals'. Eric Simms, then 20, was promoted from reserve grade for the big game to play on the right wing. Along with his Aboriginal heritage he shared Longbottom's amazing kicking abilities. And he rarely missed.

Despite their rivalry as kickers, Simms and Longbottom were great friends—and related by marriage (Longbottom was Simms' stepmother's sister's son). 'We got to know one another as teenagers and knocked about every weekend. We got to be great friends,' said Simms. Souths would solve the dilemma of what to do with two quality kickers by having Simms take the short-range goal attempts and Longbottom the long-range.

In the lead-up to the 1965 grand final, Sydneysiders went rugby league mad, and there was considerable interest in seeing if St George could win an incredible tenth-straight premiership, equalling the world record in any team game at the professional level. Almost 100,000 people descended on the area surrounding the SCG hoping to get a glimpse of the game. The gates were closed at 1 pm with an official crowd estimated at 78,000, but more than 15,000 others entered the ground illegally—and dangerously—by scaling walls and pushing through barbed wire. Spectators even climbed onto grandstand roofs, both within the SCG and at the showground next door, which afforded some view of the game.

The authorities were powerless as crowds continued to pour into the jam-packed ground. And as more people swarmed onto roofs they were eventually forced to let the overflow sit on the outskirts of the playing field to avoid people being crushed.

George Longbottom remembers the great risk he took to get into the SCG to see his brother play in his first rugby league grand final. 'There was an event [a motor show] at the showground and me and my mates paid to go in there,' George remembers. 'We then climbed up the ivy-covered wall at the back of the [SCG] "Hill".' The precarious 50-foot climb was not for the faint-hearted, with serious injury likely if you lost your grasp.

Once George had scaled the wall and negotiated the barbed wire in order to get amid the mad scrum of people on the famous hill, he then climbed more walls to get atop the toilet block roof. 'And there were heaps of my mates following,' George says. His prize for such an effort was to see his brother kick the first points of the grand final—a thumping effort from the halfway line, which Longbottom followed up by racing back to his fullback position and giving a joyful little jump in the air. By halftime, Longbottom—who was wearing his 'lucky' swimmers instead of underpants—had scored all of Souths' points after another successful long-range kick, the second one almost 60 yards long. Saints, however, led 5–4 at the break.

Saints came out in the second half with a rush. A clever short kick from Langlands had Souths on the back foot immediately and Saints' rock-hard international, Kevin Ryan, gained control and never relented. But Souths kept in touch through another Longbottom penalty goal, an amazing 55-yard kick. The newsreel commentator said he was the 'finest long-distance kicker in the league'. The curse of the commentator is long established and Longbottom—by now missing the number 1 from his back as it had been ripped off in a torrid tackle—then missed a kick from almost the same position a short time later.

After St George scored their second try Simms added a late goal to give Souths a sniff of victory with five minutes to play. But when referee Col Pearce signalled the end of play, and part of the massive crowd swarmed onto the field, Souths had failed to make up the 12–8 deficit. But their time would surely come, as Saints skipper Norm Provan predicted: 'That won't be the last grand final that [Souths] will play.'

The loss was of course a great disappointment to Souths and Longbottom but it couldn't detract from what was a wonderful season, particularly in light of the club's recent woes. Longbottom in particular had had his best year in first grade, kicking a career-high 37 goals and scoring four tries, as well as playing in his first grand final.

Souths expected to continue where they left off in 1967 but it turned out to be a disappointing year. Hit by a string of injuries to key players—including Longbottom, who played just nine matches—Souths would finish sixth and coach Purcell would be sacked. Though one of the architects of Souths' resurgence, Purcell was an abrasive character and he and Longbottom were known to antagonise each other.

Longbottom sometimes took things to heart if he was criticised at training. On such occasions he walked out of Redfern Oval following a tirade from Purcell, who let fly with further cutting remarks as Longbottom marched off. Longbottom's former teammate John Sattler said Longbottom wore his heart on his sleeve. '[Purcell would] get stuck into him and as he walked off Bernie would say, "Oh, tuck your dress in your pants, Ducks." Lummy would get really upset but eventually come back to the field.'

Purcell would, however, later praise Longbottom in a tribute piece for Longbottom's testimonial in the '80s: 'His goal kicking at times was unpredictable, nonetheless some of his efforts were outstanding and I well remember the day at Redfern Oval, in a sea of mud, in a game against St George, Lummy kicked a magnificent goal from five yards in his own territory, high true and right over the black dot.'

The start of 1967 marked the beginning of Souths' glory days. With the more amenable Souths legend Clive Churchill replacing Purcell, Souths flourished. After finishing second on the table, Souths then faced their old nemesis, St George—who, in 1966, had won their eleventh consecutive grand final—for a place in the grand final. In a hard-fought match, Souths prevailed 13–8, with Simms scoring four goals and Longbottom contributing one.

St George still had a chance to make the grand final, however, but in the grand final qualifier Canterbury ended the greatest dynasty in history, and in doing so set up a decider against Souths. For the first time since 1955 a new name would be inscribed on the J.J. Giltinan Shield awarded to the game's premier team.

The 1967 grand final was a close affair and it was almost marred by a colossal blunder by the officials. At a critical time in the game, with the scores level at 10-all, Longbottom kicked for goal, sending the ball cannoning into the left upright. But instead of the ball bouncing wide, it dropped onto the crossbar, executed a couple of small rolls then dropped over for a goal. Well, that's what it appeared to do. While one touch judge raised his flag to signal a goal, the other touch judge waved it away. After holding a conference with his touch judges referee Col Pearce ruled 'no goal'.

The decision baffled the vast majority of the crowd, including Longbottom's brother George, who was watching, this time from a paid seat. 'It was the best goal that never was,' he says. Clive Gartner, Canterbury's winger, had no doubt the ball went over the bar. 'There was no doubt in my mind that Longbottom kicked the goal. I always stood behind the goalposts when kicks were taken. I was ready to run up to halfway to re-start play … then the referee and touch judges conferred.'

Fortunately, the officiating error didn't alter the result, and Souths ran out 12–10 winners, capping a remarkable year. While Longbottom's no-goal was a talking point, so was the great intercept try scored by Bob McCarthy.

As Canterbury swept the ball wide near the Souths line, McCarthy plucked the ball out of the air and sped off, running nearly the whole length of the field. Though his hamstring went on him just before the line he had enough momentum to score.

Souths' win heralded a new era for the game, one defined by the change, that same year, from unlimited tackles to four tackles. The rule change was to ultimately see more teams chance their arm out wide—a more attractive spectacle for spectators both at the game and watching on television—rather than slowly bulldoze downfield through the forwards, or rely on ground to be gained by a fullback getting the better in a kicking duel.

Longbottom's strength as a long-range kicker was less important in the changing times, and Simms soon became Souths' preferred option—and he would become one of the greatest goal kickers the game has known. But Longbottom had achieved a grand final win and he'd find much satisfaction continuing on with Souths, albeit most often as a reserve grade player. While he would play only another ten first-grade games until 1969, Longbottom would play 37 reserve-grade games in 1968–69, kicking an amazing 53 goals in 1968 and 62 in 1969.

It was not necessarily a comedown to be playing in Souths' reserve team in the late 1960s and early 1970s. The club was so brimful of talent that even internationals played reserves. When Souths and Longbottom won the reserve grade premiership in 1968, the victorious team included such top players as Gary Stevens, Bob McCarthy, Keith Edwards, Russell Amatto, Ray Branighan, Paul Sait, George Piggins and Ivan Jones. The reserve-grade side was virtually a first-grade side in waiting.

But while Longbottom was content in reserves, he did feel cheated, with his career winding down, at not being given the honour to play his hundredth first-grade game. Time after time during 1968 he was overlooked for the first-grade team despite sitting on 99 first-grade games. Some believed the Souths selectors and club were being mean because as soon as Longbottom played his hundredth game, according to his contract, his pay automatically went up. It all came to a head one week when two players were selected to fill in at fullback ahead of him. But while Longbottom was steaming in his boots the pair were suddenly struck down with illness, and the selectors had no choice but to promote Longbottom from reserves. Some reckoned Longbottom's mates put the hard word on the pair to step aside. Others suggested a few punches triggered a rethink from the two players. Whatever the story, Longbottom got to play his hundredth game, a milestone he deserved for the years of blood and guts he'd given Souths. It the end it was another great laugh for a La Pa boy.

As Longbottom's career wound down he was diagnosed with diabetes. Fortunately, his Souths mates did their best to help him through the difficult times. Ron Coote asked him to be his offsider on his beer delivery truck in the late 1960s, and he used to travel down to La Perouse to pick him up, his truck laden with Tooth's products. Longbottom was in his element delivering beer to the South Sydney hotels where he'd later be drinking. 'It was a sad story ... I cared for the bloke and I tried to help him wherever I could. He was a huge bloke, a lovely bloke,' Coote remembers. 'The Aboriginal people were great athletes, they could do anything, great hand–eye co-ordination, great running skills too, they could run all day. And Kevin, he could run as well as anyone. His problem was the drink. He just drank too much when he was playing, he became overweight and ran out of petrol a bit too early. If he trained a lot harder he could have been anything.'

With his days as a league player over, golf became Longbottom's passion. He played off a handicap of two, and when he wasn't playing he was caddying, although that was not a lucrative venture. Back in the '60s and '70s caddies shared rooms while working at the major tournaments, and received little for their efforts. They mainly did it for the prestige and celebrations in the club afterwards.

Longbottom had been caddying on and off for Bruce Devlin in the '60s and he became his main man when Devlin played in Australia. Devlin was one of the first Australian golfers to make his name in the US. He won prize money in 36 US tournaments in a row, a record for the time. He was also an Australian Open winner.

Devlin, who eventually settled in Fort Worth, Texas, where he now designs golf courses, says Longbottom was a wise head to have around. 'He was a very dear friend of mine for a great number of years. He knew my game pretty well and was always a good man on the bag ... He was a really, really good caddy, and he knew when to stay away from me if I was in a certain mood.'

In a rare interview, Longbottom told the *Herald* about caddying for the then world No.1 female golfer, American Donna Caponi Young, during the Australian Open at the Australian Golf Course in March 1975.

'It's exactly the same as caddying for Bruce Devlin,' Longbottom told reporter Terry Smith. 'Every day she has hit two bags of practice balls and spent a long time putting on the practice greens. And I have to come down to the course first thing each morning to set the pin placements.'

Longbottom believed a good caddy was someone 'who keeps his mouth shut and clubs clean unless he is asked for advice'. He certainly was appreciated by Young who said, 'Kevin is as good as any of the caddies I have in America. He could earn a good living there.'

Longbottom continued caddying as he coached some Souths junior teams after hanging up his boots. But those close to him observed the continuing decline in his health and his financial security (at one point he was reduced to selling ice-creams in the stands at Redfern Oval). In the early '80s, Souths, in conjunction with Souths Juniors, held a benefit function for Longbottom called 'An afternoon with Lummy'.

Longbottom's liver disease and diabetes gradually worsened and the once-15-stone man withered away quickly to be a shadow of his former self. His sister Helen watched as Longbottom went downhill, and she despaired that he refused to curtail his big nights out and to inject the insulin for his diabetes.

'He couldn't handle life without going out and having a drink,' she says. 'It was very hard to see a big man fade away to a shell of himself, I saw him suffering and he didn't like it.' By the time Longbottom died—on 10 January 1986—he was just 9 stone. He was also just 46 years old.

Longbottom's funeral was held in Kingsford, at a church next to Souths Juniors. So many of Souths' great players came to pay their respects while his former teammate John Sattler gave the eulogy. It was a moving day for Longbottom's family and friends yet it became somewhat extraordinary when a young woman introduced herself to Helen as Longbottom's daughter.

'I'd never heard of her before and we've never heard from her since,' says Helen. Longbottom's mate Gabby Stathis, who knew most about Longbottom's liaisons, doubted the truth of the woman's revelation.

The *Sydney Morning Herald* ran a story on his death, saying he was one of the code's greatest long kickers and 'one of the best golf caddies in the game'. He'd also brought so much to South Sydney, reignited Souths' fortunes in the early '60s and got to bask in some of the memorable moments of the glory days.

Despite Longbottom's great career and feats there's no lane, street, park or award to honour his achievements and the inspiration he gave to all aspiring Aboriginal athletes. But while such an honour eludes him, at least he hasn't been forgotten. And memory of 'Lummy' is held most fondly by those who knew him and loved him down La Pa way.

CHAPTER SEVEN:
Ronnie Coote—From bunnies to buns

For a man who grew up in a place called Meeks Street, Ronnie Coote hasn't been shy in pursuing wealth and success. His passion to be self-supporting and prosperous started while growing up. Due to a limited family budget he was often, as a kid, walking around with 'a galosh on one foot and a sandshoe on the other'. When the Coote kids went on holiday they climbed not into the rear of a plush sedan, but into the back tray of their dad's old ute. There were many hard lessons learnt growing up on meek streets.

These days, Coote is better shod—as are the handsome polo horses he has living in nearby Milton (horses given to him years back by the late Kerry Packer). Living in semi-retirement at his country pad in Lake Conjola on the New South Wales south coast, Coote is the picture of the man he wanted to be, thanks to his remarkable football career and the business decisions he made back when his peers were less inclined to long-term thinking and more inclined to short-term drinking.

These days, the towering, powerfully built Coote, still cutting an imposing figure 40 years after his footballing prime, owns the architecturally designed McDonald's restaurant at Ulladulla. It's a far cry from the Kings Cross McDonald's he bought into in the early 1980s as he was getting a foot on the business ladder. Situated as it was in the roughest, toughest nightspot in Australia, finding a collapsed body in the toilets, dead or half alive, was a weekly occurrence. But that tough, grimy beginning was a path to fortune for Coote. Like a good running lock, he'd seen an opening before anyone else.

Now his two daughters are involved in running the business and quite often you'll see Ronnie among the undecided throng in the ordering area at McDonald's, with his granddaughter sticking to his side like a butterfly to a large tree, as they decide if they're having pickles, cheese or onions on a sesame seed bun.

As a player, Coote had two football love affairs, one amid Souths' glorious run in the late 1960s and then, when Souths couldn't afford him, one amid Eastern Suburbs' halcyon years in the 1970s. He now helps rule the roost at Easts, as a director on the board, but a piece of his heart will always be at Redfern. But is it a cheesy relationship? He has a diplomatic way of tackling this thorny issue when fans of Souths and Easts ask him which club he loves the most. 'I'll say, "Who do you go for?" [Whoever they say], I say "That's who I go for." I'd like to see both teams do good,' he says in a rare show of rugby league bipartisanship.

In fast food parlance, moving from Souths to Easts was like moving management allegiance from Hungry Jack's to

McDonald's. 'Well it was all to do with dollars,' Coote says, plain as a burger with nothing on it. 'Easts offered me a lot of money, obviously, to go there. I could have gone to Manly too. Ken Arthurson [the boss at Manly] wanted me to go there, but I didn't want to travel over the bridge, but it made sense to stay in the east with young kids and everything. My father played [at Easts] and I knew all these blokes there, because I heard their names every night at the dinner table when I was a kid.'

It was a bitter custody battle for Coote's services that festered in the early part of 1971. With Souths refusing to allow him to leave Coote more or less went on strike, sitting on the sidelines for months. At that time he was the Australian captain and had only months earlier returned from England after winning the World Cup after some torrid, brutal games. And there he was, battered and bruised and a national hero, being offered the same money by Souths that they gave him back in 1965 (a signing-on fee of $4000) when he was just a new kid off Meeks Street.

Eventually, even as their leagues club continued to fall into debt, the desperate Souths hierarchy stumped up $7000 and Coote signed on just for the rest of the year. It was Souths' lucky day. Coote led them to a grand final victory, the last one of the cherished glory days.

By the end of 1971, however, Coote had made his mind up to leave and Souths relinquished their grip on their star player. And others too. 'They'd run out of money,' says Coote. 'There was a lot of us who left. John O'Neill left. Ray Branighan left. I didn't get bitter and twisted about it. It was just one of those things that happens in football. I'd started playing with Souths since '64, so I'd had a long go with them, you know?'

You can't help but feel that it was with some bitterness Coote left the club in which he had made his name. But it's much clearer how his departure, and that of many other stars, affected Souths. It marked the beginning of a long time in the wilderness for the myrtle and red. Ahead of the 2014 NRL season Souths' last premiership remains the one won by Coote and co.

It didn't take long for Coote's golden touch to translate to Easts. In his first year, playing as captain, Coote led Easts to a whisker of victory in the 1972 grand final, losing 19–14 to Manly. Two years later he helped his new club to their first grand final victory in decades. The following year, in 1975, they went back-to-back. No wonder Coote was such a sought-after commodity. Even Queensland tried to entice him north by throwing in an offer of a free hotel in addition to his salary, a reputed $60,000 over three years.

But this time Coote couldn't be budged.

Of all the teams Coote played for he couldn't have chosen two more entrenched enemies than Souths and Easts. The two teams contest league's oldest and most enduring rivalry; one reflected unofficially by bickering and blustering between rival fans, and officially by a piece of silverware, the Ron Coote Cup (awarded to the overall winner of the two regular premiership matches during the season—if it's a win apiece the holder keeps the trophy). Souths may be considerably more successful than Easts since the first season of league in Australia in 1908, but since the cup's inception in 2007, Souths have only held it once.

While this reflects the recent fortunes of both clubs in the league, Rabbitohs' fans are not scared to emerge from their burrows to nibble at Easts' heels, and the banner reading

'Forever in our shadow' is one Souths fans like to unfurl whenever they play the Tricolours of Bondi.

Souths have only once cast a shadow over Easts in the Ron Coote Cup, however. It started with an amazing 52–12 victory in the first match-up in March 2009. Souths secured the cup with a 40–20 victory later in the season. The March display gave Souths something to crow about, and proved the trigger for some Hollywood theatrics, by way of ancient Rome. In a performance befitting a role in his film *Gladiator*, Souths co-owner, and actor, Russell Crowe, famously faced the Easts fans from the VIP box at the Sydney Football Stadium and turned down his thumb. It was an Oscar-winning performance by Crowe, and Souths.

After Souths won the next match between the two teams Coote was on hand to present the cup to Crowe, and give him some advice that would make any self-respecting Rabbitoh fan choke on their lucerne: Coote suggested that Souths should move to the Central Coast. 'I talked to Russell Crowe about moving [Souths] up to Gosford. In 2009, I spent ten minutes telling him why it would be a good thing. "The NRL will give you $8 million to relocate and you've got Bluetongue Stadium." And then he said, "Go and tell that to Nick Politis (the chairman and long-time sponsor of Easts)."'

Which isn't to say Coote has forgotten his myrtle-and-red roots. When Souths endured the pain of being kicked out of the competition following the Super League war, he stood beside Souths legend George Piggins—Souths' tough fiery hooker during the 1970s—during Piggins' pugnacious efforts to get Souths reinstated in the country's elite league competition. After Souths won the Federal Court battle, Piggins then faced the shock a short time later of seeing the club sold off to Crowe and Peter Holmes à Court by just three votes at a general meeting. 'I was shattered,' says Coote, of Souths' expulsion from the competition. 'I marched for them in one of those [protest] marches to the Town Hall. It was huge ... Whenever George Piggins rang and asked me [to help], I would be there for him. What he did was unbelievable.'

Crowe also helped Souths in those times of crisis, and he was always ready with the cash, especially as the team fought expulsion. Says Coote: 'I signed a photo of the grand final in 1971—me helping Graeme Langlands—who signed it as well. [It was up] for sale in front of 1700 people at the Sydney Convention Centre [during a fundraiser]. When I walked in Russell said, "That's going to be mine." The auctioneer asked $5000 for it, and then suddenly Russell put his hand up and said, "6, 7, 8, 9."'

Crowe's subsequent purchase of Souths has not been seen by Coote as a bad thing, even though Piggins fought the sale tooth and nail. Rather, Coote believes it has given Souths strength. 'I think Russell Crowe has been very good for them. I know George [Piggins] will hate me for saying that. But I think Russell Crowe has called it how he's seen it. What he's done, he's got the team to look like they are going to be competitive. Greg Inglis [Souths' star signing in 2011] will be a great asset to them.'

Coote knows all about Crowe's love of Souths and says a young Crowe was among the shocked crowd when Coote played in the 1969 grand final against Balmain. Souths were odds-on favourites to win, but in front of 58,825 people at the Sydney Cricket Ground Souths lost the match 11–2 after the upstarts Balmain put in an amazing defensive effort to secure their first premiership in 22 years. 'In the 1969 grand final [Crowe] sat on his father's shoulders [at the match]. He cried all the way home. He's always been a passionate Souths supporter.'

The parent to child bond is often what keeps the culture of Australian sport alive, and Coote knows it all too well. It was such a link that spurred him on during the many times he ran onto the Sydney Cricket Ground for either Souths, Easts, New South Wales or Australia. 'I have a great memory of going to the Sydney Cricket Ground as a kid to watch Australia play England. Unfortunately, Australia got beat, and after that when I finally ran out playing for Australia, and when I ran down the stairs, and looked round the ground where I sat before on the hill with my dad, it gave me a bit of a lift, you know, thinking, I'd been able to do what once I was watching others do. It gave me that little bit of fire to keep going.'

Strength, power and determination were qualities Coote demonstrated time and again during his playing years. And, reinforcing the importance of that link to his childhood, all these qualities were forged in those early years as Coote played on the grassy edges of Meeks Street. 'My grandfather bought a quarter acre block in Kingsford and paid twenty-five pound for it. He subdivided it and got his twenty-five pounds back, and from there he built a house on it. He moved out and then we moved in. That was our home, Meeks Street, Kingsford.'

The Coote ancestry hails from tough country stock. The Cootes were well-known in the Dungog area in mid-north New South Wales, where Coote's ancestors worked as wheelwrights and blacksmiths in the 1800s. Coote's dad, Jack, played for the Roosters first-grade side in the '30s; a side that set an Australian senior sporting team record by winning 35 consecutive games without loss (a record that stood until soccer's Brisbane Roar broke it in 2011). Jack Coote would play in Easts' 1936 grand final win over Balmain.

Coote's mother, Doreen, was a keen athlete too. 'My mother was from the north coast area too, near Macksville. She was a good runner, my mother, she used to compete as an athlete, and she used to go in married ladies' races at picnics they used to put on,' he remembers.

Coote obviously inherited his mother's speed and his carpenter father's accuracy at nailing things. 'We used to play footy in Kingsford on the grassed median strip in Meeks Street between the electricity poles. Your sidestep had to be good, because it was only about ten metres wide, otherwise you'd end up being hit by a car.'

It was that magic ability to judge distance and speed that became second nature to the future fast-running lock and second-rower. 'I had a bit of a knack for that I suppose. I could judge the distance from their pace and where I could catch them … I never really trained to be a runner. I'd just run in a race at school, I got to district level, but never fast enough. I was better as a distance runner like at 880 yards, because a lot of my advantage is that I could score a try in the last few minutes of the game because I had a lot of petrol left.'

Coote's around-the-legs crunching tackles are part of rugby league folklore. When the *Sydney Morning Herald*'s league writer Alan Clarkson hung up his pen in 1988, he cited Coote's tackle on Ian Brooke in the second Ashes Test at White City Stadium (London, England, on 3 November 1967), as one of his most memorable moments he'd seen in his 33 years of reporting league.

Clarkson wrote: 'Before Australia could get a stranglehold on the match in the second half the speedy Ian Brooke was put into the clear and raced downfield towards the Australian line. A try at that stage could have dented the Kangaroos' morale. But the tall frame of Ron Coote came racing across the field and took Brooke in the best covering tackle I have ever seen, knocking the Englishman metres over the sideline.'

Coote remembers the tackle as clear as a bell, as no doubt Ian Brooke does. 'We were just holding them. I just judged the tackle and broke him up a bit, you know. We ended up three or four metres over the sideline. He thought he was going, he thought he was in, but I knew I had him on the line.'

Australia won the second Test 17–11, and then retained the Ashes by winning the third Test 11–3, Coote scoring a try in each victory.

The simplicity of Coote's life growing up in Meeks Street was partly due to a lack of financial freedom. 'Growing up, in them days, there was no money around, we never went out,' says Coote. 'Father had his own business but we never had that much money. He had a car, a Holden ute. When we'd go on holidays we'd all get in the back of the ute and drive off to go camping somewhere and that would be the holiday. So, you know, it was tough going, a tough life.'

Football, however, was an escape, as Coote discovered when he started his career in 1957. 'I lived in the South Sydney area so it was only natural to play with the Rabbits. I wasn't always going to play for the Rabbits, as a kid growing up, you don't envisage you are going to play for Australia, or play for anyone, I just thought if I just got one Souths jumper I'd be happy with that.'

In 1960 Coote began playing with Souths' Jersey Flegg team (where he met and befriended future Souths legend, Bob McCarthy). Two years later he made Souths' President's Cup team and, in 1963, still in possession of the number 67 jersey, the number that came with him through the ranks, Coote was graded by Souths.

In the early years with the Souths juniors, Ronnie became great mates with another future Souths hero, Bob 'Macca' McCarthy. It seemed fortuitous that Ronnie, known as 'Solid', would become best friends with a Big Mac, known as 'The Body'. He played with McCarthy in Souths' 1960 Jersey Flegg team (under-20s) and their friendship grew on tours, both of them later to tour together for Australia.

'We were beaten in the finals by Manly, but we were sent over to New Zealand to play in a place called Shirley in Christchurch. We had a game over there and Bobby McCarthy was captain of the team. I got the pick of where to stay, which was right on the field, but everyone else got boarded out with people. Macca was 15k out of town and on the outskirts of Christchurch. Anyway, we had to be at training the next day. Macca is with the lady he's staying with at breakfast, and she comes in with this big plate. "Here's your breakfast Bob. Bacon and eggs." It was a terrific feed, it was sensational, but Macca said he couldn't eat all of it. "No you'll be right," she says, "You'll need it." Halfway through the breakfast he asks her, "Where's your husband?" "Oh, he's gone to work," she says. "Oh well," says Macca. "I've got to get to training. How can I get there?" "Well, there's a horse or a pushbike." So Macca says, "Pushbike," and all week he had to ride into town on a pushbike. He was the fittest of us by the end of the week.'

Ronnie didn't rise to the next level, the President's Cup team, in '62. His mate Macca was chosen over him, maybe because of the fitness edge acquired travelling to and fro from the lady's house in Shirley. But Ronnie made the President's

Cup team the next year and was graded in 1963 with the Rabbitohs.

That year he got his first taste of grand finals at the Sydney Cricket Ground when he played in the second-grade grand final, losing 6–4 to St George, who that year won all three grades.

Coote came into Souths' first-grade side during a changing of the guard. Coach Bernie Purcell, with his hard drive and discipline, was on the way out. The era of the happy-go-lucky players' man, Clive Churchill, the 'Little Master', was coming in. As was a happy confluence of rare talent, players like McCarthy, Ray Branighan, Paul Sait, Gary Stevens, Richie Powell, Kevin Longbottom, Eric Simms and, of course, Coote himself.

But far from first grade being a ticket to new riches out of Meeks Street, Coote found he was working mundane jobs (as a panel beater at this point) and earning very little on and off the field, certainly not enough for things like holidays. Those that couldn't accumulate enough to buy a car used to travel by public bus to training and even matches. 'I think I was getting twenty pound a week playing first grade for Souths in '64 and twenty quid a week as a win bonus. So the economics didn't weigh up, so I soon got out of panel beating and they soon found me a job somewhere else.'

Coote knew he was part of something bigger than himself, the spirit and never say die attitude of the club, a passion for tradition that would resurface with a public revolt decades later when Souths were thrown out of the competition. 'It's the story of the club, its history is everlasting what they have done, the great years, the great teams, the way they played the game, they ran the ball around, never say die and all that … You play for South Sydney for the red and green and the tradition that carries with it. That's what made you want to play.'

Success came thick and fast, and before he knew it Coote had four grand final victories under his belt, beginning in 1967 when Souths beat Canterbury (who had ended St George's quest for a twelfth-successive premiership with a 12–11 victory in preliminary final). A second would follow in 1968 when Souths beat Manly 13–9 in a match that pitted Coote against Manly's Bill Bradstreet, who two years earlier had beaten Coote to a forward position in the Australian team. Early in the game, Bradstreet punched Coote in a tackle. Moments later, Coote floored Bradstreet with 'the best right hand since José Torres', according to the commentator. Coote's act of retaliation seemed over the top but, although it happened right in front of referee Col Pearce, Coote only received a caution. He could easily have been sent off.

After the disappointment of losing the 1969 grand final to Balmain (11–2) Souths returned to the big dance in 1970 where they'd face Manly. It was the grand final made memorable by John Sattler breaking his jaw (helped by a fist from Manly's John Bucknall, that is) in the first ten minutes yet playing on.

'I still can't believe he got through … [When] I looked at him his bottom jaw was completely separated and I said "You"ll have to go off", and he said, "I'm not going off." He could hardly talk. He's just the toughest man I've ever seen.' Sattler famously saw out the rest of the grand final, which Souths won 23–12. A reporter said when he interviewed Sattler after the game the player's mouth 'swung like a rusty gate'.

Coote says his favourite grand final was in 1971 when Souths led by just 1–0 at half-time against St George after an Eric Simms field goal. In front of 62,838 people at the Sydney

Cricket Ground, Souths' forwards set up an 11–0 lead before St George fought back to 11–10 with just over ten minutes remaining.

One minute after the resumption, Piggins whipped the ball out to Stevens who tore through the ruck. Coote raced down the sideline and fed Branighan who beat three players to score. Souths led 4–0. Almost 15 minutes later, Sattler broke through, dummied inside, but passed outside to Coote who scored wide out with St George great Graeme Langlands languishing behind, lying on the ground in exhaustion. Simms converted and Souths led 11–0. St George fought back with two quick tries and the grand final was in the balance as Souths led just 11–10.

Coote remembers: 'Tension was never higher than in those final minutes.' With nine minutes to go, Simms missed a field goal. Sattler called to his exhausted men for one last effort.

'McCarthy went down with cramp, but [Sattler] ran past him and yelled "Get on your bloody feet, Bob."'

Coote says McCarthy later said of the incident, 'It was as if I'd been fired off the ground. When he tells you to do something, you do it.'

In the last scrum of the match, wily Piggins again raked the ball back and turned defence into attack. Coote ran wide to the left and when under pressure turned the ball inside to McCarthy who broke clear and then scored under the posts. Simms clinched the grand final with his kick, with Souths winning 16–10.

Alan Clarkson wrote: 'Up and down the field the battle raged with first one, and then the other, in possession, trying with their last ounce of strength and skill for that one critical break.

'It came just two minutes from the finish. Lock Ron Coote, a magnificent figure in this match, raced through out wide. Inside him was Bob McCarthy. As Coote was tackled, he passed to his second-row teammate who ambled over under the post.'

The grand final was Souths', and Coote had helped secure the win by offloading to the Big Mac, his great friend. Sattler, in another display of great courage, played through the second half with a damaged right hand.

'It was Coote's best game of the season—he tackled superbly, providing Souths with tight cover [defence] and [he was] constantly probing for the opening,' Clarkson wrote of the big lock who was famously captured by images giving hurt St George captain and his Kangaroo teammate Graeme Langlands help up from a heavy fall during the game.

Coote's football life had changed remarkably in five years. Off the field—during a time he worked as a salesman for Garfield Gaskets and was selling products to the Tooth Brewery—his life was also undergoing remodelling. 'Tooth Brewery was one of our customers and I knew some guys in there and they said "Look, we're going to put some trucks on, so do you want to get a truck, it's a really good business?" So I had a beer truck for Tooth's at Broadway for six years, delivering barrels and bottles in the '70s.'

It's hard to believe nowadays, but it was his trucking contract that stopped him from playing for Australia for almost three years. 'I had the truck in '71 when I came back from England, after I captained the World Cup team. One of the conditions to have the truck was that I could not leave it, so I couldn't play for Australia in '71, '72, '73. [Tooth's] started copping some flak about it, so they allowed me to play in '74, '75.'

While running his truck had such complications and sacrifices Coote's desire to succeed remained undiminished and he was a fierce competitor in both the sporting and business spheres. 'I probably think growing up with a sandshoe and a galosh [that] I didn't want my kids to suffer the same thing. The lessons I learnt in rugby league I took into life and running a business. And what that taught me has helped no end in what I've done.'

It was during this time that an unlikely friendship occurred: the boy from Meeks Street became friends with the richest man in Australia. Coote always knew that Kerry Packer was as much a rugby league fan as a cricket fan but he was staggered to one day see the media mogul sitting on top of the TCN 9 broadcast van at Redfern Oval wearing a white cashmere jumper, watching as Coote battled out a Saturday afternoon game.

Packer was always considered a Roosters fan through and through, but Coote says this isn't true. 'I know he was a Souths fan. He told me. He always had a soft spot for them.' But perhaps it was Packer's admiration of Coote's dashing style that saw him switch allegiance to Easts, just as Coote did the same.

Although separated by millions (of dollars), Coote and Packer shared the same earthiness and desire to succeed. Packer liked a view of sport from the ground up, and this was what Coote provided to the mogul as he was about to shake the foundations of cricket apart with the launch of World Series Cricket. First meeting the mogul up in the stands at the old Sports Ground, Coote says Packer became a regular in the Easts dressing room after games as he took a controlling interest in the club's destiny.

'I trusted him and he trusted me and we shared a good relationship,' says Coote. As Souths bled and bled after the glory days, Easts rose and rose, partly due to Packer's behind-the-scenes management. And it was Packer who was behind the eventual signing of one of the greats of football, the then Manly star, Bob Fulton.

Coote often went down to Packer's office in Park Street for lunch in the city, and soon the footballer found himself sharing a beer with the mogul in his plush residence, Cairnton, on Victoria Road, Bellevue Hill. There was the boy from Meeks Street entering the grand gates of Packer's mansion with sweeping views of Sydney Harbour to watch footy replays and give his views on the future of the league. 'He wanted to learn about rugby league, what was the best team, where would you put this player and so on. We'd share a laugh and a joke. The feelings of friendship were mutual.'

Coote also found himself in the middle of the whirlwind of Packer's takeover of cricket during 1977. Packer offered him a job as a salesman at a clothing manufacturer and he suddenly found himself organising playing uniforms for the rebel cricketers, the racy colourful uniforms that became known as 'pyjamas'.

'The problem was that a lot of the players were all overseas so we had to get their uniforms done by a tailor's order. We had one come in from the West Indies and it said "arms, three foot long" or something. We thought it must be a mistake so we sent it back. It came back again with exactly the same measurements. It was for [6 foot 8] Joel Garner from the West Indies.

'Packer,' says Coote, 'was a great bloke, a real gentleman. He'd give you advice on how to make the most of your life, about your family and what you were doing. He was a great help to me. He'd try and help you if he could.'

At one city lunch, Packer turned to him and asked what he was doing later that week. 'He said, "Why don't you take my helicopter up to Ellerston (Packer's country property at Scone) and play some golf?" So I gathered some of me mates together and up we went. It was one of the top 10 golf courses in Australia but there wasn't even a pitch mark on it anywhere to be seen when we got there. He had about 14 full-time groundsmen working on it.'

Packer never revolutionised league as he did cricket, although you feel he was itching to do so. For some reason he left it alone only to see his great media rival, Rupert Murdoch, move in on it during the Super League schism in the '90s. Packer had some bold ideas for league's future nonetheless. He put a proposal to league bosses in Phillip Street to mark the field like an American football field so people could measure the ground gained in each movement. The idea never took on at the time (although these days Packer's idea has more or less come to fruition).

Packer's Channel Nine station, however, did revolutionise the way league was marketed and played. It introduced Friday night football with its cheerleaders and fanfare. Broadcast rights were the new gold mine for league and for TV station owners, so really Packer only had to sit tight as the game came to him.

Broadcast rights are still the most significant monetary factor in the game, and they'll dictate the future of league, Coote reckons. 'The game is fantastic and I think [it] will always survive. It's a great television product and hopefully with the new television deal, the returns people are talking about, I think the game can survive and thrive on that money, but as far as club monies is concerned, that worries me. If the clubs can't supply the facilities and venues then fans will find other things to do and that will be a tragedy. I think rugby league will really evolve on television deals.'

Injury, including a broken arm, and a serious staph infection signalled the end of Coote's career in 1978. In fact, his final time at Easts almost ended in embarrassment, and would have done so if it hadn't been for his old mate Artie Beetson, who was then Easts' captain-coach. Until Beetson's intervention, it seemed the man who had led Australia to World Cup glory, helped Easts to two grand finals and Souths four, would bow out in second-grade football. 'I felt it was my duty as his mate that he should finish in first grade,' Beetson told Roy Masters. 'I felt a bit sorry for the way he went out because he was a legend in the game and he deserved a bit more fanfare. I would have liked him to go out in a grand final because it was deserving of a warrior like Cootey because he epitomised what a footballer should be like. He could play under pressure and he could play wounded. I've seen him cut to pieces and go back into the fray and not think anything about it.'

After coaching reserve grade for Easts in 1979, Coote decided his future lay in business. In 1981 he applied for a franchise with McDonald's, then only in its infancy in Australia. Powerbrokers Bob Mansfield and Peter Ritchie liked what they saw in Coote. His first outlet was at Newtown before he took over Kings Cross. Eventually he'd have three franchises. In a blink of an eye, meek times were far behind him—although Kings Cross threw up its share of grime. One night a man was shot dead right at the entrance to his Kings Cross McDonald's and Coote had to kindly ask police if they could please move the body a little bit so people could get into the restaurant.

For all his keenness to succeed financially, Coote has not forgotten what league gave him and he's keen to give back. One of his greatest achievements off the field has been the creation of the charity Men of League Foundation. Sporting many branches, Men of League—which started as an idea in Coote's head when he came across an old league player at Milton Hospital and found that he was lonely and in need of help—aims at helping rugby league people who've fallen on hard times, be they ex-players, officials, administrators, even canteen workers.

Coote, of course, is very keen to look after his own family, and he's passing the McDonald's baton on to his two daughters. Hard work, natural skills and a peppering of Kerry Packer magic powder has got him to this point in life where he can be sure his children don't have to walk around with a galosh on one foot and a sandshoe on the other. Surprisingly though, when asked about the real emotion that underlies his determination, he says it's simply 'fear'; a fear of being hurt, of getting beaten, of embarrassing yourself.

Toughness, he says, isn't innate. You learn to be tough. 'But toughness isn't everything,' continues Coote. 'You need fear.'

CHAPTER EIGHT:
Laurie Nichols—The Tiger within

Everyone marvelled at how the famous Tigers barracker Laurie Nichols only wore a singlet on his muscly torso even in the coldest of climes: while barracking for the Kangaroos by a snowbound football ground in England, or as a stiff winter wind blew across his beloved Leichhardt Oval in Balmain.

Even in Russia his hardiness became a curiosity. Nichols once emerged from customs at Moscow wearing naught but jeans and a black Jackie Howe singlet emblazoned with 'Balmain'. Suddenly Muscovites were rushing up to Nichols as if he were a long-lost royal. 'The locals thought I was some sort of apparition,' Laurie said, suddenly finding he could melt Cold War suspicions through apparel. 'They were all dressed in overcoats and assorted furs. People came up and started to touch me and I must have been photographed a dozen times.'

Later, walking with a party of tourists down a Moscow street, and still wearing the singlet, he was asked by his Muscovite tour guide: 'You not cold?'

'Not at all,' Nichols replied.

'What you do if it get much colder?'

'I just put on another singlet,' Nichols explained.

Nichols' resilience to cold extremes was forged in the bitter winters that hit his hometown of Cooma like a bare fist as he was growing up. The cold air sank into the little valley in southern New South Wales and didn't budge until the spring thaw. Ice patches would stay for months in the shade, and paths were often like ice-skating rinks in the morning. Nichols' older brother, Harry, remembers the local newsagent walking proudly down Sharp Street early one day to open his shop, whistling at the top of his lungs, when his feet went right out from under him. 'He wasn't whistling anymore,' says Harry. As the temperature plummeted to such winter extremes as minus 13 degrees, the Nichols boys would have great sport crossing the iced-over Cooma Creek, which, after heavy summer rains, often rose to cut the town in two.

But it wasn't just the cold that gave Nichols the ability to bear extremes. He grew up in the poorest of circumstances. There were 13 children born to Bill and Margaret Nichols, but three of them would die early. Raising children in those days in Cooma was tough—and it wasn't uncommon for the parents to die in middle age from pneumonia or disease—but despite the conditions and the hard lives many couples had large families.

Laurie Nichols was the fourth child, born on the last day of the year in 1922, a New Year's Eve gift to his family. Bill Nichols helped look after his big family by spending long days chopping wood in the forests around Cooma and carting it to town to feed the voracious appetite of Cooma residents for firewood. He earned just ten shillings a day.

In those early years, as the winter chills bit hard, the Nichols kids didn't even have shoes. Harry Nichols remembers travelling in a horse and dray with another family, when one of the Nichols kids looked at the feet of their fellow travellers. 'What's them?' a Nichols asked a boy. 'Them's shoes,' the boy replied proudly.

Harry says the Depression years taught the Nichols kids a work ethic that lasted all their lives, though Harry was always mindful of those that didn't work, and received government handouts. 'You didn't get dole money then,' says Harry. 'You'd go down to the police station and get food coupons. You never got money.' The boys would often skip school to work with their dad chopping wood. These were long hard days with little recompense.

There were three to four Nichols kids to a room in their small house in Lambie Street before they moved to nearby Cromwell Street. It was a case of make your own fun, or have none. They'd put newspaper into an old football casing and use it to play football at a place they nicknamed Nichols' flat, mainly because it was mostly the Nichols kids running around on it. Young Laurie made raids on neighbours' orchards, and especially liked wild hawthorn fruits. 'Never mind the thorns, just hoe into them,' he'd instruct his siblings.

Laurie also had a keen eye for rabbits, which he referred to as 'underground mutton', and he helped the family survive by shooting hundreds of them during the Depression years. Such were their circumstances the Nichols family couldn't even afford a radio.

Laurie played rugby league when he was younger and he also took to boxing, training from the age of just seven at the Cooma Police Citizens and Youth Club. He quickly showed he was adept at all kinds of quick jabs—the jabs that later were always a great television cutaway shot when he was going wild in the crowd after a Balmain try.

The policeman conducting the boxing lessons told Laurie: 'Come over here, Snowy. You can box on two conditions. One, be a good citizen and, two, when you get to my age,' about 55, 'be as fit as me.'

Nichols—whose brother Reg became a top amateur boxer, and who, according to his other brother Harry, was a 'pretty handy pug'—would say that experience helped instil in him a sense of discipline, and he kept faith with the policeman's instruction, staying fit all his life. He became well-known for doing exercises on Springwood station platform as he was waiting for the train to take him down to Sydney to watch the Tigers. Sometimes he was heckled by onlookers but he'd shout at them: 'Mate, I might be mad, but I hate people telling me; you look after you and I'll look after me.'

As a boy Nichols attended the convent school in Cooma, and played league in blue and black. During the school holidays he'd work with his dad, starting at 4.30 in the morning, bringing loads of wood to town on a dray, summer and winter. He maintained his interest in boxing and he participated in the famous bouts in the Jimmy Sharman boxing tent when boxing hopefuls were called up from the crowd to take on Sharman's troupe of hot boxers.

'I used to travel all over the place with Jimmy Sharman when I was a kid,' Nichols told the *Sydney Morning Herald*. 'I was only an amateur boxer and Johnny Shields saw me in the crowd one day. I was paid ten shillings for four fights and four hidings. I used to fight a lot but I never went on with it. I suppose because I thought that if I got badly hurt then I'd lose all my faculties, and I had my life ahead of me. I saw a lot of mates get hurt which put me off. I gave up boxing because guys used to get a few beers in them and want to fight me. So I'd swing a few punches and I'd connect and I'd be in trouble.'

Harry, who would later work on the railways at Cooma, says that Laurie became sick of being goaded in pubs for a fight, and things often deteriorated from there. Particularly for the provocateur. It was never a good idea to walk into Laurie's swift left, which fired out from his body like a piston rod. As part of his routine he'd shoot the left arm out while not looking, in a move some described as the 'no look left', which he followed up with a rapid series of uppercuts.

Nichols' first big job was at the Wool, Hide and Skin store, managed by journalist Steve Liebmann's father in Cooma, and he soon grew an interest in the wool trade. At 18 he joined the Australian Army and served in New Guinea soon after, but he was given an early discharge. While in the army, he played in a rugby league challenge match for the army's New South Wales contingent against a Queensland contingent, winning 15–9.

All the Nichols boys were thrust into the war. Harry, with his rail background, was asked to take on the task of running the railway from Darwin down to Pine Creek and Mataranka in the Northern Territory. In February 1942, he was on his way in a plane to Darwin just as the Japanese bombers were heading to the same place. 'We stopped on Groote Eylandt to refuel and while we were there we were called to the main residence and told Darwin had been bombed that morning. When we got to Darwin we saw all these people heading south.'

When he was given leave from the army after serving in New Guinea, Nichols started wool-classing work. In 1943 he married Mary at Leura in the Blue Mountains and they soon settled down to a busy life. His life was one of movement and change and from his humble base at Springwood he'd go wool classing, from Nyngan in far west New South Wales right down to wild and barely inhabited Flinders Island in Tasmania.

His love for Balmain started in about the 1960s when he befriended Springfield resident Bob Williams. Nichols, always decked out in his singlet, drank at the Oriental Hotel at Springwood, Reschs his preferred tipple. It was at the Oriental Nichols first met Williams, and through him he came to know Williams' brother Syd, who went from playing for Parramatta juniors to first grade at the Tigers. Laurie's interest was piqued to the point he started travelling with Syd to games.

'Syddie Williams, he's worth a million,' Nichols would say, one of the many catchcries he would make up for Balmain players. He also had nicknames for his family. His wife, Mary, a redhead, was 'Big Red', and his daughter Julie was 'Little Red'. Nichols and Syd Williams were 'real cobbers', says Harry.

Williams was graded with Balmain in 1966 and played in the sensational grand final of 1969, when Balmain unexpectedly beat the hotly favoured Souths by 11–2, with Williams scoring the only try of the match, diving over in the corner after he was brought on in the second half as a replacement. Nichols was punching away in the air on the hill as his mate dived over for the try.

Syd Williams starts laughing as soon as you mention Nichols, remembering his endearing qualities. He warmly recalls Nichols showing off his love for the Tigers on the long train journey home from a game, raising the Tigers' chant among the passengers all the way from inner-city Sydney to the Blue Mountains. 'Sometimes he'd be fully tanked and going off on the train. He never bought tickets,' adds Williams.

Nichols started travelling to the Balmain games with Williams in about 1966. For the first few years of playing, Williams' dad drove to the games, and he remembers the hilarious drives they had to Leichhardt Oval. 'Laurie would be in the back seat and on the way down he'd be telling us how we should play the game, and on the way back he'd be telling us how we should have played the game.'

A great air of excitement grew among the Tigers' fans as the word went out that Nichols was approaching. 'We'd often get to Leichhardt when the third-grade side was playing and it was just amazing as we walked into the ground, how slowly the murmur broke out that Laurie was there, and soon the chant went up, "Ti-GURS. Ti-GURS. Ti-GURRRS." Everyone let him through. Laurie was like Moses, he could part the waters.'

The actor side of Nichols suddenly came out as he assumed his sideline role. 'We'd go one way and Laurie would go the other, he had a little channel he could run down along the sidelines,' says Williams. Nichols almost matched the television cameramen for their sideline athleticism.

Balmain's black-and-gold colour scheme instantly appealed to Nichols, as did the working-class grunt of the Balmain area. It was as if Nichols was looking for a place in which to put his faith and the aura the Tigers engendered fully engaged his mind, body and soul. He could display his fitness, vitality and loyalty all in one show. He fell in love with the Tigers and the Tigers fell in love with him. As Williams says: 'He had two eyes: one black, one gold.' Nichols was a simple country soul and he was refreshing the city league followers with his unbridled enthusiasm.

Very soon Nichols' carry-on made him something of a celebrity at Balmain's matches. He was the most infectious of characters and for the most part shook off anyone who might fling a comment at him or declare he wasn't the full quid. On very rare times, however, he found the heckling too much to handle, according to a story related by boxing trainer Johnny Lewis.

One bloke kept shouting at him at a game, trying to confound him. 'Hey Lofty, while you're punching away could you reach up and catch a star for me?'

Nichols told him to pipe down.

But the man continued: 'Hey, Lofty, how about you reach up and grab a star for me?' The inane banter set Nichols right off. But the man came back again with the same rejoinder. This time Nichols came over and knocked him straight on the chin, and the man keeled over. 'So try and pick a star out of that bunch,' Nichols told him.

His fistic displays on the sideline became as much a drawing card as the players who took to the field for Balmain. Kids couldn't wait to get down to the sideline and shadow-box along with Nichols at Leichhardt Oval. *Illawarra Mercury* sports editor Todd Goodwin was one such kid in his younger days. A young Tigers fan from Wollongong, Goodwin and his cohorts became the shadows of the shadow-boxer.

'After conquering the big climb up the hill behind Leichhardt Oval, and going through the turnstiles, my brother, my cousin and me would give my dad and uncle the flick pass and head off to hang with Laurie for the duration of the match,' Goodwin wrote in a tribute piece on Nichols for Fairfax newspapers.

'We loved joining in when he started his drawn out "Tigers, Tigers, Tigerrrs" chant that stirred the troops, but it was even better when Balmain scored. It was then that Laurie would launch into his famous shadow-boxing routine and us kids would be standing there toe-to-toe with Laurie, throwing them right back at him with gusto. We loved it and we loved Laurie.'

Nichols talked about his 'show' to sportswriter Roy Masters: 'I can't explain why I go on like that. Something must go wrong up top. When I see the black and gold I love it. I love the boys. The sight of them running out on the field really stirs me up. I reckon my nerves are as bad as anyone's before a game.'

His obsession continued even when he wasn't at Leichhardt Oval, even when he was away shearing on remote properties listening to a crackly radio broadcast of the Saturday league games . He was stopped in his tracks once, as if he was hearing an echo. He heard something shout 'Tigers' near the shearing shed and wondered what joker was copying him. But it was just a bowerbird, or some other feathered mimicker, repeating Nichols' cry as he bellowed for the Tigers while glued to the radio.

Nichols not only supported the first-grade side. He'd often turn up for junior games or reserve grade games. He first met the then Tigers captain, Wayne 'Junior' Pearce, when he was playing in the under-23s, and he took him out to lunch. Pearce says Nichols brought out an old joke when the waitress brought him his meal. Nichols took a bite and then called the waitress back. 'Love, love, come here please, you've got to take this back. This steak is so tough it's got tattoos.' She looked at him, stone-faced, and then Nichols broke out into a big laugh.

Another order Nichols would sometimes try at a restaurant was 'I'll have my steak very rare'.

'Very rare?' the waiter would verify.

'Yeh,' Nichols would say, 'just cut the horns off and the arse and plonk it on the plate.'

Nichols's association with players developed over time until he became an integral part of the Tigers dressing room. He would be hugging, pumping up and motivating the players whether they liked it or not. Soon, for many, it was imperative that Nichols was there before they ran onto the field at Leichhardt. Pearce was one he'd pull into a bear hug, and he'd then have Nichols in his ear: 'C'mon Junior, c'mon Tigers, do it; do it Junior.' Nichols' last instructions to the players as they ran down the race to the field were, 'C'mon boys, go get 'em Tigers!'

When he was shearing out west Nichols would write to the players, seeing it as a way of keeping up their momentum, and his own. 'We'd get our mail on Tuesdays,' former Tiger Benny Elias said. 'He'd be heartbroken because he had to go off and make himself a buck ... he'd write and keep himself in tune with us to see what we were doing and make sure we were right.'

One of Nichols' proudest moments came when his mate Syd scored the winning try in the 1969 grand final. No-one expected Balmain to win even though they'd been competitive all year and gave Souths quite a shake in all the games they'd played. Syd remembers diving over in the corner to score, although at first he thought it may have been a forward pass. 'I didn't have far to run when I got the ball to cross over, but every year, as the story gets told, it seems to get further. I didn't hear the referee blow his whistle, so I thought "fair try, I'll take that".'

Laurie bolted down from the hill to celebrate with Syd in the SCG dressing room. When the boys later retired to the Balmain club for a few beers Syd, who never drank, joined in.

He soon felt sick. 'I think that was my last alcoholic drink ever,' he says.

Not many fans knew there were actually two Nichols brothers in the stands at Leichhardt. Harry stayed with Laurie in Springwood and travelled with him to the games. 'I accompanied him a terrible lot,' Harry says. One good thing about having his brother about was that Nichols was on a safe bet to get to the ground on time with his brother's knowledge of the train system. Harry says his brother always deported himself well, called everyone 'mate', and rarely took umbrage at rival fans' jeers. In fact, Nichols was often upset at his own fans if they booed at opponents. Once he became very upset when people jeered the great Wally Lewis. 'At times I get so disgusted with fans. Take Wally Lewis. I love Wally Lewis. I can't understand why they boo him. They're sick.'

Nichols' greatest friendship was with rugby league legend Arthur 'Artie' Beetson who arrived at Leichhardt in 1966 as a fresh-faced Aboriginal kid from Roma, Queensland, a centre with Brisbane's Redcliffe club who would become a second-rower with Balmain. Nichols' friendship with Beetson was forged early on when Nichols stood up for him in a bizarre confrontation in the Balmain sheds after a game.

Nichols described the incident: 'I met Artie when he had just come down from Queensland. And I had just got back from the country. I was in the toilet at Balmain and this guy says to me, "Who's that new bloody second-rower?" I said, "It's Artie Beetson." Then this guy starts laying into him and abusing him. I stood up for Artie and I told him what a great player he was and Artie himself was standing behind me and thanked me for sticking up for him. We've been mates ever since.'

Nichols, as mentioned, made up many player-related catchcries that have endured ('Paul Sirro, he's our hero'; 'Sound the alarm, it's Alan McMahon'; 'Ellery [Hanley] eats celery'; 'David Brooks destroys good looks'; 'Junior Pearce is so fierce'; 'Benny Elias says come and try us'; 'Gary Jack puts them on their back'). He also developed one for his new mate: 'Beetson beats 'em, then he eats 'em.'

It was through Beetson that Nichols entered the Balmain inner sanctum, and eventually led to him being invited into the Balmain dressing room as a motivator. Beetson had five great years with Balmain and helped lead them towards the grand final in 1969 but he was sensationally sent off by referee Keith Page for fighting during the Tigers' semifinal victory over Souths, and was thus forced to miss the final and eventually the grand final, in which Balmain won the premiership against all odds.

In an interview with Roy Masters, Beetson used Nichols as an example of what the true character of a rugby league fan should be. '[Nichols] is a rugby league supporter first, a Balmain fan second. The game is first,' Artie related to Masters in the Chinese restaurant at the Big House Hotel in Sussex Street, Sydney, as his laundry swung away on a Hills Hoist nearby.

Beetson displayed all the fight that Nichols showed in his life, never living off his reputation or fame. And his personality hardly changed. Between leaving Roma and functions with the Queen he was the same man. Beetson defied everyone who said he'd never be a forward (he became a second-rower), or that he would never play for Australia (he was Australian captain and later coach—he would also coach Easts), or that he couldn't run a business (his accountancy knowledge helped him in the role as catering manager at the Easts Leagues Club and later he ran hotels).

Nichols' only child, Julie, was 15 when she asked her dad who he loved more: Arthur Beetson or her. Nichols replied: 'Arthur is my great mate, but you are my life.'

Many years later, when Beetson came down from Queensland to coach the Roosters, Nichols was the first one there chatting and having a laugh with his old mate in the stands as Artie artfully brushed past the media throng, and got on with business, favouring his old mate. Only because Artie was there, Nichols became a member of the Easts Leagues Club as well and used their gym twice a week to train.

Harry says Beetson was Nichols' 'all-time football pin-up boy'. The two Nichols brothers became regulars at the Big House Hotel when Beetson was running it. 'We enjoyed many very interesting nights [there],' says Harry, deliberately leaving out the detail. Harry's summary of Beetson is similarly concise: 'He was a real gentleman. He gave me the impression of being a very good fellow and he never forgot his heritage.'

And Nichols never forgot his mate, almost coming to blows again at a Sydney pub when someone was badmouthing Beetson. Incensed by the comments, Nichols exclaimed: 'Hey, you're getting personal, cut it out.' The drinker told him to get lost and Nichols said, 'All right, outside now and we'll sort it out.' As Nichols was heading outside the publican rushed up and grabbed him by the elbow and said, 'Don't do it, the bloke's got a metal plate in his head.' 'I don't care if he's got a whole dinner set in there, no-one's going to badmouth Artie,' Nichols replied, but an angry Nichols was finally convinced to let the matter go.

After Beetson's career was over, Nichols was credited with getting the big forward up and running again by doing some personal training with him when they accompanied the Kangaroos on their 1982 tour of England. On the flip side, Artie was always there if Nichols got stuck in the city after a big night. Nichols stayed with Beetson at his home in Denistone and also later in Surry Hills, where he slept on the floor, with just a blanket and no pillow. A friend of Beetson's called over to deliver apples and had to step over Nichols, sleeping in the corridor, to get to the kitchen. Another time, Beetson took a call late at night and it was Nichols asking for a bed for himself and someone he called 'the Nyngan halfback'. When the pair arrived, Beetson recognised Nichols' mate as a country rugby league official and instead of a halfback's small proportions, he was close to 25 stone and nearly broke the lounge while sleeping on it.

There were times Beetson and Nichols were something of a double act. They'd go to the Mandarin Club close to Chinatown for a drink and dance, at which point Nichols would take to his boxing routine on the dance floor, surprising his fellow dancers. Another time Nichols accompanied Beetson to the Rothmans Medal presentation, league's end-of-year awards night. Nichols, of course, turned up in his singlet while Beetson arrived half-cut. 'Talk about the odd couple,' Beetson said of the big night.

Beetson was often on hand to see how excitable Nichols could be, especially when they went to the boxing together. One night, at a Jeff Fenech fight, Beetson and Nichols were sitting way up in the stands at the old Sydney Stadium. At the end of the bout, amid all the fanfare for Fenech's win, Nichols suddenly appeared in the middle of the ring to raise Fenech's arm and a huge cheer went up in the crowd. 'No-one could have ever moved faster,' Beetson said. 'I said to him later he must have had a parachute to get down there as quickly as he did.' While Nichols had the fans entranced, and some in stitches, he also had the players mesmerised, and they stuck up for him through thick and thin. Nichols was just like them in many ways, one being that they were often small wheels in a much bigger machine, and much happened in football that was out of all their control.

Balmain was a foundation club with a wonderful history. After the 1969 grand final win its next big contribution to the game was its own secretary manager, Kevin Humphreys—the man who made Nichols the club's number one supporter.

Humphreys was a man of great contradictions. He was a former Balmain front rower who moved into the world of league administration, firstly as a Balmain committeeman. A forceful speaker, he was among the new wave of league administrators who would steer rugby league into the new world of marketing, prime-time television and jazzing up the game. He became chairman of the Australian Rugby League and then the first full-time chief executive of the New South Wales Rugby League in 1976. Among several initiatives credited to him during his stewardship was the State of Origin formula, changing points for a try from three to four, and the emphasis on big-time sponsorship and television deals.

His mate Ken Arthurson, a former Manly halfback whose career ended when he fractured his skull in a match, was also an administrator and he shared Humphreys' views on how league could be progressed. But unfortunately the good work Humphreys did for the game was undermined by a scandal when, in 1977, his gambling habits brought him undone. Humphreys was found to have defrauded the Balmain club to finance his betting. The claims were originally thrown out of court but came back into the public forum after an investigation by ABC-TV's *Four Corners* program in its story 'A Big League'. Reported by Chris Masters, the brother of league coach Roy Masters, it led to a royal commission and accusations of judicial corruption. It eventually led to the scalp of the chief magistrate, Murray Farquhar, a known associate of underworld figure and SP bookie George Freeman. Farquhar was found guilty of perverting the course of justice and sent to jail. It was found that he had urged a magistrate to throw out the original case of fraud against Humphreys.

After the finding by the royal commission, Humphreys' case was sent back to court and he was found guilty of fraud, fined $4000 and given a two-year good behaviour bond. The case shook the political and judicial foundations of the state, and the government of Balmain-born premier Neville Wran, and raised questions about the wider influence of rugby league administrators and SP bookmaking. (Wran was cleared of any interference in the Humphreys case and later successfully sued the ABC.)

In his autobiography, *Arko*, Arthurson lamented the fall of his friend: 'The basic sadness I felt for Kevin in the aftermath of his downfall was that he was painted in some places as a bad or evil person. Nothing could be further from the truth.'

The Humphreys storm soon died out and he faded into obscurity. The late 1980s were wonderful times for Balmain, and by 1988 they had one of the most formidable teams ever, brimming with talented state and international players such as Benny Elias, Paul Sironen and Garry Jack, with the added exciting mix of English import Ellery Hanley. It seemed almost inevitable the team would win a premiership, but for two years in a row they were to be denied. Nichols was there with the players in the distress of losing two grand finals. The last attempt, in 1989, was particularly galling and gutting. In one of the best grand finals ever played, Canberra came back from a 12–2 halftime deficit to force extra time, and after nearly 100 minutes of play they won 19–14 to break Balmain hearts. For Nichols, the losses were terrible blows, but as usual he would never lose faith in the Tigers. 'There's no such thing as a bad Tiger,' he would say. 'Black and gold will never fold.'

Nichols became a champion fundraiser for charities and he often travelled to functions throughout Australia as a celebrity guest, be that for the opening of a new hotel in Rockhampton or the opening of a new harness track in Wagga. Everyone remarked on how well he got on with children, and he became a great supporter of the Child Flight emergency helicopter service, which had helped save his niece when she needed urgent medical attention. More broadly, Nichols became the face and good heart of rugby league wherever he went. He was worth a million dollars in generating goodwill for the league, not that everything he did was well publicised. Once, while in Great Britain, Nichols had a cake made (a blue cake, with a white 'N' on top) and presented it to the former Newtown footballer Larry Raleigh, who was watching the Kangaroo tour with his family. Raleigh had suffered a stroke in 1973 after a big head clash in a game, and Nichols hoped the gesture would bring them all some cheer. If Nichols had a saying for himself he might have said: 'Nichols, he's worth a billion nickels.'

Nichols formed a unique and unlikely friendship with leading radio broadcaster Alan Jones. When the Liberal stalwart Jones arrived from rugby union to coach the Tigers for the 1991 season, Nichols was the first one to welcome him, and happy to endorse him. 'Oh mate, it's okay,' he told a reporter. 'He's a true professional and I reckon he'll get the best out of Benny, Blocker and the rest of the boys. All the guys I've spoken to are rapt in this appointment.'

The appointment of a deadset rugby coach to a league team was viewed with astonishment by most. Ray Chesterton, in his book *Tiger, Tiger, Burning Bright*, wrote, 'the appointment of former rugby union grand slam Test coach Alan Jones as Balmain's first-grade coach was one of the most startling developments in the history of the Tigers and the game'.

In the end, Jones's three-year tenure at Balmain saw the Tigers perform moderately, but Jones added value to Balmain in other ways, Chesterton opined: 'Jones's value to Balmain extended well beyond the training track and dressing rooms. Not only wasn't he paid to be coach, saving Balmain anything up to $100,000 a season, it probably cost him money to coach.' And while Balmain didn't threaten the premiership, Jones, Chesterton said, had introduced a new feeling of 'thrilling attack' to the Tigers' play.

Julie Nichols remembers her dad's friendship with Jones, his going to Jones' home in Sydney to talk sport, or charitable causes in which they both had a hand. It conjures quite a picture. At one end of the couch there's Nichols in his singlet and thongs. At the other the excitable workaholic Jones in his chambray shirt and pleated pants. '[Dad] and Alan loved sport, particularly cricket, and Dad would often visit Alan at his house and they would talk about great matches and the players,' Julie says.

Nichols also developed a friendship with Australia's most famous boxing coach, Johnny Lewis. The two spoke each other's language—a love of boxing and rugby league. Lewis was a fanatical Newtown supporter who was devastated when his wonderful but debt-ridden team was excluded from the competition in 1983. It was a huge blow to someone who had sat and watched Newtown play since he was a kid.

Lewis had set up a training enterprise at the Newtown Police Citizens and Youth Club gym where some of the greats of Australian boxing emerged, like world champions such as Jeff Fenech and Kostya Tszyu. Into this heady mix of big-time boxing stepped the part-time shadow-boxer.

Lewis remembers the first time he saw Nichols, and it wasn't a flattering observation. His brother pointed him out in the crowd at a Newtown versus Balmain match in the 1960s as they sat in the Sheridan Stand at the SCG. His elder brother elbowed him in the ribs as Nichols was going through his punching routine. 'You see that bloke over there?' his brother said. 'I think he's got a couple of screws loose.' Lewis said, 'He looks a bit mad, but he really lets those punches go.'

After a different match, Lewis was introduced to Nichols and they both struck up a friendship. Nichols soon became a regular at the Newtown gym into his late 70s, still punching the bags. 'When I first met Laurie, I felt like I'd known him all my life,' says Lewis. 'He was far from being an idiot, he was fun and the greatest guy you'd ever meet and also extremely loyal. He wouldn't put someone down to be funny, he was very clever.'

Nichols asked Lewis if he could come along to the Newtown gym to train with Lewis's boxing team. Very soon he was punching away at the bags alongside Fenech and, later, Tszyu, who was born Konstantin Tszyu (pronounced 'zoo') in Serov in the Ural Mountains. The power-packed 165-centimetre Russian tyro—whom Lewis considered the best fighter of his era—became one of Nichols' little favourites. Tszyu could hardly speak English when he immigrated to Australia in 1992, and little by little got his head around the language and Australian strine. Certainly a lot of the sayings Nichols came out with had Tszyu scratching his head.

Nichols' and Lewis's friendship continued to grow, and they were regular lunch partners, often meeting down in Sydney's Chinatown where they loved to sit at the bar of the Covent Garden Hotel at the bottom of Hay Street. Sometimes their respective wives would join them. Nichols became part of the entourage when Lewis and his boxers went overseas to boxing matches in places like Las Vegas. Some accused him of jumping on the glory of others. But such claims were met with a rapid response from Lewis, who said Nichols paid his own way overseas and just loved lending his support. If Nichols' presence in Vegas was big-noting, Lewis told an interviewer in 2000, 'those athletes would read him right away. There's not a phoney bone in Laurie's body. He's a beautiful loyal bloke. Even Kostya got that vibe in the early days when he didn't even have a real grasp of English and knew stuff-all about league.'

Tszyu—who inspired the Nichols catchcries 'Kostya, Kostya, who's next on the roster' and 'Kostya, Kostya, he'll cost ya'—became world light welterweight champion in 1995. His professional record would end up as 31 wins and two losses, as he unified the WBC, WBA and IBF titles, becoming one of Australia's greatest boxers. Punching for him all the time from the sidelines was Nichols.

Tszyu remarked (when his English improved): 'Laurie was not just good friend and good fan of mine, he was inspiration. Before I came away he was at my gym training every day. I am young and this guy who was much, much older than me was working the heavy bags furiously and shadow boxing. It was inspirational, it gave me extra energy to train.'

Lewis's opinion of Nichols' form was that he was a good boxer and that 'if he hit you on the chin he'd rattle you'.

Just as Nichols travelled with Lewis's boxers, he joined (again paying his own way) the Australian rugby league team when they played overseas. His first trip was the 1982 Kangaroo tour of Great Britain. The added bonus on that trip was having his mate Artie Beetson not too far away. When the Poms caught sight of Nichols they soon dubbed him 'the hooker' because of his shadow-boxing.

Manly stalwart Peter Peters remembers travelling from Edinburgh in a car with Beetson to watch the Kangaroos train in Leeds before the third and final Test on the 1982 tour. 'We hired a small BMW with Artie the driver, myself as navigator, and his loyal mate, Laurie Nichols, in the back seat. Despite the freezing weather Laurie was in his famous Balmain singlet and screaming his one-liners such as "Artie Beetson picks 'em up and eats 'em". I was terrified as Artie negotiated his way through the fog at breakneck speed across the border into Yorkshire, and Laurie reckoned with all the weight in the front, we were a "two-wheeler".'

Nichols was there again on the 1986 Kangaroo tour of Great Britain, where he became great friends with Australian halfback Peter Sterling's dad, Max. Sterling wrote: 'It's well documented that the British public were intrigued by this Aussie "madman" shadow-boxing on the sidelines in freezing conditions at each match. The fact that they could see how welcome he was by anyone associated with the official party, and most importantly the players, gave him immediate credibility despite their curious glances.'

And it wasn't just the Australians who took him in. After one Test, former British forward Colin Hutton gave him his Great Britain tie.

Commentator and rugby league legend Rex Mossop remembered seeing Nichols in situ at a game during the 1986 tour when Australia played Hull in Yorkshire. 'The game was played on a day when at 2.30 pm the temperature had barely reached freezing point, and was in the process of going lower still. As the teams came down the chute the large crowd started laughing. There, standing near the gate, was Laurie, punching the air with his fists, dressed in long pants and singlet, performing his usual routine.'

Nichols, though, was finally beaten by the weather gods, catching pneumonia. 'I had to lend him my jumper,' Beetson said. Nichols didn't have one.

While on tour Nichols would often make time to nip over to Russia—where he'd stunned the Muscovites with his sartorial decision-making—or France. One time in Paris he became incredibly lost when he came across a street called Chappell Rue. Thinking it had some connection to Australian cricket's Chappell brothers, he went for a jog down it and soon lost his way. He later explained what happened: 'I thought it was Greg and Ian's street, [so I figured] "I'll be right". I got twelve miles away from the hotel before I called for the stretcher and had to borrow the bugs bunny for the train ride back.'

The landscape of rugby league changed immeasurably in 1995 and passionate league fans like Nichols were made to suffer. The game they loved, and many of the teams they adored, were about to be torn in two.

Ken Arthurson was travelling on a bus with the media when the news came through that News Limited was planning a breakaway competition that would come to be known as Super League. Raids to poach ARL teams and star players had begun with News already having claimed to have 'won the game'.

But there would be no outright winner. News Limited's push led to a split, with two competitions running concurrently in 1997 and 1998—a Super League competition and the incumbent ARL competition. A compromise was reached ahead of the 1999 season but in the wash-up many teams were then, and in the coming year, forced to merge to meet the criteria of the new competition run under the banner of the National Rugby League (NRL). The cash-strapped Tigers found themselves in an invidious position and the Balmain board took the dire view they had to either merge or be kicked out of the competition. Merger talks first took place with Parramatta before they turned to Western Suburbs.

Any talk of a merger was anathema to Nichols' deep-seated love of the Tigers. Three board members resigned after the Tigers board decided to push for the merger with Western Suburbs. Swimming legend Dawn Fraser, Nichols' old mate, split with the diehards and went for the merger. Other players close to Nichols also backed the merger, including Wayne Pearce and Paul Sironen.

The emotional meeting at Balmain's headquarters late in 1999 went well into the night but at the end of the vote there was resounding support for the two teams to merge. Nichols stood up to oppose the move but couldn't continue, breaking into tears. It was as if his whole make-up, his reason for being, was under threat. His life support had been taken from him, and he could not fathom why such pressures had been imposed on his favourite club and forced it into such a compromise.

The vote of 295–99 votes in favour of the merger was a show of faith in the future, and it brought an immediate $8 million cash injection into the merged entity, the Wests Tigers. Dawn Fraser said, 'History has been made again in Balmain tonight. We have to get on with the job and we will do a good job.'

Wayne Pearce declared: 'Common sense has prevailed and the Tigers will live on.'

The Balmain chairman, John Chalk, put it bluntly to the press as he was leaving the meeting: 'What else could we do? We'd die if we didn't do it.'

Nichols was pressed for a comment outside the meeting but he just hung his head as he told Channel Ten: 'It's a very, very sad night.' The amount of conflicting emotions running through his body was tearing him apart. Some of his greatest friends supported the virtual death of a club he lived for—how could this be?

Johnny Lewis saw Nichols the following day when Nichols turned up to the Newtown PCYC for boxing training. 'People say Laurie came to accept the merger, but I tell you he never did. I know when it was first announced he was in the front seat of my car and he cried all the way to the gym. He was absolutely distraught. He said "How come we are so tough, but can be so weak? How could they do this?" It just got too much for him.'

Nichols mulled over the situation for months. He constantly wondered what to tell the players in the club as the new season approached and the merged team was about to take the field. But on the fateful week of Nichols' death he decided to make peace with the terrible insult to his club, by visiting the players during their pre-season training at Leichhardt.

After asking Wayne Pearce if he could address the players Nichols stood up in the February heat on a field he could almost call his own and started speaking in a quiet voice: 'The first thing is, I'm wearing this shirt,' he said, pointing to his Balmain singlet. 'But we're Wests Tigers now, okay? The thing that we've got to get into our heads is that we are a new club. We've got to support Wests Tigers, not just Balmain or Wests. I can't wear this anymore, 'cause fair enough, our name has changed.' With that the players clapped and slapped Nichols around the back as he went into his punching routine they were all too familiar with, but they couldn't believe he was prepared to consign his beloved Balmain singlet to the dustbin.

As the Wests Tigers were launching their season the following day, Nichols was sitting down with at the Marigold Restaurant in Chinatown. Along with members of the Lions Club of Sydney Chinese Inc. he was discussing a fundraiser to help a young amputee, Anna Rauscher, who needed funds to go to England to get a prosthetic leg to pursue her dream of being a model. Alongside Nichols was his new partner, Eva, with whom he had set up home after the death of his wife, Mary.

Suddenly Nichols got up from the lunch to go to the toilet. When he came out he collapsed, with blood spilling from his mouth. A large ulcer had burst in his stomach. His stunned friends ran to his aid but it was too late. Laurie Nichols was dead, just 33 days into the new millennium, and just days before the new Wests Tigers were to take the field again.

At the time Johnny Lewis was in the US preparing Tszyu for a world title fight. Nichols hadn't gone on the trip because, as he told people without elaborating, he had a 'small problem'.

Lewis had cushioned Nichols' disappointment by suggesting he was better off waiting for the next fight anyway, as better opponents were around the corner.

It was late at night in the US when Lewis took a call from Alan Jones. 'Johnny, we've lost Laurie,' Jones said in a low voice full of hurt.

Lewis would come to believe that Nichols died of a broken heart—the break occurring when Balmain agreed to merge with Wests. At the time he heard the news, though, he was simply floored. As a mark of respect, Tszyu's team put up a photograph of Nichols on the fighter's dressing room wall before the bout. 'That was something that touched everyone,' Lewis said. Ten days after Nichols died, Tszyu went out under the bright lights of the Mohegan Sun Casino in Uncasville, Connecticut, to take on Mexican Ahmed Santos for the WBC light welterweight title. Tszyu took a while to warm up, but like Nichols he dug deep, and in the eighth round he had the Mexican on the back foot and sent him to the canvas twice before he finished him off with a knockout. Tszyu was world champion and, no doubt, Nichols was dancing around him in spirit.

A huge number of people gathered for Nichols' funeral at Our Lady of the Rosary Catholic Church at The Entrance in New South Wales. Among the mourners on that hot February day were Alan Jones, Dawn Fraser, Artie Beetson, Benny Elias, Keith Barnes and Peter Sterling. Nichols' nieces and nephews formed a choir and filled the church with their wonderful voices. Balmain fans and supporters made a guard of honour as Nichols' coffin was taken by his league mates, including 'big Artie', to the hearse. As the procession passed along the Central Coast streets to the Palmdale Funeral Home, punters came out of the pubs and raised their glasses.

Jones, who gave the eulogy at the funeral, spoke of Nichols on his radio show the next day: 'I made the point that greatness is not a function of who your parents were, where you were born, how much money you made, how many titles you had or how much influence you enjoyed. Greatness in a life is a function of the greatness of the individual spirit and heart, and Laurie's was enormous. It is true to say Laurie Nichols transcended rugby league.'

Nichols, of course, made a huge impression on his own family. His nephew Jack, Harry's son, always held his words closely, but especially remembered what great fun his uncle had been. 'Laurie's view on depression was this: go and have a warm bath, and if that doesn't work, go and try and help someone. That always brings out the positiveness in you,' Jack says. 'His philosophy was that if you do something good you don't need to tell anyone, because everyone already knows. The same went if you were a good player, you don't have to go on about yourself, everyone can already see it.'

Nichols' attitude in life was to unleash the Tiger within.

CHAPTER NINE:
Nathan Blacklock—
Running free in Tingha

Two young boys are scoffing down their breakfast porridge, sitting, not at a table, but on the tin roof of a shaky wooden home. From their vantage point they can see the landscape emerging as the mist rises from the valley on a cool autumn morning. The big rocks, forest and creeks that they see in the distance will be their classroom today. The mother of one of the boys has come out looking for them and scratching her head. There are numerous children running in and out of the house and it's full of noise.

One of the boys turns to his mate. 'Ready to go cuz?' he says with a big smile. 'You bet,' his cousin replies. They climb down the ladder they'd put up at the back of the house, push their empty bowls quietly on to the edge of the verandah and take off west into the cypress pines. They won't be seen again for the rest of the day.

In the forest, they come across all kinds of fun and food: swimming holes, lizards running up the big rocks, kangaroos (*bungar*) darting between the trees, and they call on the rabbit traps they've laid in the bush. Sure enough, they'd caught a few. One of them climbs high into a big tree and comes down with some wild fruits from the canopy and they gorge themselves. They know their fruits by their aboriginal names, *bumbul* (pomegranate), *bunyah-bunyah* (bread fruit) and *geebung* (gooseberry). They remember the knowledge passed on by their elders on how to find honey. Capturing a bee that's flown to the edge of a pond for a drink they attach a small feather to its legs and watch it fly off. They can spot the feathered bee in the air and it leads them to their tree honey pot. One of them finds a wild plum bush and they've got lunch. If they hear a curlew or a mopoke in song they take it as a bad omen and clear out. A collection of rabbits grows around the hips of one of the boys.

They make their way over the rolling hills to a farm that has slides and swimming pools and the owner lets them in and they spend the afternoon there. They run, wander and explore and by the end of the day, as they present themselves to the back porch, they are tired and can run no more. A huge rousing is only stopped when they present the rabbits and wild fruit for everyone to enjoy, and they are let inside and told not to go wandering off again without permission. But they wander over and over again.

The two boys are Nathan Blacklock and his cousin Preston Campbell, and they will become two of the fastest, hardest to catch players in rugby league at the start of the new millennium.

It's all hands on deck in the Tingha Tigers' den in early 2012. Another arm of league ancestry is in the making. The sister of

Canterbury Bulldogs rugby league star Ben Barba is marrying the brother of Gold Coast Titans star Preston Campbell, and everyone's thinking ahead beyond the wedding reception to how well their progeny may be able to weave and run if they take up the tackling game. Ben Barba can't make the wedding because the Bulldogs won't let him out of their pre-season training camp, but he's sent up a message on DVD for the newlyweds. The girls are fussing over table decorations while the men wheel in supplies for the guests at the Tingha Sports & Recreation Club.

Outside, club secretary, general handyman and Tigers stalwart Dick Hayden is putting the finishing touches to the bowling green, artfully cutting the grass in diagonal patterns as Tingha hosts an intra-town bowls tournament that you can bet your life will end in a few quiet beers at the bar. At about 3 and a half kilometres each mow, Dick reckons he's walked around Australia almost one and half times since he first took on the job many long years ago. 'Right now. I'm just on the other side of Mildura,' he says with a big throaty laugh. Everyone here is hard at work and everyone except for the cleaner is a volunteer.

Nearby, the Tingha Sportsground awaits another season where the Tigers faithful will hit the sidelines to barrack vociferously for their team in the Group 19 competition. From juniors, some playing in bare feet, to women's tag league, to the big Group 19 battles, every game is supported with the same Tigers' passion. The sports club is the centre of the league team, and league is the centre of the town's life.

The township is a higgledy-piggledy collection of homes nestled in the open hills on the banks of Copes Creek (named after a 1800s Scottish settler camped by the banks of the creek and sang 'Hey Johnny Cope'). Large granite rocks dot the paddocks as if giants once played marbles with them on the land. The locals give these prehistoric rocks, some of them balancing precariously, familiar names like 'koala', 'gorilla' and 'turtle'. It's a quiet place and you mightn't feel it worth stopping if you were driving on the back road to Guyra from Inverell. A small cluster of colonial buildings hang on in the main street, and Wing Hing Long's famous old general store (once run by Chinese immigrants, now a museum) sits on a bend in the road. A large fire in the early 1900s destroyed many of the town's old buildings.

Tingha is not far behind nearby Woolbrook as one of the coldest places in Australia outside the Snowy Mountains. At certain times in winter the temperature can plummet to minus 14 degrees Celsius. A heavy frost often blankets the town and water pipes ice up and burst.

This is Ngarabal and Anaiwan country, home of the Northern Tableland Aboriginal people who call the area Nucoorilma, after the native apple tree. All the diverse inhabitants of Tingha from different Aboriginal tribes and European and Chinese heritage gather as one to barrack for the Tigers. It's through league that everyone shares a common history.

Tingha was called Armidale Creek in the tin-mining days. It was given the new name of Tingha, an Aboriginal word meaning open plains, which just happened to have the word tin in it. Most of the streets are named after gems found in the area such as Diamond, Sapphire, Topaz, Garnet, Agate and Amethyst streets. The landscape, with cuttings in the side of the river and dams used to run sluices, bespeaks the frenetic tin mining activity that once invaded the area. It was once full of 700 Chinese people with their stores, opium dens and joss houses (temples), a busy thriving town where fortunes were won and lost. Now most of the younger generation have to leave town to seek their fortunes.

Football in Tingha started in the 1890s. The first rugby players wore striped shirts and sported long waxed moustaches and vied for the Wilson Cup among teams from the region. There were a few rugby teams in Tingha; one of them was called, quaintly, the Tingha Mushroom Football Club. They were 'the knights of the leather' and played 'open, fast and strenuous football'.

But a wildfire was blowing. League fanaticism ran through the country and by 1928 the men who had once played union all their lives were given a stark new option. As one, as if a common emotion was aroused, they all plugged for league. It was the day Mushrooms turned into Tigers.

The Tingha Sports & Recreation Club is a miracle in itself. Reborn after a fire in 1986, it rose again to show that goodwill can't be extinguished. The terrible blow came as a shock to the quiet community with the loss of a great amount of memorabilia, some of it old gold trophies that melted into the dirt. After many fundraisers and working bees the club rose again from the ashes, as a testament to Tiger power.

Dick Hayden has been club secretary and all-rounder for nearly 20 years. He insists the club is not owned by any one person, but rather by the whole community. He talks about the Tigers with a true passion and every season he holds hope that it will be a famous year. He loves to slap someone on the back and say 'good on ya, boy' for encouragement, as his wiry frame busily gets around the club.

The faces of Aboriginal players slowly filtered through to the ranks of the Tigers as the barriers in other parts of society slowly came down. Three names stand out in Tingha's proud modern rugby league history, and all three are Aboriginal: Owen Craigie, Preston Campbell and Nathan Blacklock. (Well, there was another one. Their mate Peter 'PJ' Ellis also broke into Sydney's first-grade ranks, but he rarely gets a mention.) Dick's over the moon that Blacklock has returned to coach the Tigers for 2012, and he's brought with him a new eagerness to be involved. Blacklock, of course, carried the nickname Tingha when he played in Sydney with St George and later St George Illawarra.

Hayden, a plumber by trade, is himself an old Tiger. He left Tingha to play in the Newcastle competition in the late 1960s and then represented Newcastle in its under-21 side when he was just 18. That's before the Tigers' call was too strong to ignore and he returned to play in the then Group 5 second division. The Tigers won the A reserve and junior competition in 1970. One of Hayden's opponents was a young John Cootes, the priest who played for Australia and then set up a successful furniture business.

'Father John' played for the Armidale Rams and in one game the Rams were putting the fear of God into Hayden's Tingha team by a whopping 105–0 when Tingha tried to call off the punishment. But Father John said, 'Play on, good things may come your way.' And they did. Tingha scored 20 points in a rush, with the score ending up a tad more respectable at 110–20. Father John was a great country and western singer and sometimes he'd bring out his guitar for a singalong after a game.

Tingha went into recess from 1971 to 1976 when they couldn't muster a team. Hayden explains: 'It's only a little town and kids come and go.' There've been four recesses in the Tigers' history, each one a heart-thumping blow to their pride. But Tigers never say die and the club had too much history to fall by the wayside. Most juniors from Tingha play for West Inverell before returning to town to play for the Tigers later in the senior competition. The club has enjoyed its share of glory. Between 1967 and 2009 the Tigers have celebrated 22 premierships in various divisions. The team's biggest victory by far was in the Group 19 grand final of 2009, the team's first-ever Group 19 premiership (Group 5 was merged into Group 19 in 1980). No-one thought Tingha could host such a big occasion and there were concerted moves to take the grand final away from the town and have it played in Inverell. But Hayden and his club dug their claws in and refused to budge. More than 6000 people crammed into the Tingha field, and the club took $36,000 at the gate and through hospitality as the Tigers ran over the competition hotshots Guyra 46–14. The club hired an aeroplane with a photographer to take an aerial shot of the historic match and crowd.

In 2011, Tingha had four teams in the finals of various divisions, a great effort for a town of just 800 people, dwarfed by neighbouring Inverell, which has about 16,000 people. Now Nathan Blacklock, one of their favourite sons, has come back again (he's done it a few times) to give the Tigers a push along.

But Tingha doesn't boast. You won't find big cabinets full of trophies to memorialise their great players and honour their amazing deeds. You wouldn't know that anyone of note ever came from the town. As you look about the Tigers' den, there are mainly bits and pieces on Group 19 battles, and very little about the boys who went on to wow Sydney and play for Australia. And that's the way they like it. No-one is allowed to get ahead of themselves in this town. They keep things quiet and close to the chest. But their history keeps on inspiring the youngsters like a volcano that bubbles up, always ready to explode.

Blacklock shakes his head when he thinks of what he got away with when he was a youngster in Tingha. He once explained that if he didn't get out, his mum would have had him mowing everyone's lawns. His smile is wide and it rarely leaves his face. It's enduring. He holds his big soft hands together and remembers those great days running free in the bush when he was young. You sense he longs for those simpler days again, away from the public gaze.

'That was life when I was young; chasing rabbits, making my own fun, going down to the dam, I'd be doing stuff all day, picking up wild fruits … blackcurrants, wild plums, you'd be full by the end of the day.'

Talking about his partner in fun, Blacklock says Preston Campbell 'was like a little packhorse. He was the best little rabbit carrier ever'.

Blacklock's mum, Sue, is a strong Christian, a member of the Uniting Church with a degree in theology, but she speaks her people's language and her Aboriginal culture is foremost. She instilled a sense of duty in her son, despite his wild streak. She's a respected elder in Tingha and her warm spirit is one of the guiding lights in the town. Apart from looking after her own crew, now comprising 35 grandchildren, she's fostered numerous children in her home to help other families struggling with whatever crises they've confronted. Her house, now a brick one, is still as busy as ever.

Under her watchful eye, a young Blacklock set out on his voyage to manhood. That he was fast there was never any doubt. That famous solo effort for St George Illawarra in the 1999 grand final against the Melbourne Storm—when, like a runaway train, he scooped up the ball and ran three-quarters of the length of the field, slicing through the might of Melbourne to score under the black dot in front of a world-record league crowd of 107,999 people—was proof of his explosive talent. So was the time in 2001 he ran down the sideline for the Dragons against Balmain, chipped the fullback, regathered and scored, before celebrating the spectacular last-minute, match-winning try with his signature cartwheel and backflip. But while these wonderful tries became rugby league folklore they belied his simple start in the game.

Blacklock's late father, Merv, and his father's brothers played for the Tingha Tigers. Merv was a guiding light for him, and his sudden death in 2001 was a devastating blow to Blacklock as he was about to embark on a Kangaroo tour of England. It was a tumultuous time, leaving his family in the depth of their mourning, and journeying alone with his grief to cold England, but Blacklock felt he had to do it to keep his career going. And he was fulfilling his father's dream. So the way he saw it, he had to go. However, after all that, he played in just one Test on tour.

In his other Test appearance, Blacklock scored two tries against Papua New Guinea in Port Moresby. It was ironic, he was good enough to play for Australia, but not considered good enough to play for his home state.

Blacklock took his opportunities when they fell at his feet, and he adopted a can-do mentality that helped him get a foothold in the big time in Sydney. He first went down to Sydney in 1995 to play for Easts but he only played five first-grade games. He'd been playing five-eighth or in the centres with the Roosters but when he went to the Dragons in 1997 he was asked to play on the wing. That was a pivotal moment, and when he took his chance in this unfamiliar position his career took off. After appearing for the Dragons only once in 1997, he played 22 games in 1998 and scored a remarkable 20 tries.

'I tell the young guys you have to put your foot in the door and be willing to take the opportunities that come along, just don't reject something because it doesn't suit you. A lot of players aren't as good as they think they are,' he says, talking of when he took his chance to play on the wing.

By the end of 1999 Blacklock was the league's top try-scorer, a feat he repeated for the next two years. This was something not achieved in Sydney league since 1927. He'd become a try-scoring machine and was always there at the right time with safe hands, and fast legs, to collect the ball.

The gymnastic efforts of Blacklock and his mate Anthony Mundine brought the wow factor to the Dragons' games during the 1999 season. It was a big year for the Dragons. At the end of the 1998 season they'd officially merged with the Illawarra Steelers and it took many rounds for the new team to gel, something not helped by lingering divisions between the joint venture's foundation clubs.

Former Canterbury legend and NSW Origin player Andrew Farrar was with the Steelers side when the joint venture was formed and he became the new assistant coach to David Waite. He saw a young Blacklock making his mark. He was instantly impressed by his skills, and he believed he could have played anywhere in the backs, even fullback, if he wanted to. Although his defence was not the best, he knew where to place himself so he didn't let the side down.

'He was fairly quiet and fairly shy when I first met him. But that was the way it went with him, you started off slow and then things warmed up and you started to get to know him. We had a special bond. He was a really intriguing personality.' Soon Farrar, who hailed from Cowra, was calling Blacklock 'Ting', shortened from his nickname, Tingha.

'Ting could sniff out a try like no-one else,' he says. 'There was something uncanny about how he could be in the right place at the right time, he just had great skill levels. Every time Ting got the ball you knew something was going to happen. You knew he was fast at training, well, he was four times faster when he was playing on the field.'

Given his form, Farrar was confident Blacklock would score an Origin jersey in 1999 or 2000. 'I was sure he was in the calculations of selectors but it never came through, that was very disappointing.'

St George Illawarra played exciting, sometimes magical football in 1999 and, despite just scraping into the finals, won through to the grand final. But ultimate glory was taken from the Dragons bitterly and cruelly in the final minutes of the year's biggest match despite them, at one stage, leading 14–0. That was when Anthony Mundine knocked on in his attempt to dive over the line for a try; a try that, had it been scored, would probably would have put the game beyond doubt. But with just three minutes remaining, and with the Dragons leading 18–14, Dragon Jamie Ainscough came in high on Storm winger Craig Smith just as he went to ground the ball over the line. The Storm were awarded a penalty try, the first in grand final history, which allowed the Storm's Matt Geyer to take the conversion from right in front of the posts. The St George players were gutted as Geyer added the extras to give the Storm a decisive 20–18 lead. The match proved an eternal source of hurt for Dragons fans and players.

Farrar laments the grand final that got away. 'I think that is the only time you will ever see a grand final decided by a penalty try. Because it was so late in the game we had no chance to make it up,' he says. 'You just shake your head. It was devastating.'

He feels that the divisions in the team between the previous rival clubs didn't help the situation. 'Look, it was a game of two halves and just before half-time we had a chance to score but that didn't come off. There was a little bit of "us and them" in the team. It might have been a contributing factor in not getting over the line.'

St George couldn't back up their 1999 form the next year but Nathan could, scoring 25 tries to become the leading try-scorer in the league again. His career was powering along but he still kept missing out on an Origin jersey, even in 2001 when he was again on his way to being the competition's leading try-scorer (he'd end up with 27 tries from 28 matches) for the third consecutive year.

The close of that year was a climactic one for Blacklock, his year of doubts. Rugby union was scouting for new talent and Blacklock was on their wish list. And the loss of his father still weighed heavily. 'He was very sad his dad didn't get to see him play in the green and gold,' says Farrar.

It all came crashing down on him emotionally after he returned from the Kangaroo tour, and by mid-2002 Blacklock asked for a release from St George Illawarra. It was a difficult time and it was heartbreaking for him to leave a club that had done all in its power to nurture his career. As he told journalist Paul Suttor on announcing his retirement, 'I owe my life to the

Dragons. They've made me who I am. It's like a family, it's like me leaving home for the first time. I'm a bit sad. I'm doing my best to stay strong.'

The death of his father and then the breakdown of his relationship, from which his son, Kyle had been born, was eating away at his ability to play tough competitive football week in, week out. And then there was the bitterness of constantly being ignored for the NSW Origin side.

'At the time I said it didn't worry me but it killed not knowing that I wasn't going to get picked after playing well. It really made me think, I've got no future in league, I got overlooked so many times,' Blacklock said.

As Dragons CEO Peter Doust set him free from his contract, Blacklock also signed a departure clause stipulating that if he came back to league he could only play for the Dragons. That was the way he wanted it. He left the club as a three-time Dally M Winger of the Year.

Within a few months Blacklock had signed up for a new career in rugby union, taking on a two-year deal, and a fresh start, with the NSW Waratahs. But despite some strong games in the 2003 season, including an amazing try against the Bulls from Pretoria, South Africa, he had no rapport with the union culture and eventually ran into trouble. He was dropped to reserve grade for disciplinary reasons and later Rugby NSW said it would not prevent the 'mercurial' Blacklock leaving if he wanted out. He took little part in the rest of the Waratah's season.

St George Illawarra jumped at its chance to get its favourite winger back and soon Blacklock was gliding along the sidelines for his old team, scoring eight tries in the first four games of the 2003 season, this time under the guidance of coach Nathan Brown, his old playing mate.

In an article in the *Sydney Morning Herald* entitled 'Walk Slowly, Run Fast', he explained how the death of his father still haunted him. As he told Jessica Halloran, 'I miss just seeing him fix the car, just out doing something, having a yarn, a cup of tea, just those sorts of things. I guess he's always going to be there in spirit, he's always around, looking down on me, which is good.'

Blacklock was often seen pacing about near his home, walking the beach. Some people saw him as this restless soul, although really all he was doing was walking as he had done all his life. He liked being on the move. And if he needed to recharge his batteries he'd head straight back to Tingha.

His cousin Preston Campbell's career started not long after Blacklock's. But they both chose different paths. Campbell's dad, Tom, drove him every weekend from Tingha to Newcastle in his early football playing days. Eventually, Campbell scored a contract with the Cronulla Sharks and made an instant impact. By 2001, he was voted the Dally M Player of the Year, sharing the limelight with his cousin Nathan (awarded Winger of the Year) on league's grandest stage: two Tingha boys voted the best in the game in the same year.

But the sudden fame appeared too hard to handle. By midway through 2002 Campbell had been dropped to the Sharks' reserve grade side and he was battling depression. On one night late that year he drove his car into a tree. Blacklock spent the whole night keeping a vigil in hospital praying for Campbell's recovery. It had all unfolded so quickly, from fame to tragedy in a year. 'I had to be there for him,' Blacklock said. Campbell, with help, recovered and later joined the Penrith Panthers and the Gold Coast Titans, playing successfully in the top grade right up until 2011. He was one of the integral movers in starting the annual All Stars match between an Indigenous All Stars team and a National Rugby League All Stars team. He also established mentoring programs for Aboriginal youths while based at the Titans' head office on the Gold Coast.

Blacklock, meantime, finished his second stint with the Dragons at the end of the 2004 season and accepted a stint with Hull in England for the 2005 season. The then 27-year-old quickly made an impression, scoring three tries in his first game. 'Hull's supporters are going to get their money's worth with this man around this season,' Hull's coach, John Kear, exclaimed. 'He's a genius.' Blacklock played a second season for Hull in 2006 and in his two years with the club he scored 33 tries in 47 appearances.

England struck a chord with him. 'I loved the history and culture in general, people were different. They just live simple over there. Should have gone there earlier,' he said. It was a time he made many good friends, including star English player Richard Horne, and got reacquainted with old ones. During Blacklock's time with Hull his old coach Andrew Farrar was with Wigan, and Farrar had his former star over to stay when things in Hull hit a lull, as they often did.

After finishing with Hull, Blacklock returned to Australia and by 2009 he was back helping the Tingha Tigers. But he couldn't stay still. His next playing gig was with the Aberdeen Tigers in the Hunter Valley after he got a job in the mines, handling heavy machinery and placing explosives. 'I've always loved it—blowing things up, can't say no to that,' he joked. He then moved on to captain-coach the Muswellbrook Rams and while there he decided to get more involved in football and any programs that advanced his people's cause. 'A lot of [Aboriginal] kids can go far but it is up to them,' he says. He believes there are lot more opportunities now for younger players to enter the game with traineeships. He warns them not to fall for the temptation of big nights out if they've finally made the big time. 'But I don't put too much pressure on the guys, in the end rugby league is a game, not a profession,' he says.

Blacklock is a new man these days. With a mobile at hand, he has more responsibility, loves playing golf, and gets to keep a close eye on his son, Kyle, who also loves golf. Back in Nucoorilma, he's at peace.

Aboriginal people wandered over the place they call Nucoorilma hunting and gathering and living at one with the land. The Ngarabal and Anaiwan territory ran from south of Tingha up north to past what is now the Queensland border. They didn't have much time for coastal Aboriginal people or the Kamilaroi people out on the western plains. When a boy had gone through the initiation ceremony at the bora ground and was ready to marry, the elders found a wife for him, usually from the tribes up north. It was an intricate marriage system that was only occasionally broken. Any couples flouting the traditional marriage rules were in serious trouble.

Nucoorilma was the place of marriages. It was place for nurturing in the benign climate of the tablelands with its abundant water and wildlife, like wallabies and kangaroos. After a wife was selected a gunyah was built for the couple and flowers were arrayed around the small hut in anticipation of her arrival. She would arrive with food specially prepared by her family. When she became part of his family she would find it hard, with her husband being away for many months while out hunting with other males of the tribe. The women often gave birth alone.

The tranquil life enjoyed by the area's Aboriginal people—who had no king or queen and lived by a code promoting 'equality, sharing and acceptance', according to a University of Sydney project about life in Tingha—was thrown apart with the arrival of white settlement as squatters took over their hunting grounds for grazing cattle and sheep from the early 1800s. The Ngarabal and adjoining Wirrayaraay tribe had made some peace with squatters and were camped on surveyor Henry Dangar's outstation at Myall Creek, on the road between Delungra and Bingara. Some of the tribesmen had gone off to collect bark for the station manager while others in the community, mostly women and children and one old man, were camped near the homestead. The north-west plains had been awash in blood for almost a year. A campaign by Major James Nunn had set off drives by squatters to wipe out the Aboriginal people from the rich grazing lands of the region. Nunn had been responsible for several atrocities, one near Moree and one at the headwaters of Slaughterhouse Creek with mounted troopers involved.

On 10 June 1838 a posse of 11 white stockmen arrived after travelling up north looking for Aboriginal people to revenge a raid on their stock. At Myall Creek, they came across the camp of mostly women and children. The Wirrayaraay had nothing to do with the slaughter of livestock further south. The tribe had entered into a peaceful partnership with Dangar's workers. The white posse rounded up 28 Aboriginal people and took them to a stockyard where they were killed with swords and their bodies later burnt. A couple of boys and two women survived. One of the overseers told authorities about the slaughter and police later arrested the stockmen. A huge outcry followed as the men were put to trial, with much of the public believing white men should not be tried for killing blacks. Originally set free and then later found guilty at a second trial, seven of the men were hanged for the murders. It was the first time in colonial history that white men had been found guilty in a court for murdering Aboriginal people.

It is believed that following the massacre the white party then went after the Aboriginal men from Myall Creek, who'd been advised to flee, and killed them as well. Running from the original massacre were two little boys, one of them saved by the white overseer who pushed him back into the hut when the others were being rounded up. One of the boys running for his life was an ancestor of Nathan Blacklock's.

(Nearly 160 years later, Sue Blacklock, Nathan's mum, played an instrumental part in creating a large rock memorial at the site of the massacre at Myall Creek. It became not a memorial to the horrors of white settlement, but a light in the reconciliation movement, a real touchstone in the efforts to understand the suffering of Aboriginal people. The site is now on the National Heritage List, and it helped instigate a surprise. Out of the woodwork, some of the descendants of the perpetrators of the massacre came to offer their hand of sorrow and reconciliation to the Wirrayaraay.)

As white settlement eventually took over the Liverpool Plains in the 1800s, the Aboriginal people were forced onto ever smaller areas to live and some came to agreements with squatters to stay on their traditional lands. This occurred at Tingha, under the conditional lease run by Captain Sydney Darby, and nearby on the property of Bassendean, south-west of Tingha, where a large clan of Aboriginal people lived, most of them taking the last name of Munro. Aboriginal people in the area often took the names of the station owners including Sullivan, Boney, Murray,

Gardner, Blair and Baker. Small ad hoc reserves were created for Aboriginal people to camp in the 1850s.

Aboriginal people were totally ignored in the Robertson Land Acts of 1861 as most of the north-west that was not under lease was carved up into small 320-acre lots for small farmers. Some squatters gave shelter to different tribes, but most Aboriginal people found themselves moving from reserve to reserve. Such was their plight in the 1860s that Dr McPherson, on seeing Aboriginal people on the Northern Tablelands, made a grave prediction: 'Drunkenness with attendant evils, exposure to cold and wet nights, tuberculosis, hydatids [tapeworms], venereal disease, the diminished body vigour resulting from occupying and sleeping in damp, dark and ill-vented hovels, incumbent upon their civilisation, have all conspired to destroy the tribes and soon the few remnants will be gathered to their fathers and we shall know them no more.'

What Dr McPherson didn't realise was that the Aboriginal people were enduring all the terrible acts and conditions thrown at them. He was actually witnessing a great act of survival, not a race on the brink of extinction.

In 1892 there were reported to be just 80 full-blood and 50 half-caste Aboriginal people living in the Inverell-Bingara area. It wasn't until 1893 that official reserves near Inverell were created for Aboriginal people, one at Pindari and one at Tingha. In 1894 it was reported that the Tingha reserve had 'an old half-caste woman and some of her daughters. She has cattle of her own and keeps sheep'. Half-caste Aboriginal people faced a tough life and many were spurned by both their white and Aboriginal families. The rule for acceptance of a half-caste in the tribe was that they 'were not too fair and had Aboriginal markings on their feet'.

Quite often Aboriginal people were moved on from Inverell to Tingha. Even in 1938, an Inverell alderman complained about the council's decision to move to Tingha a number of half-castes living by the river because of fears they would disturb the peace if they stayed. In the early 1900s, missionaries arrived and the people's lives changed again. The early Methodists started their preaching and supported the Aboriginal people in their fight for rights. Many of the converted indigenous people met up for conventions in northern New South Wales.

Another reserve was created south of Tingha, almost 10 kilometres away at Long Gully, but there was little available water and authorities required visitors to seek permission to visit Long Gully–based relatives. Not surprisingly, people deserted the place en masse.

The wheels of change moved slowly for the Aboriginal people in Tingha. It took nearly 30 years for authorities to decide where to put four new homes for Aboriginal families, as debate raged over whether they should be allowed a place by the river or the town common. Reconciliation was a long and painful process. When a group of academics from the University of Sydney arrived in the late '60s to report on Tingha's Aboriginal community they were astonished to find many Aboriginal people living in tin- and kerosene-can humpies dotted in the scrub. The researchers described the conditions as 'unliveable': 'Holes in roofs, no doors, no windows except for holes cut in galvanised iron walls, no electricity, no water and no sanitary services.'

The team estimated Tingha's Aboriginal population to be about 200–400, and of those only one man was employed full-time.

'Women fossicked for sapphires or tin to get by,' they recorded. Thirty-four of the group were on the pension. These were the conditions not in outback Northern Territory or in the desert tribes, but dead centre in one of the richest agricultural areas in Australia. Despite their desolation, the researchers found the Tingha community resilient and 'a strongly tribal people'.

Poverty produced all the typical ills as time went along, such as alcoholism, violence and then drug abuse. Eventually, with the creation of the Anaiwan Land Council and subsequent government money, proper housing was finally built for the Aboriginal population. But there was another turning point, something else assisting the Aboriginal people on this difficult journey. It was something that gave them hope, belief, often a bit of controversy, and sometimes a reason to party. It came with no strings attached (just a ball). And they took to it with great heart. The Tingha Tigers Rugby League Club became one of the inspirations for a downtrodden people to restore pride.

It was only natural then that when Linda Burney, an Aboriginal woman and then–NSW Labor Government minister, wanted to tackle the issue of domestic violence she turned to league. Borrowing an idea from the Normanton Stingers Rugby League Club in far north Queensland—which ties club behaviour to behaviour at home—the minister set up Tackling Domestic Violence, a unique program in which teams signed up to the code and won a $5000 sponsorship deal in the process. If they broke the code it had ramifications for their playing life, from suspensions to bans. Soon the message of 'No more excuses, no more lies and no more cover-ups' was being shared among 900 players and 22 regional communities in NSW.

Nathan Blacklock and David Peachey, another brilliant Aboriginal footballer who played most of his career with the Cronulla Sharks, became ambassadors for Tackling Domestic Violence and travelled throughout NSW. It's been acknowledged as one of the most successful grassroots programs introduced into Aboriginal communities. The new NSW Liberal government agreed to fully fund it. Community announcements on stopping domestic violence are run during the footy season.

Blacklock has also been an ambassador for a federal literacy campaign in indigenous communities. Just as importantly, he's helping some of the youngsters in Tingha keep their feet on the ground. He teaches them the old ways, the bush ways. He also wants to set up a gym in Inverell to teach healthy lifestyles. He's motivated, but he's always wary of the mobile phone.

'I got to get away from this phone, people are chasing me all the time,' he says, sipping the last of his caramel latte in a cafe on Inverell's busy Byron Street.

These days it's like he's constantly being tugged at. By the spirits of his people and knowledge passed down, by the fans tooting on this autumn day even when he's having a coffee in town. The constant handshakes from fans even though he hung up his boots nearly a decade ago.

But overlooking it all is the watchful, wary eye of his mother, Sue. She has a wonderful presence. There is a solidity and fortitude there, watching what her boy is up to, keeping that eye on him, making sure he doesn't run off too far. Then after polishing off his favourite coffee, Blacklock's quickly lost in the Saturday morning rush on Byron Street and, like his ancestor at Myall Creek, he's running, not for his life, but towards it.

CHAPTER TEN:
Holy Foley and Origin origins

It's State of Origin night and the imposing concrete facade of the Cassowary Coast Regional Council office in Innisfail rises into the heavy tropical air, a resolute force ready to withstand the poundings of the severest cyclone. Inside, in the dimly lit foyer, the names of the fallen from military conflicts are held securely on rolls of honour, and then, as if a secret hand is guiding you, old wooden doors open automatically to reveal a long hallway.

Way down the end, behind the reception desk, there are no pictures of past mayors, or famous visiting officials, or plans for the next major city development. Rather, there are cut-out images of cane toads crawling all over the display board. You could be mistaken for thinking you have entered Toad Hall, the fountainhead of cane toads, the epicentre of croaking. Such is the passion Innisfail has for State of Origin and rugby league.

Innisfail is a brave town that has fought off many cyclone emergencies. Cyclone Larry was a direct hit in 2006. Then category 5 Cyclone Yasi, which looked like a huge fireball on satellite imagery, only just missed the town in 2011 after suddenly veering south and devastating Tully. After the destructive winds and the relentless rain, the people slowly returned to business and life. As much as anything else that meant awaiting the next rugby league season.

League has been the sport of choice for north Queenslanders since the early 1900s, and it's rather hard for southerners to understand how league has hopped so confidently north.

Over the decades, Innisfail's small population (about 8000 in 2012) has produced some of league's best players, including internationals Lionel Williamson, Trevor McDonald, Kerry 'Bowie' Boustead and Billy Slater. There have been great clubmen too, like Greg Bandiera (Newtown, Easts and Balmain), Ron Tait (Queensland, Toowoomba, Rockhampton) and North Queensland Cowboys players Ty Williams and Scott Bolton. Many Innisfail players were behind the creation of the Cowboys. Several others have played first grade in the National Rugby League or at Brisbane club level. It's as if the rich red arc of volcanic soil around Innisfail is the perfect sprouting ground for top sportspeople (like former world triathlon champion Brad Beven, who grew up at nearby Mirriwinni).

As the deciding Origin match of 2012 draws near, with the Maroons gunning for another series victory to make it seven on the trot, everyone is on edge after the 'Cockroaches' of New South Wales scared the life out of the 'Cane Toads' outfit in the first two games, winning the second. A lone New South Wales supporter who migrated north to be an Innisfail businessman has had the gall to trawl the shopping centre looking for blue tissues to hand to his mates later in the night, expecting a Blues triumph.

Innisfail's famous modern prodigy Billy Slater is out injured for the decider, taking some of the gloss off the game for the local enthusiasts who love to watch his dynamic runs from fullback. But the ardent Queensland barrackers still expect another Origin series victory.

At the Brothers Leagues Club, the home base of Innisfail's rugby league team, known as the Leprechauns, there's hardly a person in sight—big or little—on entering its vast hall with only hours to go before kick-off. Rather than a sea of Maroons supporters there's just the odd lawn bowler settling in for the night after a hard day on the greens. An absent member has just missed out on a $1250 jackpot in the club badge draw.

Brothers secretary and former Leprechaun Paul Laffin explains the lack of patrons: 'It's Wednesday and they're all at home watching the game on television with screens as big as this,' he says, tapping a large glass table. 'You should be here on Saturdays after the local league game. Then, it's packed.'

In the foyer of the Brothers Leagues Club sits the glass cabinet housing tributes and memorabilia to the greats such as Williamson (who's now a football coach and school officer at St Augustine's College in Cairns), Boustead (who moved on to selling real estate in Brisbane) and the still-active Slater. Williamson's Australian jersey and cap sit on the bottom shelf of the cabinet. Boustead, the remarkable winger who played for Easts in the early 1980s, for Queensland in the first Origin game, and who was once the youngest-ever Kangaroo at 18 years and 310 days, is remembered in a timber-framed portrait. And then there's the space where Billy Slater's memorabilia used to be before it went on 'holiday' (though it's since been retrieved).

A hoon took the signed and framed photo of Slater from the foyer's glass cabinet late one night. The loss of the photo was like losing an icon from a church altar. Unfortunately for the alleged thief, he'd signed himself in on entering the club and it wasn't long before Laffin and a beefy, above-sized Leprechaun tracked him down to a caravan park at nearby Flying Fish Point.

Laffin and the Leprechaun stood outside the caravan and demanded the man's attention. He eventually emerged and Laffin encouraged him to stand aside with the beefy Leprechaun while he searched the rented van. The man pleaded his innocence, but when Laffin suggested the police might take on a more thorough search, the memorabilia appreciator retreated inside and pulled out the photo. 'God knows what the police would have found if they'd gone into the caravan,' says Laffin.

Far North Queensland is a wild place that shows no signs of being tamed. Boulder-filled rivers are engorged with foaming waters from months of torrential rain that rush down from the tablelands to the coast. Swathes of rainforest in the Misty Mountains, and up on the cooler Atherton Tablelands, are home to some of the most remarkable and diverse examples of flora and fauna in Australia, including the tree kangaroo. On the coast the cassowary has its last foothold on Earth where the rainforest meets the beach. Mount Bartle Frere, the highest mountain in Queensland, sits like Kilimanjaro above Innisfail, its top quite often circled majestically by a ring of cloud, its apron of valleys releasing cool beautifully pure water downstream. The rainfall at the summit is so high that it is rated one of the wettest places in the world. In the wet season it buckets and buckets along the Far North and it's not surprising that Tully chose a large concrete gumboot to celebrate its status as the town with the highest annual rainfall in Australia.

In the early 1900s, land was easily accessible in the area for migrants willing to put in the hard work of establishing and running sugarcane farms with all the seasonal variants. The fire that was lit in the belly of the people of the Far North for rugby league started soon after, when life was tougher, when people survived on the hard work of farms. Migrants started life afresh, arriving from such diverse places as Italy, Spain and Germany, adding to the early settler mix of Scottish, Irish and English. The migrants didn't turn to their traditional game of soccer for it often brought out too many old rivalries. Along with sugarcane, it was rugby league that bound them together.

For decades, fans would navigate flooded roads in bad weather just to watch a game of rugby league. The various competitions from the early 1920s eventually ended up in the battle for the ultimate treasure, the Foley Shield, named after North Queensland's father of league, Arch Foley. The Shield competition was started in his honour a year after he died, aged just 59. The Foley Shield replaced the Carlton Cup as a round robin trophy between three pools of North Queensland teams, with the grand final always to be held in Foley's hometown of Townsville, where he was the founding member of Townsville Souths. Foley had fostered great business and sporting contacts along the length of the east coast (at least to the New South Wales border), including a future prime minister, and Robert Menzies' long-time treasurer, Artie Fadden, who was an accountant in Townsville.

In 1914 Foley moved his team, Souths, from rugby union to league, making a statement that league was destined to be north Queensland's top sport. He was a lively five-eighth representing the northerners many times, including as captain against Toowoomba, rated in the 1920s as one of the best teams in Australia. North Queensland defeated the Toowoomba side twice during tour visits in the 1920s. Foley also played for Queensland against New South Wales in Sydney in 1914. After his playing career ended in 1922, he went into coaching and officialdom, and became president of the North Queensland Rugby League. Foley saw early the wisdom of maintaining the support of the league powerbrokers in Brisbane and Sydney, making it possible for a North Queensland representative to often have a say in Queensland and Australian team selection. Foley's hard work meant the league talent pool of the north could never be ignored.

In a letter he wrote to the *Townsville Bulletin*, North Queensland Rugby League selector J.C. MacGregor expressed his dismay when Foley announced his retirement from league officialdom in 1935, saying he was one of the ablest men the code had known, and held in high esteem by Queensland and New South Wales league officials. After Foley's visit south with his associate and brother-in-law Charlie Stone, MacGregor wrote: 'Such have they impressed the Southerners that the North Queensland league enjoys a wonderful reputation among them all.'

Their visit also paved the way for a visit by the touring England team in 1928. Foley coached the locals that day and they led the visitors 16–15 at half-time before the English ran away with the game in the second half finishing 30–16 winners.

Foley, who would later become a publican and own two hotels in Townsville, mortgaged his own home to build a grandstand at the Townsville Sports Reserve to entice big teams to the north. And it became a tradition for the English Lions to play in front of Foley's grandstand. These were all important building blocks that would one day pave the way for the NRL to grant a licence to the North Queensland Cowboys.

After his death, Foley's widow paid 60 pounds for an elaborate, wood-carved shield, made in Townsville by F. Heatley and Sons. Etched into it were the words, 'Memorial Arch Foley Shield'. The shield celebrated the diversity of the north's great timbers. The mounting was 20 centimetres thick and made of silkwood. The body was made of Maryborough pine, red bean, black bean, Leichhardt tree and silver ash. White cedar was used for the capping and the figure of a footballer is etched into the silver of the middle badge. The shield became the Holy Grail for northern footballers and a testament to the north's craftsmanship.

When the Foley Shield kicked off it had two zones: the northern zone, which included Innisfail, Cairns, Babinda, Eacham and Tully, and a southern zone of Mackay, Ayr and Townsville. A central zone of Home Hill, Herbert River and Charters Towers was added the next year. The two top teams played in Townsville in the grand final. Several towns moved in and out of the competition over time or, in the case of Mount Isa, often changed zones.

The Foley Shield took all of north Queensland's attention in its heyday. Australia might be playing England in a Test, but when Innisfail played Eacham or Mount Isa played Cairns, all eyes were cast that way. The games between Innisfail and Cairns were often the most competitive.

Kerry Boustead summed up the Foley's appeal in the foreword to *Up North... The Foley Shield Story*: 'The Foley Shield played a big part in the North Queensland community structure and was invaluable in providing the league stronghold which was instrumental in North Queensland gaining a berth in the national competition. Representative jumpers were earned, not bought, at your local sports store. They were carried on the field and thus worn with pride. A Foley Shield win would mean a long trip home, as the victors would pay a visit to each watering hole on the way and verbally replay the game, just one more time, so no-one was unsure of the outcome. One week from Townsville to Innisfail (normally a five-hour road trip) was conceivable.'

Boustead played for Innisfail in a Foley Shield final in 1977, but lost to Mount Isa. He remembers a large truck parked at the end of the field, side on, to help accommodate the large crowd with people clambering aboard the big B-double.

Boustead grew up on a cane farm at Silkwood, an hour south of Innisfail. His family were of Scottish ancestry. His brother Ian played league and at the age of just six Boustead was already telling his mother, Judy, that he wanted to play—and not for the under-7s, but with his brother in the under-12s.

Judy Boustead reached a compromise whereby he would play in the under-9s. 'They put him at fullback so he'd be out of the way and wouldn't get hurt, but before long he was running through the other teams,' Judy remembers.

Boustead, playing for Innisfail Souths, had played Foley Shield for Innisfail in his early teens but all eyes were on his brother Ian when he played for Queensland against New South Wales in 1976. But Boustead wasn't far behind his brother. After representing Queensland schoolboys, Boustead made his debut for Queensland to play New South Wales in the interstate series of 1978. The baby-faced winger surprised everyone with his great tackling and his ability to bring down giants like New

South Wales centre Mark Harris. He also scored some amazing tries for the Maroons.

He was elevated straight into the Australian side to play New Zealand in the midwinter Australian tour of 1978. At the age of 18, Boustead was the youngest person since Charles 'Chook' Fraser, in 1911, to play for Australia. His selection wasn't about blooding him for the future, either. He was thrust in at the deep end and immediately justified his place in the experienced team, something he'd done consistently during his fledgling career. He was man-of-the-match in the first Test in Sydney and starred with two tries in the second Test in Brisbane.

Every major team in Sydney had their chequebooks out to try and secure Boustead for the 1979 season, but the efforts of Easts' coach and league legend Bobby Fulton prevailed. Queensland tried to stop his transfer but were unsuccessful. The row at least helped ignite a reconsideration of interstate matches, namely which state players should represent. Interstate matches had become a one-sided joke. New South Wales had won 50 of the past 54 interstate matches leading up to 1980. Queensland senator and Queensland league chairman, Ron McAuliffe, pressured the league to reinvent the interstate fixtures, and a one-off 'state of origin' match was proposed for Lang Park in Brisbane on 8 July 1980.

Up until 1980, if you played in New South Wales you represented that state. So the vast wealth of Queensland talent often played for New South Wales, and it was not uncommon for players to have played for both states. Queensland often found it was playing against a virtual Test side. On the night of the first Origin game, Roma-born Arthur Beetson captained the Queensland side and Queenslanders warmed to the concept straight away.

Already, four years earlier, the New South Wales team has been coined 'Cockroaches' by former Australian halfback Barry Muir. He was Queensland coach at the time and while on tour to New South Wales he was sitting in a run-down Sydney hotel watching a television replay of the interstate match his team had played earlier. 'There was one of those rabbit-ear aerials on top of the TV with this cockroach sitting on it,' he remembered. 'It was on the [aerial ear on the] New South Wales side [of the screen]. Then when the Blues changed sides at half-time, it did too. I thought, that's what they are, bloody cockroaches.' He used the term at training and it endured. As a comeback, a New South Wales player later coined the term 'Cane Toads' for the Queensland team.

Muir was one of the best halfbacks in the game in the early 1960s and he had a connection to the Far North, coaching Ayr after hanging up his boots. He was also one of the proponents for the State of Origin series, incensed that Sydney clubs could buy up the best Queensland players and then get them to play for New South Wales.

Boustead remembered the build-up to the first Origin match in Brisbane: 'Each day we'd walk through the city and each day the crowds grew and grew. That's when we started to get a feeling that it was something special and we started to realise how much the state needed a good performance because we hadn't won for a long time.'

Boustead scored the historic first try for Queensland and there was bedlam among the 33,000 fans as Queensland ran out winners 20–10. Its side boasted a young Mal Meninga and a young Wally Lewis, both of whom would become Origin heroes.

'It was fantastic, but the crazy part was, I played for New South Wales the week before and I had cans and apples thrown at me. Obviously, the mood had changed somewhat,' Boustead remembered. The Origin concept was off to a flying start and a young man from Innisfail was at the centre of its success. Many years on, Billy Slater would again fly the Innisfail flag in Origin.

Boustead had a long career, playing for Easts and Manly, and representing Australia 25 times, and being an Origin combatant until 1984. By that time it had become a three-match series and had eclipsed the old interstate formula, proving a massive television hit. Boustead eventually took an executive role with the new North Queensland Cowboys but resigned, disgusted when the team joined up with the rival Super League competition in 1997.

As Boustead rose to another hemisphere in league, back on home soil in Innisfail the battle for the Foley Shield still raged. And following it all was an enthusiast of Foley folklore in Bob Faithfull, who played in some of the roughest and wettest Foley games in the Far North.

As a fan slowly stirs the air above his head in an Innisfail cafe on Origin night, Faithfull explains why the Foley Shield was such a drawcard. 'You'd get anything up to 10,000 people to the grand final, all of the players capable of playing down south,' he says, with 'south' meaning Brisbane and south-east Queensland. Faithfull could have played down south himself but knocked back an offer to play for Toowoomba because he 'fell in love' and settled down.

Some of Faithfull's happiest playing days were the early ones. 'When I was a young fellow I played five-eighth at Gordonvale, and we were in the Cairns competition, and in one year we had eleven of the thirteen in the rep side (North Queensland), that was a bloody excellent effort.'

The competition was very tough, he recalls, and the popularity of the Foley Shield was helped by the lack of competition. 'There was no union or [Aussie] Rules and soccer was unheard of. In the '50s'—back when Faithfull would play with Billy Slater's father, Ronnie, in Innisfail—'the crowds would roll up in bloody big numbers.'

Innisfail has been home to several league teams in its history. The main ones were Uniteds, Southern Suburbs and Railways. Players were chosen to represent Innisfail from these smaller teams. Eventually, Innisfail Brothers—the Leprechauns—became the main senior team.

When Faithfull came down from Gordonvale to coach—and finding himself getting used to games being held in driving rain—he moved around, taking coaching gigs at Mourilyan, Southern Suburbs, Ravenshoe and then Richmond.

For his coaching role, he received ten pounds a week in wages and free board—which was a great earn back in the 1950s. But often he had a tough time getting a team together as many were away working on farms or off on jobs up on the Tablelands.

Coaching also required knowing what made players tick, and it wasn't always the same thing. 'We had a bloke up in Ravenshoe,' remembers Faithfull. '[His name was John] Kerrigan, a good fighter, a good half back, and he followed me down here [to Innisfail] and he [was with us] to play Tully in a Foley Shield game. Anyway, he was down in the dumps, sitting with his head in his knees. I said "What's wrong, John?" He said, "I'm crook." And Noel Rees was the president then (of the club), and he came up to me and said, "Just watch this." He had an Aspro. He went over to Kerrigan and said, "Quick, swallow that." Well he went out to play and played the best ever game in his life. There was a bloke nicknamed "Basher from Babinda", a big solid bloody canegrower; Kerrigan wanted to fight him and get into him. You never seen anything change a man like that just because he thought he took a pill—[but] it was only an Aspro.'

It was a hard and tough competition and Innisfail didn't make their first Foley grand final until 1960. That year, led by captain and coach Jim Paterson (an eight-time Kangaroo representative, who'd accepted a massive £800 deal to captain-coach the team), they defeated Herbert River 12–9. Paterson—who'd been coached by two of Arch Foley's sons in his early days in Townsville—added another string to his bow that would have warmed the heart of Arch Foley; he coached the North Queensland team to beat the touring Great Britain side in 1966.

While most players stayed in the Far North, quite a few went on to glory in Sydney (so going further than 'south'), and many played for Australia or for club sides in England (a long way north-west). Among those who went 'south' was Innisfail-born Ron Tait. Tait now lives on the outskirts of Innisfail near the railway line and has lost a fair bit of tin from his roof over the years from cyclones. A cassowary occasionally emerges from the bush over the line and it's common for a few peacocks to make a nuisance of themselves on the roof. The former electrician has retired after a life lived around league. Even his honeymoon was sidetracked by football. He'd accepted a job to coach and play for Rockhampton in 1960 and had to leave a day after his wedding. He and his new wife celebrated on the train journey down to Rocky.

Tait's career was supported by the Christian Brothers in his early years. His senior career started when he was a young teenager and he was given a remarkable chance to play for the Newtown side in Toowoomba in 1951. He was given free board as part of his transfer deal and within a week he had a job. 'That was pretty good for then,' says Tait. Toowoomba was a nurturing ground for many northern footballers.

Tait made the Toowoomba representative side as a five-eighth and played in the Bulimba Cup against the cream of footballers in south-east Queensland. He earned four pounds a win, and £100 if his Toowoomba side won the competition. 'It was all football in those days, everything I did centred around that,' he says. He played in Toowoomba until 1959 and on his return to Innisfail he received another offer he couldn't refuse, this time to captain-coach Rockhampton. One of the selectors in Brisbane had urged him to take the role to boost his chances in representative football. He was on course to play for North Queensland and Queensland, which he duly did. It seemed an Australian jumper was only a hop, skip and jump away.

While in Rocky, Tait received a phone call from the Australian Rugby League in Sydney telling him to pack his bags because he'd been selected to play for Australia. They told him to book a plane seat to Brisbane. He couldn't believe his luck. Due to leave later the next day, he raced down to the *Rockhampton Bulletin*'s office the next morning, expecting to see his name in bold type in the Australian team list in the newspaper. He stood back in shock when he couldn't see his name anywhere. He walked disconsolately out of the office.

Everyone in the north reckons Tait was a certainty to play for Australia after his great performances for Queensland against New South Wales. Some reckon there was a mix-up, that Tait's mate, Alan Gil, someone who resembled him, mistakenly received the nod at the last moment. Ron believes there was some behind-the-scenes chicanery between the time he was told to pack his bags and the time he learnt he wasn't in the team.

Three people selected the Australian team. 'It only takes three men to make an international. There was a lot of politics in it, you know,' says Ron. He thinks the Australian selectors were trying to get as many players down to training just in case some didn't turn up.

He returned to Innisfail the next year and was among the great Innisfail sides that won the Foley Shield. He also had the great result of defeating France when he played for North Queensland. He was able to enjoy some international glory.

When he played for Queensland he was up against the likes of such greats as Johnny Raper, Reg Gasnier and Ron Coote in the New South Wales team. "We all used to get together for a good grog-up after the game. They (the New South Wales players) were gentlemen off the field. On the field, well, let's say they didn't like getting tackled.'

Tait retired from football at the age of 32 in 1968. His electrical business in Innisfail got off to a high-voltage start because everyone in the district knew him from his league fame.

Another Innisfail player who came to the fore in the twilight of Tait's career was Adrian 'Storky' Astorquia, Billy Slater's great uncle, who played for Innisfail in the early '60s before moving to Sydney in 1969. He was first lured to play for Western Suburbs by tough fellow Queenslander Noel 'Ned' Kelly, but the deal fell through. Future league supremo Ken Arthurson had spotted Astorquia in a North Queensland match, and urged him to head to Sydney and play for Manly. When Astorquia finally got to Sydney he looked for Arthurson and asked him: 'What do I do now?' Arthurson deadpanned: 'Go to training.'

Having always played in the backs in his career in Queensland, Astorquia was surprised, and in unknown territory, when Manly put him straight into the second-row. Manly legend Rex 'Moose' Mossop—who'd become a commentator famous for his so-called 'Mossopisms', statements that could have several raucous meanings—advised Astorquia to 'tackle the man a foot early'. Astorquia practised it and suddenly found himself leaping through the air to surprise the opposition player with the ball. Mossop also advised him to weave more to break the defence, and Astorquia quickly saw the benefits with some 50-yard tries. Astorquia spent most of his time in reserve grade for Manly, playing two first-grade games.

Astorquia was almost the age of his nephew Ronnie Slater, Billy's dad. He was a late arrival in Juan and Connie Astorquia's marriage, born in 1943, almost 18 years younger than his nearest sibling. But Astorquia had the honour of later setting a few firsts. He had a hand in two Foley Shield victories for Innisfail, 11 years apart. His first triumph was in the 1964 side and although he didn't play in the grand final, he was a mainstay of the Innisfail team the whole year, later selected in the North Queensland side, which won the Queensland divisional championship three years in a row up until 1965.

Astorquia returned to Innisfail after his stint in Sydney in 1975 and captained Innisfail to another Foley Shield victory, this time with Billy's dad, Ronnie, alongside him. The nephew-uncle combination put Townsville to the sword with Innisfail running away with it, winning 15–4. Among the Townsville opposition was former Manly player Johnny Bucknell, the man who infamously broke Johnny Sattler's jaw in the Sydney grand final of 1970. 'I think the celebrations went on for two weeks,' Astorquia remembers of the 1975 victory.

Innisfail's second-ever Foley Shield victory was won 11 years earlier in 1964, when they defeated Townsville 30–8. In the side was future Australian Test player, Lionel Williamson. By this time, Jim Paterson had returned to his home of Townsville, so in the 1964 finals he lined up against Williamson and Ron Tait.

Williamson was a mystery player to many people. He suddenly appeared in top-class football with little playing time in the juniors. Everyone had been asking 'Who is this Lionel Williamson?' Williamson was one of five brothers from a cane farm at Daradgee, just north of Innisfail. He'd spent his early years doing the hard yards on the cane farm, labouring in the fields and later working in the South Johnstone Mill. His family were devout Scottish Catholics and he heard the calling, signing up for the priesthood, not league, when he was 17.

But life in a seminary confounded him. 'I couldn't hack the Latin,' he says. He quit after two years and headed back to the cane farm and league in Innisfail. He won the player-of-the-carnival for the under-18s tournament in Townsville, and within a year he was elevated to Foley Shield football. He was only 19 when, a relative unknown, he played in his first Foley Shield game against Mareeba. Who was this kid? Well, after he scored three tries the commentator on Cairns radio station 4CA declared, 'We know who Lionel Williamson is now.' During the first year in the Foley Shield, Williamson enjoyed running off Ron Tait's precise passes to score many more tries.

As Williamson would discover, Foley Shield was big news in the Far North. Whole towns came to watch matches, and the games had great spirit about them. 'It was like farmer against farmer, or farmer against townie. It was good healthy rivalry,' Williamson says.

Sometimes, however, the rivalry got a little heated, particularly when money was on the line. Williamson remembers a pair of Foley Shield games against Mount Isa, the first when Innisfail was unexpectedly rolled when they travelled away to Mount Isa. "We were expected to win easily, but we'd all been having a party the day before and they gave us a flogging,' he says. 'When Mount Isa returned to play us at the coast we gave them a hiding and they were real dirty claiming we had lost on purpose in the previous game and that we'd been foxing to get a price (there was plenty of betting on Foley Shield games) out there.'

Though Williamson was rewarded for his efforts with selection in the 1964 Queensland side, just one year into first-grade football, he was soon gone as fast as he had appeared. During the off-season he accepted an offer to play in England with Halifax. He then had two seasons with Bradford: From the humid air of North Queensland to the often snow-covered and icy fields of northern England in the blink of an eye.

But, needing an operation to have gallstones removed, Williamson returned to Australia. And once back he stayed and settled into the Innisfail life once again. It was a wise move. His interstate and international career took off exponentially. He played a vital role in two World Cup campaigns and became a mainstay of the Kangaroo touring sides for the next seven years. Williamson made the Queensland side in 1967 and then was selected in Australia's World Cup squad the following year. He scored two tries in the final against France as Australia won the World Cup 20–2 in front of 54,000 people at the

Sydney Cricket Ground. His teammates included such league legends as Bobby Fulton, Eric Simms, Johnny Raper and fellow Queenslander and immortal, Arthur Beetson.

Williamson was renowned for his strength and fitness, attributes he derived from putting in back-breaking work on cane farms and sugar mills to earn his keep. Cutting cane, carrying it to bins, lugging railway sleepers, shovelling gravel onto trucks for hours at a time in the hot tropical sun; it was a physical life. 'When we were working in the mill, everything was a contest to see who could do a task quicker; we weren't shovel-loading rocks for half an hour, that was for half a day.' The work turned him into a small man-mountain, but with speed, and he had one of the firmest grips in the game. He rarely dropped a football.

There was a number of times when he had to show his cane farm–earned mettle in tough games against New South Wales. He was marking the great winger Ken Irvine and giving him some punishing treatment in an interstate clash. Williamson says Irvine complained to his burly New South Wales teammate Noel 'Ned' Kelly and urged him to go over and square up with Williamson. Kelly came over to Williamson to rough him up, but as soon as he saw him said 'Blow you, see you later', without laying a hand on him.

A large transfer price was placed on Williamson for his move from Queensland to the big league in Sydney. Canterbury tried to secure him but baulked at the price, which was $7000 from the Innisfail club, with an extra $4000 placed on the transfer by the Queensland Rugby League. Newtown instead came to the party and Williamson became a Bluebag, playing with them until 1974, with the likes of Tom Raudonikis in the team. Williamson won international plaudits in two World

Cup campaigns. It was on the 1973 Kangaroo tour of England that Williamson's muscle was brought in at a vital time to help clinch the Ashes for Australia in horrendous conditions. Australia had lost the first Test of the tour, and then won the second Test, setting up a massive decider at Warrington. Ice covered the Wilderspool field before the game, and a mountain of straw was laid on the pitch to thaw it out.

Australia brought in two tough tackling Souths players, Ray Branighan and Paul Sait, in a brazen attempt to tackle England out of the game. The ploy worked. With beefy Williamson also on the attack, England were hit by a mountain of muscle. 'I used to just bulldog them over the sideline,' says Williamson, using all that cane farming–acquired grunt. Australia prevailed 15–5 in the northern cold. It was a great tour for Williamson and Australia. Later on the tour, the Kangaroos defeated France in two Tests, returning home with 17 victories from 19 games.

Rugby league historian Ian Heads said Williamson was one of the most unappreciated of Australia's wingmen. 'Of stocky build and short on genuine pace, the likeable Queenslander compensated with perhaps the best pair of hands that any winger has ever had, and the happy knack of being in the right place at the right time. He was a fine player,' Heads wrote.

Williamson also made an impact in interstate football, which was a different beast to today's Origin blockbusters. The series up until the early 1980s comprised four games in two weeks: two games in Brisbane followed by two games in Sydney. Players would arrive on a Monday in Brisbane, train on a Tuesday, and then play on the Wednesday. They'd back up with the next game on the following Saturday and repeat the clashes the next week in Sydney. It was nothing like the weeks of preparation that go into today's State of Origin, which is a tri-series played over two months, with a three-week break between games.

When Williamson was preparing for the state clash in Brisbane there was little public fervour. City monuments certainly weren't lit up in maroon, as they are today. The Queensland team in the late 1960s was housed in a modest hotel in Fortitude Valley in Brisbane and in Sydney they were given quiet digs at Hotel Bondi. No-one in the crowd wore representative jumpers or dressed up in funny wigs. After a match, the players would head off with their interstate rivals for a beer together.

Williamson says club, state and Kangaroo jerseys were devalued when they put them on sale to the general public. 'You couldn't buy a jumper back then, you had to earn it,' he says. And back then footballers played for pride, not for financial reward. After a four-match interstate series in 1968, Williamson received just 30 dollars as a bonus. (By contrast, in 2012, State of Origin players received just over $12,000 a game.) It was the same when he travelled overseas for Australia. He was paid 60 dollars a week, 40 of which stayed at home for his family. In 1973 he received a bonus of $200 after returning from several months playing overseas in England and France.

Williamson's old teammate Jim Paterson says North Queenslanders faced a tough task getting into the Queensland state side, facing some regional prejudice. 'We (North Queensland) were beating Brisbane heavily in those days and [the league bosses in Brisbane] didn't like that. They'd forget about you when it came to picking the Queensland side. It was easier sometimes to get into the Australian team.'

Williamson's football light had burned well into the 1970s, but at the same time the light of the Foley Shield was slowly fading. As the competition went on, teams slowly moved to other league groups or withdrew. One of the most famous talents from the last days of the Foley Shield was referee Barry 'Grasshopper' Gomersall. He went from refereeing under-18s games, Foley Shield, and intense Palm Island matches in the north, to refereeing State of Origin for six years up until 1988. According to author Graham Stockwell, Gomersall rated the Foley Shield final third behind the Brisbane and Sydney grand finals in importance.

After 1996, the Foley Shield became a round robin competition played over three days in Townsville. In 2013—by which time only three teams contested it, Cairns, Mackay and Townsville—it was put into 'hiatus' as its future was, and continues to be, debated, 64 years after the first Foley Shield game was played.

On the eve of the 2012 Origin decider, Blues fans were hoping for a miracle, that their side could break the long drought. But all around Innisfail, cane farmers were burning their crops, a farming ritual (to reduce leafy extraneous material) that's dying out as more environmentally friendly green cane harvesting comes to the fore. But as the sun set in the west it turned the glow of the fires into a large maroon pall that billowed high in the air, wafting south. In this sporty state soaked with league talent, it wasn't a good omen for New South Wales.

Sources

General references:
Collis, Ian and Whiticker, Alan, *Rugby League Through the Decades*, New Holland, 2011.
Heads, Ian, *True Blue: The Story of New South Wales Rugby League*, Ironbark Press, 1992.
Dollin, Shawn, Ferguson, Andrew and Bates, Bill, (compiled by), 'The Rugby League Project: career statistics on players'.
Whiticker, Alan and Hudson, Glen, *The Encyclopaedia of Rugby League Players*, Gary Allen, 1999.

Chapter One: From the Wild – The Cleals
Interviews:
Don 'Bandy' Adams, Bob Barker, Harvey Cleal, Ronnie Coote, Bob Fulton, Kerry Hales, Stan Jurd, Wayne Kratzmann, Ray Lindsay, Craig Mordey, Ann Newling, Tommy Slater, Greg White.
Articles:
'Big Les has a beef', Dorothy Goodwin, *Sydney Morning Herald*, 19 September, 1987.
'Fulton promotes the other Cleal', Alan Clarkson, *Sydney Morning Herald*, 11 May, 1982.
'Northern Division takes on Great Britain', *Northern Daily Leader*, 6 June, 1979.
'Old soldier Beetson will keep pledge', Geoff Prenter, *Fairfax*, 31 August, 1980.
'Packer just a good club supporter', *Sydney Morning Herald*, 25 September, 1987.
'Premiership is guided by God and the Cleal brothers', *Coffs Coast Advocate*, 8 September, 2006.
'Second Cleal just Waiting', Ian Heads, *Fairfax*, 14 June, 1981.
'Teamwork the essence of Easts 11-man try', *Sydney Morning Herald*, 24 August, 1982.

'The big centre clash, Mick versus Noel', Tom Bishop, *Sydney Morning Herald*, 6 April, 1980.

Chapter Two: 'Humble' Eric Weissel and 'unstoppable' Harry Sunderland

Interview:
Bruce Weissel.

Articles:
Much of the information for the 1929 Kangaroo tour and other Ashes tours was taken from reports penned (as his second or third job) by team manager Harry Sunderland and published in *The Brisbane Courier*. These are a selection of them:

'A spirit of unity', Harry Sunderland, *The Brisbane Courier*, 8 August, 1929.
'Australia Wins Torrid Test Battle', Harry Sunderland, *The Brisbane Courier*, 20 June, 1932.
'Brilliant Win', Harry Sunderland, *The Brisbane Courier*, 13 September, 1929.
'By Six Points', *The Brisbane Courier*, 11 November, 1929.
'Team morale Essential', Harry Sunderland, *The Brisbane Courier*, 20 November, 1929.
'Team of Stars', Harry Sunderland, *The Brisbane Courier*, 28 October 1929.
'The Best Ever', Harry Sunderland, *The Brisbane Courier*, 9 October, 1929.
'The Kangaroos', Harry Sunderland, *The Brisbane Courier*, 31 August, 1929.
'Visit to New York', Harry Sunderland, *The Brisbane Courier*, 14 October, 1929.
'With the Kangaroos', Harry Sunderland, *The Brisbane Courier*, 11 November, 1929.

Other articles:
'Australia Wins', *Cairns Post*, 7 October, 1929.
'Australia Wins', *Sydney Morning Herald*, 23 July, 1928.
'Eastern Suburbs Beaten', *Sydney Morning Herald*, 10 July, 1928.
'Faithful Dogs', *Sydney Morning Herald*, 22 September, 1927.
'Saturday's Game was Pink Tea', L.H. Kearney, *Courier-Mail*, 21 June, 1950.
'Weissel Brilliant', *Canberra Times*, 18 April, 1932.
'Weissel May Not Play', *Sydney Morning Herald*, 3 June, 1930.
'Weissel's Definite Appearance', *The Brisbane Courier*, 18 June, 1929.
'Weissel's Retirement', *Townsville Daily Bulletin*, 8 March, 1933.

Other sources:
Carr, Andy 'My good comrade of the rugby league', Centenary Conference of Rugby League in Australia, 7 November 2008.
Caskie, Patricia, *Cootamundra 1901–1924, Past Imperfect*, Anwell Enterprises 2000.

Cootamundra Local History Society Inc.

Sheehan, M.V. (Sinbad), Bradley, *The Maher Cup Story*, information from the chapter 'The greatest five-eighth', J.A. Bradley and Sons, 1963.

Chapter Three: The Maher Cup
Interviews:
Tom Apps, Ted Curran, Gary Elliott, Bill Kearney Jnr, Ian Kirk, Eric Kuhn, Col Ratcliff, Barrie Stanford, Fred Strutt, Terry Sturt, Patrick 'Scoop' Sullivan.

Articles:
'Back from the bush', Joe McGraw, *Rugby League News*, 1 August, 1927.
'Flouted', *Sydney Morning Herald*, 7 August, 1929.
'Footballer to travel by plane', *Sydney Morning Herald*, 22 July, 1935.
'Football Victory', *Sydney Morning Herald*, 27 June, 1924.
'Maher Cup at Young', *Sydney Morning Herald*, 13 June, 1930.
'New Maher Cup rule', *Queanbeyan Age*, 16 June, 1925.
'Protest in Maher Cup Competition', *Sydney Morning Herald*, 12 August, 1927.
'Stir in Country Football', *Canberra Times*, 7 August, 1929.
'The Maher Cup, a wonderful record', *Queanbeyan–Canberra Advocate*, 12 August, 1926.

General references:
Madigan, John, *The Maher Cup and Tumut*, Wilkie Watson Publications, 1995.
Sheehan, M.V. (Sinbad), Bradley, *The Maher Cup Story*, J.A. Bradley and Sons, 1963.

Other references:
Sullivan, Patrick 'Scoop', 'The Maher Cup', his address to a Maher Cup reunion.
Weeks, Jack, 'A brief history of Group 9 rugby league'.

Chapter Four: Tom Kirk
Interviews:
Alan Froome, Ian Kirk.

Articles:
The bulk of the match reports for Tom Kirk were taken from the newspaper clippings collected by the Kirk family during Tom's career. There are too many items to list individually. Most reports were taken from *Truth, Daily Telegraph. Labor Daily, The Referee* and the *Sun* in the 1930s and 1940s. These are cited in the chapter. The major journalists were John 'Dinny' Campbell, J.C. Davis, Claude Corbett, W.F. Corbett (Claude's brother), Ross McKinnon and Viv Thicknesse..

Other articles:
'Curtailing SP Bets', *Sydney Morning Herald*, 29 April, 1938.
'Farrell not guilty on ear-biting charge', *Sydney Morning Herald*, 5 February, 1946.
'Henry Porter, prop forward', *Sydney Morning Herald*, 10 September, 1947.
'Hoosman Beats Narvo', *Army News*, 13 November, 1944.
'Player named by McRitchie', *Sydney Morning Herald*, 7 August, 1945.
'Reducing Fines', *Sydney Morning Herald*, 2 May, 1938.
'Restricting SP betting', *Sydney Morning Herald*, 5 October, 1938.
'Sluicing at Shepardstown', *Sydney Morning Herald*, 13 July, 1929.
'SP Betting', *Sydney Morning Herald*, 23 July, 1938.
'SP Drive', *Sydney Morning Herald*, 16 May, 1938.
References:
Hassett, Annette, 'Along the creek' *in History of Shepardstown, Grahamstown and Mt Horeb*, Wilkie Watson, 1999.

Chapter Five: Clem Kennedy
Interviews:
Quintin Graham, Mary Kennedy.
Articles:
'Englishmen too heavy', *Sydney Morning Herald*, 13 May 1946.
'Footballer would have been capable boxer', *Army News*, 1 July, 1945.
'From the scrum', *Sydney Morning Herald*, 29 May, 1946.
'Great statesman, Great sport', *Rugby League News*, 20 July, 1946.
'Goliaths no problem to Tom Thumb half-back', *Daily Telegraph*, 11 July, 1944.
'Kennedy to consider Young offer', *Sydney Morning Herald*, 9 April, 1948.
'Kennedy may transfer to Newtown', *Sydney Morning Herald*, 13 February, 1948.
'Kennedy Misses Test Chance', *Sydney Morning Herald*, 28 June, 1946.
'Mt Carmel's fine record', *Sydney Sun*, 7 August, 1937.
'Rugby team will be delayed here', *Daily News*, 30 April, 1946.
'State half in brilliant bid for Test', *Sydney Morning Herald*, 15 April, 1946.
Other references:
Anathasou, Professor James, 'An Anzac Tribute (to Clem Kennedy)', 16 April, 2011.
Heads, Ian, 'Clem Kennedy remembers, Little Man Big Heart', from *The Juniors: the best for the best*, Playright Publishing, 2000.
Heads, Ian, *Never Say Die: The George Piggins Story*, Pan MacMillan, 2002.
Hudson, Tony, 'The Story of Clement Kennedy'.
Mordey, Bill, 'Clem Kennedy, The Mighty Atom', *Daily Mirror*.
The Rabbitoh Warren, online web chat site.

Chapter Six: Kevin 'Lummy' Longbottom
Interviews:
Russell Amatto, Les Bridge, Ronnie Coote, Bruce Devlin, George Longbottom, Helen Longbottom, John Sattler, Gabby Stathis.
Articles:
'Miss Keller and gum-leaf band', *Sydney Morning Herald*, 12 April, 1948.
Wilkins, Phil, 'This Goal is not on record', *Sydney Morning Herald*, 17 September, 1967.
References:
Randwick: A Social History, NSW University Press, 1985.

Chapter Seven: Buns and bunnies
Interview:
Ronnie Coote.
Articles:
'Coote may help Easts rule roost', Alan Clarkson, *Sydney Morning Herald*, 29 January, 1972.
'Coote rejects Qld', *Sydney Morning Herald*, 28 January, 1972.
'Coote rejects Souths terms', Alan Clarkson, *Sydney Morning Herald*, 27 January, 1971.
'Coote-South dispute is still on', Alan Clarkson, *Sydney Morning Herald*, 4 February, 1971.
'Fulton joins Easts', Alan Clarkson, *Sydney Morning Herald*, 15 October, 1976.
'Twelve minutes', Alan Clarkson, *Sydney Morning Herald*, 19 September, 1971.
References:
Masters, Roy, *Inside Rugby League*, Pan, 1992.
Tom Brock Collection, Mitchell Library.

Chapter Eight: Laurie Nichols
Interviews:
Harry Nichols, Johnny Lewis, Syd Williams, Julie Besgrove (nee Nichols), Todd Goodwin, Craig Mordey.
Articles:
The information was gathered from newspaper articles collected by the Nichols family over several decades, mainly from the *Sydney Morning Herald, Daily Telegraph, Cooma-Monaro Express* and *Daily Mirror*.
Chesterton, Ray, 'Remembering Laurie Nichols', *Daily Telegraph*, 27 July, 2007.

Other references:
Arthurson, Ken with Heads, Ian, *Arko: My Game*, Ironbark, 1997.
Channel Ten's coverage of merger between Wests and Balmain.
Chesterton, Ray, *Tiger, Tiger Burning Bright*, Playright Publishing, 2000

Chapter Nine: Nathan Blacklock
Interviews:
Nathan Blacklock, Andrew Farrar, Dick Hayden.
Articles:
'Tingha bids NRL goodbye', Paul Suttor, *Illawarra Mercury*, 5 June, 2002.
'Tingha chases four-year record', Paul Suttor, *Illawarra Mercury*, 15 March, 2002.
'Walk slowly, Run fast', Jessica Halloran, *Sydney Morning Herald*, 19 July, 2003.
'We are the Champions', Jessica Halloran, *Sydney Morning Herald*, 2 May, 2009.
References:
Fennell, Mrs Marian, Grey, Lex, in collaboration with the Aboriginal people of Tingha, *Nucoorilma*, The University of Sydney, Van Leer Project, 1974.
Horton, Dr David (editor), *The Encyclopaedia of Aboriginal Australia*, Aboriginal Studies Press, 1994.

Chapter Ten: Holey Foley and Origin origins
Interviews:
Adrian Astorquia, Sue Astorquia, Bob Faithfull, Jim Paterson, Tommy Slater, Ron Tait, Lionel Williamson.
Articles:
'Arch Foley's death at 59', *Townsville Daily Bulletin*, 22 December, 1947.
References:
Stockwell, Graham, *Up North: The Foley Shield Story*, Queensland Rugby League, 1996.

Acknowledgements

There were so many butcher shops in the New South Wales South Coast village of Thirroul that there was little hesitation when they wanted a name for the town's new rugby league team: they called it The Butchers. That was 100 years ago, when Thirroul was a coastal weekend getaway, dotted with worker's cottages set among dairy herds grazing under the escarpment. The most famous person to live in Thirroul was novelist D.H. Lawrence and he couldn't help but mention a rugby league game in his writings. Some of the young men who kicked off the game of rugby league in 1913, though, would soon be swapping footballs for guns on the other side of the world. Another Thirroulian and history buff, Gary Elliott, provided some wonderful detail on Maher Cup matches and Test matches, played in Sydney, that he saw as a young man.

A solemn sculpture of a slouch-hatted Digger sits near Thirroul station. His stare marks the loss of innocence that the terrible war years brought. But it is as if, at times, the Digger is slightly woken by a sound, which has rattled his ears for decades: of Butchers training just across the railway line. If the men from the area who went to war thought of something while they were away, they probably dreamt of returning to play with, or to support, the Butchers.

Thirroul has changed a lot since 1913. Today a footballer may enjoy a vegie burger from one of the many cafes, as much as his mate might like a meat pie from Flemings bakery. But one thing has remained firm—the Butchers line. From six-year-olds up, the Butchers are cajoled to run and tackle harder, as trainers sprout the wisdom taught over the ages. It was inevitable Thirroul, my own home, would be fertile ground for league stories. Like many places in New South Wales and Queensland, its history is steeped in rugby league.

Sitting at Thirroul's Beans Talk Café, I was yarning with my relative Anne Ellicott, a Thirroulian through and through, mentioning how my project included a history of the Maher Cup. 'I know a good Butcher you could talk to about that,' she declared. His name was Ted Curran, and he gave me a wonderful account of the time he wrested the Maher Cup off Young for his team Temora. Anne's advice started an avalanche. Before long I had a list of ex-Maher Cup players who had left the country for life on the coast, and were eager to tell their stories. Someone suggested I should talk to 'Kirky', a former country player whose dad was a supreme goal kicker in the Sydney comp in the 1930s. One day I was parked outside a house in Thirroul where I was delivering my son for a play over. Suddenly there was a knock on the car's window. 'You looking for me?' 'Who are you?' I asked. 'Kirky' he said. I'd been trying to track him down and it turned out his grandson was the boy my son was visiting. 'Kirky' (Ian Kirk or 'Kicker') lived just a few streets away. Generously he loaned me his family albums that helped me piece together the story of his footballing hero father, Tom.

One day at Thirroul school, I was talking to Heather Froome, the mum of one of my younger son's friends, and I mentioned the league book. 'My granddad played league,' she said. 'Oh really, what was his name?' I asked. 'Keith Froome,' she replied. Played league? He was a former Australian captain, I later found out! Heather was always very humble. Her father, Alan pieced together a short recount of his dad's life. So there we were: my two sons, friends in the same school with two great-grandsons of a couple of league greats, and more stories unfolded.

The book grew and grew and a journalist friend of mine from Harden, Gabrielle Chan, suggested a few old timers might let me into a few secrets of how Harden–Murrumburrah held on to the Maher Cup for so long. Tom Apps gave the secret away. In the second half of the game they always ran towards the end where the pub was located, and went there straight afterwards.

Former player Mick Bristow kindly sent me a book on the Maher Cup from the place where the Cup sits in its final resting place of Tumut. Newspaper editor Patrick 'Scoop' Sullivan from Gundagai shared some sacred lore from his beautiful country haven by the Murrumbidgee filling in many gaps in my Maher knowledge. Scoop has proved a wonderful associate in the writing caper, helping me with my first book on country racing—what's our next project, Scoop?

I was down in my old holiday haunt of Adaminaby in the Snowy Mountains when Adaminaby stalwart Leigh Stewart was telling me how much he loved Balmain's Larry Corowa, when I casually mentioned I may write something about the exuberant Balmain fan Laurie Nichols. 'You know he came from Cooma (just down the road) and his brother's still alive.' Thanks to Leigh I tracked down nonagenarian Harry, who had recently renovated his Cooma abode, and sat down for some time with him and his son Jack before they lent me, without hesitation, a collection of cuttings and bits and pieces on Laurie's life.

Another holiday favourite in far North Queensland offered up a bevy of stories. Innisfail is the home of a player once voted the best in the world, Billy Slater. When I tracked down Billy's great aunt Sue Astorquia at the Innisfail Advocate, she kindly put me in touch with old league player and trainer Bob Faithfull, who lent me his book on the Foley Shield and gave me some great stories on Foley folklore. Billy's uncle, Adrian Astorquia, who led the way for the Slater clan in top flight football, playing for Manly, provided some great detail on Foley lore, as did former players Ron Tait and Lionel Williamson. Leprechauns club boss Paul Laffin kindly showed me some of the North's treasured league memorabilia.

Rabbitoh Clem Kennedy had always stuck in my mind as one of the neglected players of league. League writer Ian Heads helped me find Clem's widow, Mary. Mary Kennedy kindly showed me Clem's football memorabilia and we had a long chat over tea about her late husband's great life. Mary even got her photocopier rumbling for me.

Russell Amatto, a former Souths player, kindly lent me some material on the life of Kevin 'Lummy' Longbottom, including some testimonials of the former Souths fullback and amazing goal kicker, and Russell's wife put down some facts and figures on Lummy's life.

I did a north-west NSW tour to research my chapters on the Cleal brothers and Nathan Blacklock. Harvey Cleal kindly spent a few hours out on the porch at his home in Warialda talking about his famous sons, Noel and Les, and I could picture them playing outside the house as youngsters, one of them destined to play for Australia. Later in Inverell, I managed to track down Nathan Blacklock after going to his mum's house in Tingha and finding no-one there. Suddenly the phone rang as I was walked dejectedly back to the car. It was Nathan. 'You looking for me?' he said. 'Sure am,' I replied. 'I'm in a cafe in Inverell waiting for you,' he said. Nathan kindly spent some time talking about his career amid a busy Inverell Saturday morning where every second person wanted to shake his hand. When mum Sue walked up she gave me a keen stare as if she already knew me. The ever-busy club man and Tingha Tigers enthusiast Dick Hayden was a great source of material for the chapter on Nathan.

On a weekend away to listen to the band The Church play at Milton on the NSW South Coast, I'd lined up an interview with Ron Coote, who lived nearby. Ronnie kindly gave me two hours of his time at his McDonalds franchise at Ulladulla. I politely declined many offers of hospitality. For some reason later when I told older ladies who I had interviewed, they always managed a cheeky smile.

Bruce Weissel was very helpful to me in tracing some history on his famous father, Eric. I was also helpful to Bruce. Together we worked to locate some old jerseys of his father's that had gone missing. Mission accomplished Bruce! Betti Punnett from Cootamundra Historical Society sent some material on Eric Weissel's early life. Librarian Andy Carr from the State Library of NSW kindly sent me his conference paper on Harry Sunderland that he'd prepared for the Centenary Conference of Rugby league in Australia.

My former colleague Brad Walter, a senior sports writer on the *Sydney Morning Herald*, and a fellow Thirroulian, was always good for a chat and to bounce ideas off. This made for a good relationship when, as both coaches of young Thirroul football teams, we had to divvy up bits of Thomas Gibson Park for training areas during the week.

Publisher Pam Brewster was a great source of encouragement as I worked to complete *Uncommon Heroes*, as it weaved and dodged through several concepts. I would also like to thank my family for their support in this grand adventure. The resources of the Mitchell Library in Sydney and the National Library of Australia, through the Trove facility, helped no end in helping bring the project to completion.